PRASE FOR A *

'Rachel shows masses of heart a
challenges but also in her ab
insecurities for all to see. We all have an inner critic and body
dysmorphic disorder is more common than one would think.
It's high time it was out there and discussed. Rachel's frank
and funny style shines a light on this difficult subject and
will help many people to feel seen and inspired.'

Melanie Sykes, broadcaster

'Rachel writes with a witty honesty and, at times, hard-hitting
directness about her anxieties. Her dogged determination
with her running and cycling is an uplifting example of
how exercise can trigger such positive feeling.'

Josie Dew, cyclist and author

'A rollercoaster that any aspiring runner or cyclist can
relate to. From the catastrophic lows of injury to the soaring
highs of chasing down your goals – it's both magical and
exhausting all at once. You find yourself rooting for
her even more the second time round.'

Nat Scroggie, *This Vet Runs* blog

'Will resonate with readers who suffer from body dysmorphic
disorder and other mental health challenges.'

Miriam Díaz-Gilbert, author and ultrarunner

'Honest. Brutally so. Rachel's account of dealing with injury
and the despair in which she finds herself is a searing
account of mental and physical torment.'

Jeff McCarthy, *RunEatRepeat* blog

PRAISE FOR *RUNNING FOR MY LIFE*:

'I love this book for showing how, with sheer determination and dogged tenacity, you can overcome great difficulties ... She might even persuade me that one day I too could love running.'

Louise Minchin, TV presenter

'It's so inspirational to read how Rachel's discovery of a passion for running helped her to overcome her mental health struggles. It's heartwarming to learn how Rachel has been able to prove to herself that she really can achieve things that she would have never believed were possible.'

Jo Pavey, long-distance runner and medallist

'A searingly honest account of Rachel's amazing journey ... I'd thoroughly recommend this book to runners everywhere.'

Tom Williams, Global COO of parkrun

'What a heartfelt, moving, honest journey of self-discovery ... this is a book you have to pick up.'

Sissi Reads blog

'*Running For My Life* is a rich, colourful and brutally honest account of one woman's fight to beat her mental health demons.'

The Very Pink Notebook blog

'Full of heart and beautifully told ... inspirational, melancholy and often very funny, it's kind of a road map of the inner soul – I loved it.'

Liz Loves Books blog

'Written wittily, honestly and with a "take no crap" attitude, I could feel the warmth of [Rachel] as a person in her writing. Anyone who is hungry for change, looking for "the light" or even running their first marathon and needing a little insight: this book is FOR YOU! I loved every chapter.'

Lipstick & Trainers blog

A MIDLIFE CYCLIST

My two-wheel journey to heal
a broken mind and find joy

RACHEL ANN CULLEN

BLINK
bringing you closer

Published by Blink Publishing
80–81 Wimpole St,
Marylebone,
London W1G 9RE

www.blinkpublishing.co.uk

facebook.com/blinkpublishing
twitter.com/blinkpublishing

Trade Paperback – 978-1-788-701-84-6
Ebook – 978-1-788-701-85-3
Audio – 978-1-788-703-20-8

A CIP catalogue of this book is available from the British Library.

Typeset by seagulls.net
All illustrations © Shutterstock
Printed and bound in Great Britain by Clays Ltd, Elcograf S.p.A.
1 3 5 7 9 10 8 6 4 2

This book is a work of non-fiction, based on the life, experiences and
recollections of Rachel Ann Cullen. Certain details in this story, including
names, have been changed to protect identity and privacy.

Every reasonable effort has been made to trace copyright holders of
material reproduced in this book, but if any have been inadvertently
overlooked the publishers would be glad to hear from them.

Blink Publishing is an imprint of Bonnier Books UK
www.bonnierbooks.co.uk

For Mum – because you are and always were enough.

CONTENTS

PROLOGUE

I am riding a bike through tiny paths, weaving in between rice fields. I look across to my left and a farmer is diligently tending to the crops in his field. A Vietnamese woman cycles towards us on what looks like a 1960s retro high-handlebar bike. It reminds me of the classic scene from *E.T.* when the boys ride up into the sky. She is wearing a traditional Vietnamese conical hat, which is tied underneath her chin with a floral scarf. I can see a pair of battered old shoes sitting in the rusty basket on the front of her ancient push bike and an enormous bundle of harvested grasses is miraculously tied to the back. As she passes me I catch her eye and her virtually toothless smile is almost the same width as her hat.

I can hear nothing other than the sound of my own wheels turning and the occasional barking of a dog. I realise in this moment that I am experiencing happiness, that this is it. A feeling of peace and tranquillity fills my being, and I know that – right here – riding a bike through one of the most serene and truly peaceful places I have ever known is filling my heart with joy. There is no stress or anxiety here. The farmer quietly tending the rice crops in his field isn't in a battle with himself, or weighed down with the burden of the daily grind. The pocket-sized Vietnamese woman cycling along, transporting her massive bundle of crops with a pair of battered old shoes in the basket of her relic bike, doesn't appear to be battling any inner turmoil and I doubt she has been making enquiries with a local psychotherapist to tackle issues relating to her self-hatred. She looks as content riding her retro bicycle through the paddy fields as it is possible to be.

It makes me think of my own wrangling with my ever-present angst and my busy, chattering mind, which tries to tie me in endless knots and wrestle me into headlocks most hours of most days. *Anxiety?* That doesn't exist, here. *Worry?* Worry about what? *Noise?* Both internal and external noise are simply not a part of this reality.

I'm riding my Trek Hardtail bike through Vietnamese rice fields and I feel absolutely and truly peaceful. It's a kind of peace that transcends anything I have ever known. I push down on the pedals and realise that I am *IN* the tranquillity. I am *A PART* of it. I am *HERE*. In this moment, nothing else matters. My worries cease to exist. My anxious chatter about the 'hows' and the 'whys' and other disproportionate concerns about life's frustrating minutiae is – for once – completely silenced.

I am riding my bike and I feel as peaceful and as present as I can ever remember being. Of course, I've experienced similar feelings whilst riding my bike back home, but something about the beauty of this place cements what I already knew: that this is a special moment for me and that my long journey to arrive here has all been worthwhile.

I think back to my life back home and to the bombardment of '*must-haves*'. I fell for all that, once. Even now, I sometimes struggle to extricate myself from the barrage of tiresome propaganda. I look at the other school mums in the playground and I can't help but compare myself and my life to theirs. It is surely a flaw of our society that we are now programmed to want more, and – even more worryingly – to *be* more. I wonder when we all became so consumed with 'self' and on a constant mission to pick ourselves apart.

* * *

I'm cycling at speed down a rough mud track somewhere along the banks of the Mekong, on our route through Cambodia. The mud here was completely saturated just a few days ago when the monsoon rains hit, but it has dried up quickly in the baking thirty-five-degree heat, leaving hardened ridges where yaks and mopeds have left evidence of their passing. My wheels become momentarily stuck in a deep groove and I skid, almost thrown from my bike. Thankfully, I manage to keep myself upright.

I'm one of the 'fast ones'. I'm at the front of the group, riding just behind our Cambodian biking guide. He is forging a route for me as I push on over the rough terrain, wrestling with my handlebars over the corrugated burnt orange ground.

I'm loving riding at speed across this land. Every minute I'm concentrating hard, working out the best route to avoid the myriad deep pits, grooves and potholes in the dried mud track. Occasionally, there is a pool of orange, muddy water where the relentless sun has not yet managed to dry out the ground underneath. Sometimes, I swerve around the stagnant water, but other times I have no choice but to ride straight through it if there is no way around. The water splashes up on my face and I can taste the earth in my mouth.

A frail, sun-baked man walks towards me on the track. He is pushing a flimsy-looking cart, which is being pulled along by the skinniest pony I have ever seen. I can see all its ribs protruding and its knee bones look enormous in proportion to the rest of its skeletal body. The cart is piled high with planks of wood, which must be at least fifteen feet long. I wonder how it is moving forward at all. This is his track and this is his job for today, along with his cart and his skinny pony. And I am cycling past him at speed on a mountain bike, dodging the grooves and holes which his flimsy cart has made over the past few days, weeks, and no doubt much longer.

How am I here? I'm approaching my fifty-second mile of the day on this mountain bike – and I feel fast and free. Already I feel like I know this bike intimately. I understand how the gears work and when to shift them to suit the ever-changing terrain; I trust myself to swerve around any obstacles, even to navigate my way on to small boats (to cross the Mekong River) and back off again, cycling up rough, steep banking. All of this I can do and I wonder, when did this become my reality? When did I know all these things?

I love the feeling of my heart pounding like this.

I have learnt so much about myself since I discovered how to ride my bike. I'm so grateful for challenging myself and for realising that I can do this. Because without that, I wouldn't be here, experiencing true joy.

INTRODUCTION

FEBRUARY 2017

It's five weeks since I've been able to run.

In the big scheme of things, it's no biggie: I'm very aware that people do have *real* problems! But the thing is, running has been my Prozac, my therapy, my lifeline, my sanity, my solace, my best friend, my quiet time, my escape route, my go-to place, and my default setting for some eight years now.

How ironic then that for an indeterminable length of time (and I honestly have no idea), I won't be able to run. My body won't let me. And based on the past five weeks, it's going to be a painful experience. I feel vulnerable, insecure, not quite right, off-kilter. It's like a piece of me has – well, if not died, been temporarily placed in a deep, comatose state. That piece of me brought me joy and sanity.

And I want it back.

It's difficult to describe what running is to me. It became something far bigger than I'd ever anticipated following the very first marathon I ran, back in 2011, when my daughter

Tilly was just seven months old. Why? Because running the London Marathon symbolised everything that I believed I could never be. As an overweight teen, I'd been told that I wasn't the 'sporty type'. Who then expected that later in life, I would be able to run a marathon – *any marathon* – let alone at the very time when I'd also come face-to-face with my biggest fear: motherhood?

Running gave me a feeling of self-worth, a sense of achievement despite my physical and mental health misgivings, and a sense that things I hadn't at one time considered possible were entirely within my grasp. And so, rightly or wrongly, I labelled myself 'Rach the Runner'. It gave me a newfound sense of identity, belief and of belonging, from a place where I'd had none.

I keep having flashbacks to some of my many running adventures. I remember exploring Barcelona on broken legs the week after the Yorkshire Marathon in 2014 following a dream race and probably my greatest ever personal running achievement. I picture myself running effortlessly up snowless ski slopes in Font Romeu on my thirty-seventh birthday and the joy of discovering the Paula Radcliffe trail, which weaves around the high alpine mountain tops. The excitement of exploring some flatter routes around beautiful Lake Matemale and spotting running legend Mo Farah as he flew around the otherwise-empty track at the Font Romeu Altitude Training Centre. I remember how surreal it felt to sit down on the grass and watch him run in a way I have never seen any human run before, whilst inhaling an obscenely large Danish pastry (well, I *had* just run twelve miles at altitude).

And what about those nauseating speed sets running along the sea front in Mallorca? My Other Half took the girls into town on the bus whilst I set off running alongside it like a bat out of hell, much to the fascination/amusement of the other bus passengers.

'Is she really running into Port de Pollença?' a mystified bus passenger asked him.

'Erm, yes. Yes, she really is!' was his reply.

You see, it wasn't a big deal at the time, only a part of my normality. I just run: I just … *ran*.

Standing on the start line of the Dubai Marathon in January 2016 and running under what felt like a repressive heat lamp with a dodgy thermostat for 26.2 torturous miles. Precisely *how* I managed it after a long-haul flight and waking at 4 a.m. to stuff down a banana on the morning of the race escapes me. Thankfully, I emerged still breathing on the other side of the finish line.

But hang on a minute. That's not the full picture, is it Rach? The clues were already there. You see, I didn't achieve the time I was hoping for at the Dubai Marathon and the morning after the race I woke battered and broken, berating myself for such a 'poor performance'. *How could you be so slow, Rachel? Why didn't you run faster? You should have tried harder. Why didn't you try harder? NOT GOOD ENOUGH, RACHEL. MUST DO BETTER.*

MUST TRY HARDER.

I may have been in pieces physically following my very best efforts on that day in the blistering desert heat, but devastatingly, my Bastard Chimp – the cruel, inner voice who taunts me – had me well and truly beaten. Mentally, I was on my knees, in a stranglehold, and I had no way of escaping.

'I'm just going to do a few recovery miles along the Palm,' I mumbled to my long-suffering Other Half, who was soaking in the bath after experiencing his personal horror at the very same marathon, just hours before.

'You're doing *what*?' he replied, completely stunned. 'Rachel, you ran a tough marathon yesterday, in insane heat, after virtually no sleep and with jet lag. Your legs will be completely wrecked! What on earth are you even considering going running for? THAT'S INSANE!'

'Oh, I'll be fine! My legs don't feel too bad and anyway, it may loosen them up a little. See you in a bit – I won't be long!'

And so I coerced my aching, blistered feet into my godforsaken, dusty trainers and I knew that it was all wrong. *Wrong, wrong, wrong.* The truth is so painful to acknowledge at times and that morning, I knew with absolute certainty that in putting my trainers back on and making my legs run again *THE DAY AFTER THE MARATHON*, I was potentially damaging myself. But the Bastard Chimp had won.

Muscles are incredible things: they work hard and break down, only to rebuild and repair to become even stronger than they were before. But there is a limit. My legs couldn't possibly recover from the damage of the marathon by forcing more painful miles out of them the very next day. And for God's sake, I could barely walk, let alone run! Tears streamed down my face as I hobbled six miles – in agony – along The Palm from our luxury resort. *Why did I do that? How could I do that to myself?*

Reflecting on all the highs – and the many lows – of my running experiences feels like I'm on an emotional trapeze. I swing from one platform to another, from moments of sheer elation to the depths of despair, with nothing to catch me as I fly through the air in between.

I've already processed many thoughts around the *whys* and *hows* of my inescapable and irrefutable loss of running. I've asked all the questions and I've cried in frustration at the apparent lack of answers. But I need to finally start being honest with myself about what running has become to me and how I find my way back from this place.

Did I push myself too hard, too soon, for too long?

Yes, I did.

Did I balance my running with other cross-training activities to strengthen and support my body and to help prevent overtraining?

No, I didn't.

Did I rest adequately (or at all), making sure that I refuelled properly after hard training sessions and races?

No, I didn't.

Did I race too much?

Yes, I did.

Did running feed my demanding and incessant Bastard Chimp as it bounced up and down in front of me, shouting, 'You're still not good enough, Rachel, or fast enough, or just … enough! TRY HARDER!'

Yes. Sadly, and devastatingly, it did.

Did I manage to tame the very same Bastard Chimp as it bullied me into bashing out many more miles and races than my body wanted to run?

No, I didn't.

The chimp won.

Is this the result?

Yes. I'm quite sure that it is.

* * *

'We've been learning about something called "The Power of Yet" at school today, Mummy,' Tilly says, tucking into half a sausage roll as we amble down the lane on our walk home from school. It's one of the many perks of living near a farm shop.

'Really? And what exactly is "The Power of Yet" then, Tills?' I ask.

'Well, if you can't do something, then you put a "YET" at the end of it,' she explains, sounding like a trainee teacher in a young child's body whilst devouring her pork and pastry combo, 'and then it means that you just can't do it ... YET ... but you WILL be able to do it at some time in the future.'

'Wow! That's a great way of looking at things,' I reply, genuinely impressed with the whole notion of this 'turning obstacles into challenges' and 'stamping out defeatism' vibe.

'So, I cried in maths today when I couldn't work out why number 9 was the odd one out of the numbers 9, 12, 20, 36 and 45, when Delilah could.'

I temporarily switch off from her continuing chatter and drift into some dusty old mental arithmetic corner of my mind, where I frantically divide and subtract and race through my (very) basic knowledge of prime numbers before finally concluding that this is a test designed for six-year-olds.

How hard can it be? *Shit! What's the answer to a six-year-old's mental arithmetic quandary?* I also drift back to a time when I had believed certain things about myself that were untrue: *I'm no runner ... I could never be 'A RUNNER' ... I could never run a marathon ... I couldn't possibly exist without taking mental health medication ... I can't possibly find my way out of a lifestyle which has me trapped ... I'm not up to motherhood ... I'm just not capable of doing ANY of these things.*

'... But then I thought that I just don't understand it *yet,*' she continues, exaggerating the 'yet', delivering it slowly and deliberately, as though talking to someone of significantly inferior intellect, '... and that I *will* understand it *some time in the future.*'

My mind is still racing to work out the answer to my six-year-old daughter's mental arithmetic conundrum when I also consider the fact that I have applied the very same theory to myself and to my own previously self-imposed limited beliefs:

I can't run a marathon YET ... but perhaps I WILL run one, at some time in the future.

I can't call myself 'a runner' YET ... but maybe I will be able to, at some time in the future.

I can't consider the possibility of existing without my mental health medication YET ... but hey, that might be possible for me some time in the future ...

'Right, right. I see,' I reply, still rifling through *The Dummies Guide to Basic Algebra* in my head as she continues telling me about her day.

'The Power of Yet'. Not making the grade ... yet. Not quite hitting the mark ... yet. Not understanding the hows or the whys ... yet. Not reaching the 'qualifying standard' ... yet. Not getting there, wherever that might be ... yet.

Yet, yet, yet. And yet ...

It's a big and generous concept, 'The Power of Yet'. It's intended to stop children quitting before they've battled with their own internal belief systems and to remind them that sometimes the answer isn't always easy, and it doesn't always jump out from the page. It teaches them that the qualifying standard might take many, many attempts – including multiple failures – and that giving up isn't the right option. Word on the street is that 'Struggle is good!' and 'It ain't cool to quit, kids!'

But then it got me thinking: when is enough ever enough? When does 'The Power of Yet' turn on us and become some big old shitty stick with which we beat ourselves? What if the right thing to do IS to quit? Move on. Leave it there. Accept our limitations. What happens to 'The Power of Yet' then? Furthermore, when are *we ever* enough? When are our accomplishments, achievements, feathers-in-caps and certificates on the walls ever enough? When are we thin *enough*, or pretty *enough*? At what point do we declare ourselves rich *enough*, or successful *enough*? Are we forever doomed to kneel and worship at the altar of 'The Power of Yet', deeming ourselves – and all of our achievements – to be (offensively scrawled in red pen) 'could do betters' and 'must try harders'? What if we *have* tried our best? What if that *is* as close as we can possibly come to hitting the bull's-eye?

What if – despite slogging our guts out – we simply can't do or be any more?

What then?

You see, I've spent years in a silent, daily battle with The Power of Yet's arch enemy, 'The Curse of Enough'. I've spent decades chasing, wrangling and head-locking a little Bastard Chimp inside my head which told me that I simply wasn't good enough ... *yet*. I wasn't fast enough ... *yet*. Not thin enough ... *yet*. Not pretty enough ... *yet*. Not successful enough ... *yet*. NOT GOOD ENOUGH ... *yet*. I was under the misapprehension that some illusory, unidentifiable moment would occur in my future when I would reach this place – this pinnacle, this mecca of contentment – but that time was never here and never now.

'The Power of Yet' has been a double-edged sword for me. It has brought me great success; it has motivated me to try harder. *Want to knock an hour-and-a-half off your personal best marathon time in the space of two years?* Use 'The Power of Yet' – it really works! The medals, the certificates, the victories, the achievements ... 'The Power of Yet' doesn't know when to stop.

But what about enjoying the journey? What about putting a lid on our endless fascination for the desired outcome and noticing the small, momentary glimpses of joy along the way? Years of being catapulted between 'The Power of Yet' and 'The Curse of Enough', feeling like some stunned Wimbledon tennis ball being strewn around Court No. 1 have taught me to TREAT WITH CAUTION. And now I'm here – I'm broken, and I'm unable to run.

My mental health is swaying like a rickety old bridge across a gaping crevasse because I didn't understand that I would be chewed up and spat out by 'The Power of Yet' and I would then fall foul of 'The Curse of Enough'. I didn't realise my sense of self-worth would never come from achieving a certain uber-fast marathon time and genetically, however hard I train and no matter which convoluted, gruelling marathon training regime I follow, I can only ever achieve a certain level of physical fitness and I will only ever be able to progress to a pre-determined peak. At some point, I would have to accept my limitations and I would be wise to declare, *'Yes, Rach. All you've done – the progress you've made, the medals accumulated and the prizes you've won, the incredible experiences you've had – it's enough. You've done enough.'* But sadly, it hasn't happened that way.

The Dubai Marathon – which I finished twenty minutes slower than my personal best 2014 marathon time – devastated me. I saw it as a huge failure for me and a regression from that elusive moment at some point in my future when it all makes sense: when I would finally be *enough*. It caused me to damage myself and to push myself to the point of breaking. It resulted in floods of tears and me knowing that what I was doing was no longer about pushing through invisible barriers, courtesy of the virtuous 'Power of Yet'. It was about self-flagellation and punishment instead.

I ran as hard and as fast as I possibly could on that day. With every cell of my being, I battled for just over twenty-six gruelling miles and I crawled over the finish line in three hours and thirty-seven minutes. I conveniently forgot that only a few years before, this would have been a huge personal victory for me: *Fucking hell, I've just run a sub-3:40 marathon!*

But, 'The Power of Yet' combined with 'The Curse of Enough' stole my moment.

And what about running being a solution for my mental health difficulties? What about that? I thought I'd found an answer: I genuinely believed I'd found it. *NO MORE PROZAC FOR ME!* Having been diagnosed as suffering from bipolar disorder early in my twenties, I've had my fair share of mental health demons to battle. Running was the one thing that prevented me needing to pop my daily SSRI happy pills. I'd proven that ever since training for the 2011 London Marathon. You see, for me it was never just about the running in a physical sense. It was about discovering my mental strength and my own resolve to find a place deep inside myself I'd never known existed before. I'd spent twelve years on mental health medication. That's over a decade of my life popping pills which I truly believed I needed (and for a short period of time, I probably did) whilst self-medicating with alcohol and living a life which I didn't want to be mine. I gave running all the credit for this miraculous transformation in my mental state, whilst giving myself none.

'So, did you work out the answer then, Tills?'

'To what?' she asks, temporarily distracted by her sausage roll.

'Your maths puzzle. The random numbers and why number 9 was the odd one out.'

'Oh yeah. It was because 9 is a single digit, the others are double digits.'

'Of course, I was just about to say that,' I lie.

Here I am, trying to solve a child's algebra puzzle by involving complex multiplication, subtraction and square roots. No doubt my six-year-old daughter was doing the same thing with her genetically similar, overthinking mind. But the answer was so simple that we could barely see it.

I'm sincerely hoping that one day she will come home from school and tell me all about 'The Power of Enough' because sometimes the answer is so simple: trying your very best *is* good enough. I'm realising, just like my own daughter, I still need to learn this lesson.

I can't run and I am – at this precise moment – filled with fear. I feel lost, vulnerable and devastated. So, what am I going to do with all of this? Am I going to wallow and wilt whilst sobbing into my sofa cushions, eating paprika-flavoured Pringles? (Yes, probably!) I've cried irrational, melodramatic tears; I've spontaneously combusted at the frustration of my running being taken from me without any explanation.

I *love* running. *I love MY running*. It pulsates through my entire being and makes me feel alive. But this is a journey that I'm going to have to learn from. Despite my tears of frustration and through my desperate 'Tilly, you'll have to run junior parkrun by yourself today, sweetheart, because I don't think I can run 2km with you ...' sobs to my daughter, I need to turn this into something strong and positive, something that I can use to grow and to build from and as a fuel to propel me, missile-like, into the next phase of my life.

But I have no idea what that looks like. I'm learning, and I'm trying to find my way ... again. And I'm documenting the journey of my progress and my setbacks. Some days, I feel mentally strong and defiant. Others, it's as though at the slightest nudge, I could crumble into a pit of mental health woes and outrageously disproportionate fears. Those are *my* fears and all of this is now a part of my journey and my reality.

I must somehow navigate my way along a tightrope which spans the deepest, darkest crevasse between 'The Power of Yet' and 'The Curse of Enough'.

I just daren't look down.

1

LOSS

It's exactly eleven weeks – or seventy-seven days – until the London Marathon 2017. *How's my training going?* It's going shit. I've already vented my frustration at having two weeks' worth of KFC family bucket-sized '*Do you want to go large with that?*' flu rampaging through our household, knocking me sideways, off my feet and away from any semblance of any 'real' marathon training, or any training at all.

And then it gets worse. I kicked my own backside so hard playing some misconceived game of marathon training catch-up, I've now brought on an injury to my lower calf/ Achilles area. This caused me to go all *E.T.* and 'phone home' on Thursday morning's run as I stood by a wet, lonely bench high on Norland Moor with sad, heavy eyes, waiting for my long-suffering Other Half to pick me up, just three miles from my own front door.

It has been a mere THREE DAYS since the *E.T.* incident and subsequent emergency physiotherapy appointment at which he – Magician Dave – said to me, and I quote – 'So, you WON'T be racing the Dewsbury 10k on Sunday then, Rach, will you?'

I don't answer.

I *do* believe in miracles, and I *do* turn up to the start line of the Dewsbury 10k road race. I *know* it's a silly gamble, but my fragile running ego forces me to take the risk.

I set off knowing the grumblings are still there, but by only one mile into the race, the pain is intensifying. At two miles, there is nowhere to go and so I limp off the course and make an about-turn, facing the Walk of Shame back to the start. Runners stare at me as though witnessing the Resurrection, as I trudge slowly back down the high street in the wrong direction, towards the centre of the toilet bowl that is Dewsbury.

'Are you OK, there?' a kindly marshall asks, as I lumber pathetically by.

'I'm injured,' I say, feigning a sorry smile, whilst hobbling melodramatically and pointing to my left leg.

A St John's ambulance pulls up next to me and a particularly keen hi-vis-adorned First Aider shouts out of the window, 'Do you want a lift back to the start, love?'

'Yes. Yes, please, I do!' I reply, as the prospect of shuffling a further 1.5 miles back down the Dewsbury U-bend isn't altogether appealing – and certainly not in (short) shorts and a thin running vest, albeit one of the *real runner's* variety to which I have become so accustomed.

I hop on board the non-emergency ambulance and reluctantly make polite chatter with the First Aid crew, who look grateful to have something to do. Having barely broken a sweat, I turn down their kind offer of an emergency sports drink and confirm that I don't need bandaging up or pushing anywhere in a wheelchair, which seems to dampen the mood slightly.

Once safely dropped off at the race start/finishing area – and now shivering profusely – I bump into Andy, a local runner I know who also happens to be hampered by injury. He offers me his warm XXL winter coat and the oversized arms swing down around my knees like a lazy octopus. We chat about our respective injury-induced misfortunes whilst another lovely friend, Claire, and her baby Amber walk over to join us. Claire's husband is racing today. She hugs me as I stand, cold, helpless and without words in Andy's octopus overcoat, and it helps, but I am still devastated.

Claire and I traipse across to Wetherspoons, where I dunk one of my small complimentary biscuits into a large mug of free-refill coffee. The hot coffee warms me up, whilst the small sugar hit makes me feel incrementally better and helps to ease my non-running sorrows. The boys have joined us now and begin to chat about their race times, tactics and performances.

'It was definitely much colder than last year,' my Other Half says to Claire's husband, Tim, just seconds before inhaling the second half of his bacon sandwich in one bite.

'Yeah, and the start was absolutely packed!' Tim replies, clearly jittery and still buzzing with race adrenalin. 'It took me at least a mile to work my way through the crowd and find any rhythm.'

I glance over at baby Amber, who is smearing cold beans across everything in the immediate vicinity, and my adrenalin-free heart sinks as I so desperately wish that I could join in their running chatter.

Once back at home, I sit down and I begin thinking:

Who am I if I can't run? Who am I if I can't run? I simply don't know the answer. *How does it make me feel? What is my state of mind? How will being unable to run around the Yorkshire hills impact on my mental health? What will I do if this lasts for much longer?*

Of course, this may seem a little melodramatic (I've been told that I can be inclined towards 'catastrophising') and rather hasty, as I don't yet know the full extent of my left limb's blatant refusal to play along with my London Marathon hopes and aspirations. But these are questions that I will ponder over the coming unspecified period of cross-training, rehabilitation and ... REST (NO, NOT *THAT* WORD!).

It does admittedly make me want to shrink and recoil in my own skin to think that I'm already struggling with a small overtraining injury and with the certain knowledge of an indefinite period without running, whilst there are plenty of people who are experiencing greater irritations in life – their very own warts on an otherwise peachy backside. And yes, there most certainly are far bigger problems to be facing in the world, right now. But still, rational thought doesn't always seem to help – if indeed it ever does. Mental health issues don't usually respond in such a convenient manner, so I've found.

I will put some more thought to this and to the glaring flaws this highlights in my own emotional ability to handle the prospect of an unspecified period of significantly reduced running, if I can even run at all. And I will ponder on why this minor bump in the road is already threatening to send me into a headspin of such epic proportions. I'll have plenty of opportunity to think about that over the coming days, weeks and – dare I even say it? – months ahead. I do know that I'm terrified. I'm terrified of not running because that's what I love to do, but mostly I'm terrified of what's already going on inside my head. I can feel everything changing and my equilibrium is shifting. It's like being a house built on the very edge of a cliff, just waiting for a landslide to come and sweep me into the sea. When will I succumb to the waves? Is this a waiting game of erosion and eventual destruction?

I'm terrified of facing the realisation that running wasn't the answer after all. I'm panic-stricken at the prospect of my self-worth being reduced to a collection of shiny medals or the number of hours and minutes it has taken me to run from a designated point A to a finishing line at point B. I'm also horrified that I didn't see this coming. I hadn't imagined that so much of my mental wellbeing hinged on my ability to run and the upward trajectory of progression I once enjoyed. *What happens when I peak, or plateau? What happens if I can't run?* I never considered the possibility.

I have been under the misguided belief that Prozac and running are mutually exclusive: it was always one or the other, for me. I saw running as being the complete mental health replacement tool-kit I needed to stay safe from the horrors of my bipolar disorder *without* mental health medication. So, logic dictates that *without* running, my subconscious, illogical mind keeps telling me that I will need to go back onto mental health medication. And I don't want to. I don't want to believe that this is something I can't control. Running helped me to manage and wrestle with my demons before. What will happen now? How will I fight them without resigning myself to medical intervention?

And – to be very clear – I most certainly DO NOT see the need to go onto mental health medication again as any kind of weakness. For me, in the early days of my diagnosis whilst at university, and for many others in the longer-term management of their condition (like my mum, for example), medication is the answer. It's exactly what they need to create equilibrium from an unstable, erratic place. But the challenge for me is that I've *proven* that I can manage my own condition, haven't I? I haven't *needed* to take mental health medication for eight years now, so it must be possible for me to manage this myself. But when I have done this exclusively with running, and my almost constant progression, what happens when that stops? My mind has a virtual meltdown at the prospect that there could ever be a replacement 'fix', or that my sanity may be safely managed in any other way. This is where my head is at: the unknown. What could possibly replace running as my mental health 'fix'?

I just don't know. I don't have any answers.

2

NO. RUNNING.

I'm up with the larks to see Magician Dave for spells and contortions as my physiotherapist tries his best to unpick this holy mess I've made of my leg.

I turn up at the Miracle Centre and his polite – if slightly officious – receptionist makes me a bowl-sized flat white. I'm not sure whether I'm in a physio's waiting room or Starbucks, but I'd be happy with either, right now.

'How is it?' Dave asks in his unmistakably Irish twang and I begin to splutter through the ridiculous tale of my having undone precisely ALL the patching together he'd achieved before my ill-conceived attempt at the Dewsbury 10k road race.

He is patient, understanding and kind. He doesn't stand before me with condescending tones of 'Well, *that was really clever, wasn't it, Rachel?*' or repeated, disapproving sighs. He knows me well enough now to be absolutely confident that either of those responses may incite me to drive straight home and go out for a rage-fuelled run (yes, he also knows I'm THAT stupid).

He pulls and pushes my limbs as I move this way and that.

'Can you push your RIGHT hand towards the LEFT corner of the room' … 'And your LEFT hand down the INSIDE of your RIGHT thigh.' … 'Good. And your RIGHT hand down to the floor to touch your RIGHT foot.'

Suddenly, I'm in an expensive game of Twister. Or the Hokey Cokey.

I'm given my orders: rehabilitation exercises (I hang onto his instructions as though hearing the Words of God himself), 'other' non-impact training. Oh, and I must do NO running.

NO. RUNNING.

'Did you hear that correctly? I said NO. RUNNING.'

Those words, 'NO' and 'RUNNING', suddenly hit me and I grapple with myself for being so utterly ridiculous.

'Let's see how it is in a few days' time – a week at the most,' he says, as I try to comprehend what he is saying. By then, he reassures me, I *may* be able to reintroduce some very short, steady 'jogs'. I look at him incredulously, as though he's just told an old lady to 'fuck off', and my head still spins with unanswered questions:

When will I be back running? I want a time and a date. Possibly even a place.

He can give me nothing.

Will I lose my fitness? Will I lose all that I've trained so hard for over the past seven years, just because of one silly little 10k race which pushed me too far?

I'm too afraid and too ashamed to ask.

What will I do instead? What other training shall I do to (a) fill the void of my beloved running and (b) stay sane? I hate most fitness classes, I *can't stand* swimming (I get far too cold and I always want to wee as soon as I get in the pool) and I fall off bikes (although admittedly, not static gym ones – at least not yet).

What about all the races I'm booked to take part in on the run-up to the marathon? Does Magician Dave not realise that these are all a necessary part of my marathon training? What does he expect me to do, just write them off?

And what about the London Marathon itself?

What on earth am I going to do about the fact that I'm supposed to run the London Marathon in ten weeks' time?

And finally, what about the London Marathon?

I so desperately want to be on that start line in April, which I'm very aware is just a few short months away, and this question spins around my head and eclipses all others.

* * *

Following my devastating physio appointment, I head over to the gym at work the very next day. My head is filled with resentment, anger and rage. I'm now riding the wave of a Kubler-Ross Change Curve: I've already visited 'shock', moved on to 'denial' and now I'm arriving at 'frustration'.

It's suddenly like being in a bad episode of *Blind Date* from 1996. I begrudgingly make eye contact with Contestant Number 1 – the static gym bike. *He isn't too bad,* I ponder. *Maybe we could grow to like each other?* It seems I'm left with no option but to go on a date with him …

It's lunchtime and myself and the static gym bike enter the *First Dates* restaurant. We have a pleasant chat and appear to have a few things in common. '*He seems nice,*' I tell myself, whilst fully aware that anything with the word 'NICE' attached to it is in fact thoroughly shit.

I glance across the room. There's another woman on a date with *my* treadmill. She doesn't love the treadmill like I do, I can tell – she isn't even interested in him. But she's on a date with him and I'm not. I'm stuck in the corner with dull arse 'Mr Nice' static bike for company.

The clock ticks slowly by. Offensive, red pixelated minutes and seconds pass in front of my tear-filled eyes as I turn up the volume on my oversized headphones. D:Ream's 'Things Can Only Get Better' suddenly blasts into my ears. *Oh, for fuck's sake!* I silently shout to myself as I work up to face my second endurance set on the bike – another eight minutes of hard effort – without sliding off the plastic seat.

The dinner date between non-runner and the treadmill has just ended. She's flounced off, not even giving a backwards glance, whilst the belt is left spinning slowly, as though it wasn't ready to be left on its own, just yet. Another day – when I had the luxury of choice – I would have dumped this static bike with its slippery seat and soulless interval sessions in a heartbeat and hopped aboard my beloved treadmill. I'd say, '*Listen, Treadmill. I know it hasn't all been plain sailing. And you know that I love running outside in the sunshine infinitely more, but in here, you are my one true love. Can we please just patch things up and make it work?*'

But today, I'm with the static bike and there's no escaping that fact.

I come to the end of my interval session, which I've split into purposeful, manageable chunks. I've worked hard, I've sweated (rather a lot, to be honest) and I feel a sense of achievement that I've acquainted myself with the bike and I've stuck it out.

I look at the clock and see that it's time for me to head back to my desk. And then, just as I'm about to head out the door, the static bike shouts over, '*So, shall we do this again sometime, then?*'

'*Yeah*,' I say, miserably – glancing wistfully at the treadmill with watery eyes. '*Yeah, let's.*'

I feel like crying inside.

3

I HATE CYCLING

2009

I've finally conceded: I have agreed to go out on a 'steady evening ride' with one of my long-standing personal training clients and her group of local cycling buddies. I don't know why I've eventually caved in – possibly the build-up of peer pressure following endless weeks of, 'Oh, come on, Rach, you'll be fine! You're easily fit enough and you'll probably kick our arses on the hills!' and then reassurances of, 'We won't be going on any silly routes, or riding very far. Honestly, it will be a very tame ride, and anyway, we'll look after you!'

They are a small group – or 'clique', if I have my more sceptical head on – of maybe five or six local women, all good friends in the little rural village where I now live. It's been a struggle to establish myself in this close-knit community since setting up my personal training studio here, eighteen months ago. Everyone knows everyone else's business around here and it was quite a thing, my arrival, and the plonking of a brand-new shiny fitness studio in what was previously a derelict old shit-encrusted chicken shed. It took some time for my 'New-Age' way of thinking to catch on (Personal training? Hmmmppff! Who needs a bloody personal trainer, anyway?)

Once we got over those unhelpful early barriers, I began training Maggie, the dairy farmer's wife, on a weekly basis. She's a bubbly, chatty type with her finger very much on the local pulse — assuming there is one. From knowing about the latest Dock Pudding competition (a local delicacy made from the leaves of a specific kind of dock plant, combined with nettles, oatmeal and some other bits and pieces to no doubt try and disguise the presence of any of the above) to the goings-on down at Snippers, the village hairdresser's, and the unfortunate young trainee who has recently been knocked-up by her delinquent boyfriend and has just started to show.

Maggie is a few years older than me and not what you'd perhaps expect for a ye-olde-worlde dairy farmer's wife. She is a corporate machine on the sly, which may explain her vast range of (mainly fuchsia) designer handbags. But she is also a true-grit Yorkshire lass who isn't afraid to – excuse the clumsy farming pun – 'muck in' with the endless daily tasks her quietly spoken husband diligently cracks on with for seemingly most hours of every single day and no doubt most nights, too.

She is a biker – a mountain biker, she tells me. I have no interest in this as a sport, or any kind of fitness activity, but I can sense that she enjoys telling me about the Girly Biking Clique's latest Wednesday Night Ride, or the debauched biking weekend they recently enjoyed in the Peak District, where there was '… more drinking than riding (chortle chortle)' as Penny finished off two whole bottles of Chardonnay … ALL BY HERSELF! But somehow still managed to complete their planned daily thirty-mile mountain bike rides, apparently unaffected. EEEK! It sounds like my idea of merry hell – a few clutter-packed camper vans and a bunkhouse filled with pissed, cackling women but she insists I must come along next time and I'd SIMPLY LOVE IT!

I know I won't.

The group have been meeting up and going out on their mountain bikes every Wednesday night for a good number of years, Maggie tells me. All of them live within a two-mile radius of each other and they have all frequented – and survived – the piss-up bunk barn/mountain biking weekend experience several times over. I'm the New Girl in Town and it feels like it's my turn to be brought, kicking and screaming, into the local Girly Biking Clique's fold and to be inaugurated into their gang.

And it starts tonight.

'Remember, I've said I'll go out with Maggie and her biking buddies tonight,' I venture to my boyfriend Chris, who has been unable to engage me in any kind of conversation about mountain biking/cycling/bikes of any description since we met just over a year ago. That's his thing, not mine. He accepts and (kind of) respects the fact, although he does highlight one glaringly obvious flaw to me at the eleventh hour: the simple fact that I don't have a bike. Hear that again: Shit! I don't have a bike!

'But don't worry, Rach, you can use mine,' he offers, generously.

I've never taken much notice of his mountain bike before. I don't know the make or the specifications. In fact, I don't know ANY makes or ANY specifications of ANY bikes. In my naïve, innocent, non-cycling mind, a bike is a bike ... is a bike. That's all there is to know, right?

'Oh, that's great, thanks,' I say, feeling a heady mix of relief and at the same time increased anxiety: relief because I'll be able to keep my word and go out with the Girly Biking Clique on their Wednesday evening bike ride and increased anxiety because (1) I don't have my own bike; (2) I've never even ridden Chris's bike before and I know absolutely nothing about how any of it works; and (3) I will have to keep my word and go out with the Girly Biking Clique on their Wednesday evening bike ride.

I no longer have the best possible Get Out of Jail Free card ever – 'Oh, I'm SOOOO sorry, Maggie. I can't come along tonight, because – well, I don't have a bike to ride!'

Shit, shit, SHIT.

Chris spends precisely twelve minutes talking me through how everything works, from changing gears to the sensitivity of the 'Avid Juicy' brakes, something about locking out the front suspension ... oh, and a dropper post (?) I forget absolutely everything other than how to use the brakes and I ask him to lower the seat for me because I will need to at least be able to balance my big toe on the ground when necessary if I'm going to get back from this thing alive.

'There should be enough charge on the lights,' he says, confidently. 'I used them on my ride with Paul on Monday night, but I'm sure you won't be out for hours with the girls, tonight, will you?' he concludes, with a stifled laugh. I agree. They're meeting me here at 6 p.m. and I'm anticipating I'll be back home with the bike locked up, having showered and changed into my PJs, sitting with a large glass of rosé, chilling out in front of MasterChef by 8 p.m. at the latest. Glancing out of the window, I can see very little other than my own reflection: dusk has long since fallen.

'Cool,' I say. 'Just remind me how to turn the lights on again, would you? And are they meant to flash?'

He looks at me like I've just taken a dump in his cycling helmet, or in cycling wanker talk – the 'lid'.

4

TRAPPED

1998

I'm locked in the tiny bedroom in my shared student house overlooking the narrow backstreet, which is lined with dustbins. I know the backstreet well.

I'm kneeling up on my mattress, which I have taken off my bed, because I spend a lot of time down here, and it's easier on my bony knees. I'm staring into a small round mirror which is propped up against the window pane, listening to the sounds of the other girls in the house having showers and slamming doors. *'Bathroom's free, Selena!'* one of them hollers just before another door bangs, making my drafty bedroom window rattle and my little round mirror fall over. *Fucking hell!*

I'm nibbling fruit and nut cereal, which I've placed in a tiny pile next to the mirror on my windowsill. I graze on the bran flakes and the dried fruit, but I always leave the hazelnuts, even though I like them. My eating has become more erratic and irregular lately, and I'm relying on my endless supply of dry breakfast cereal for sustenance so that I don't need to leave my window – or my mirror – for any longer than is absolutely necessary.

The house is completely silent, now. The front door has slammed shut and I can hear the girly chatter and laughter slowly fading as my housemates walk away from our house and up towards the Student Union. They didn't bother asking if I was joining them, today. I'm not surprised, though: that stopped a long while ago. They just leave me to it – I'm (thankfully) invisible, in here.

I'm relieved that I finally have some peace and I can concentrate again without being distracted. Focusing on my reflection in the mirror, I can see all the tiny veins, blemishes and open pores on my skin, which looks red and raw. I have already washed my face several times today, and then slathered thick layers of moisturising cream over my papery skin, which doesn't know when its epidermis is going to be stripped bare once again. My face feels sore and tingly; dry and oily all at the same time. And I have some open wounds where I was convinced that imperfections were lurking and needed digging out. The few fingernails I have (most are chewed down to their wicks) have made semi-circular, bloody indents in my skin, clearly demonstrating my efforts to rectify my many glaring imperfections.

I feel sad almost all the time, but it doesn't feel like sadness – it just feels like emptiness, as though I'm entirely hollow inside.

Some days, I must leave the safety of my bedroom and go to places like the university (only for compulsory seminars,

I'm invisible in lectures) and the local shop (for absolute necessities like fruit and nut cereal and, occasionally, some bread and milk). On those days, I go through my usual deep cleansing routine, but then I try to mask the damage I have done to myself by applying thick layers of gloopy beige make-up. I know that my skin looks painful and hideous, and I am fully aware that I have damaged myself. Many times, I need to clean all my make-up off and begin the whole rigmarole again because I simply can't cover up the mess I have made of myself: no amount of concealer or foundation can disguise the bloody imprints of my fingernails or the sore redness of my now angry-looking skin.

When I'm forced to eventually leave the sanctity of my window, and I haven't been able to rectify the visible damage I have done to myself, then panic sets in. *How can I leave the house? What will people think when they see me? How can I possibly face the seminar group, today? Will I recognise the look of disgust in their eyes when they see what I have done to myself? Will ugliness accompany me everywhere? Is this my constant companion, now?*

It feels as though I have succumbed to this being my life, and I have accepted that this is how I will now fill my days. I find it increasingly difficult to concentrate on anything at all, from my Law degree to the social goings-on which I am no longer a part of. This thing that has engulfed me has robbed me of it all, and I no longer have the energy to fight back.

The skin-picking is getting worse, and there are many times when my face, my neck and my fingers throb with pain. I can feel my body trying to heal itself, desperately forming scabs where I have hurt it. But then I go and do it all over again and tear at the sores, simply unable to accept that I now have ugly scabs on my face. My only response is to try and rip them from my body, and to fight the onset of ugliness which has hunted me down and now has me trapped.

I can't see a way out.

* * *

THURSDAY, 9TH FEBRUARY 2017

I'm heading to the gym to try again with my new best friend, the static bike. Reluctantly, I complete three sets of my recently discovered indoor cycling interval sessions, and miraculously, I manage once again not to fall off the slippery seat.

I follow this by shoehorning myself onto the one remaining exercise mat, in between a man who is attempting abdominal crunches using some plastic rocking contraption from the 1990s and a woman who looks worryingly uncomfortable on a stability ball. The old guy smiles at me and says, 'Any excuse for a rest, eh?' as I sit myself down on the mat next to him, desperately wishing I were running instead of this.

Funny bastard.

In frustrated silence I complete my futile rehabilitation exercises, and then it's on to my yoga class. I feel fat and heavy as my Bastard Chimp is having a field day without running to 'manage my weight'. This is the ridiculous, bullshit mantra I've been telling myself for the past fifteen years: *YOU NEED TO RUN TO NOT BE FAT, RACH. WITHOUT IT, YOU'RE THAT SEVENTEEN-YEAR-OLD MARS BAR-MELTING*

LOSER AGAIN ... I can't believe how quick my Bastard Chimp is to jump onto this cruel and painful bandwagon after such an offensively short time without running. It makes me sad to think that these thoughts have never really gone away. I thought they had, but it looks like I was wrong. Being unable to run even for this embarrassingly short period of time has brought to the fore a whole raft of mental health issues that perhaps – and please excuse the awful pun – I have been running away from. *Is that the truth?* Maybe running has simply been a sticking plaster over the deep-rooted, soul-haunting glitches I know about myself that I don't honestly want to tackle. That possibility was made abundantly clear this morning, when an innocent comment by a six-year-old girl sent me into a headspin of epic proportions.

In preparation for my eagerly anticipated ONE MILE test run, I rush downstairs half-dressed. I'm still wearing my slightly questionable gingham pyjama top, but I've changed into Lycra running tights. Admittedly, it's a strange combination. When I take off my pyjama top to replace it with a thermal running layer, the innocent six-year-old points to me and says, 'HA HA! You've got a FAT TUMMY!'

Time stops. I stand completely still, and I'm rendered motionless in my stunned state. I can feel my head beginning to pound. It's melting into a confused, emotional rage that I couldn't possibly have foreseen. I fly upstairs, shut myself in the bathroom and weep uncontrollably, as my Other Half tries to reassure me quietly through the locked door that his six-year-old daughter would call a broom handle 'fat' given the opportunity (she has three selective adjectives, the other two being 'stinky' and 'poopy' – either of which would have been preferable to 'fat' for my irrational brain).

With tears still stinging my eyes and streaming down my cheeks, I head out of the front door for my one-mile test run. I feel like Fred Flintstone's car: barely moving forwards on clunky, semi-spherical, Stone Age wheels. My emotionally drained state doesn't help matters, but I reach the end of my ridiculously condescending single mile of slow, downward trudge and berate every second of it. My legs feel heavy and cumbersome – and they hurt. I don't 'ease' into it, and the tightness never loosens its grip – not one bit. It feels like I'm running on two wooden legs that are not – and never were – meant to be mine. WHERE HAVE MY LEGS GONE? I WANT THEM BACK!

Heartbroken and deflated, I slump into the passenger seat of the car as my family picks me up just a single mile away from our house. The girls are subdued in the back. I can feel that they are cautious of me, and they feel unsure how I will respond. Maybe they are wondering if I will explode/ break down into inexplicable tears again. *Is she going to have another meltdown?* I can imagine their six-year-old minds contemplating, weighing up the risk of a repeat performance from earlier. *Is she calm again, now?* I can see their young eyes questioning.

I feel sad: I wish I knew the answers. And I wish I knew how to protect them from these thoughts and feelings – my ugly companion for the last twenty years.

We drive home in silence, where I try my best to move on from the 'Fat Tummy' incident, which continues to taunt me. My young daughter doesn't need to live my angst, and she shouldn't have to even try to understand why I have a meltdown over an otherwise innocuous, silly comment. Unfortunately, on this occasion, I couldn't protect her as I would have liked. Normally, my running helps me to do that.

5

HELP!

'*Your tummy looks fat in that ... Your tummy looks fat in that ... Your tummy looks fat in that ... Your tummy looks fat in that ...*'

The words of a six-year-old little girl play on constant repeat in my head. They ring in my ears and echo all around me as though I'm trapped in the longest, darkest tunnel. I can't switch it off, and I don't know how to mute the sound, but that's just the tip of the iceberg. I know what's been happening to me lately, and it's far bigger and scarier than this one tiny, isolated incident, which doesn't in any way qualify me as suffering from body dysmorphia. Not at all.

Feeling 'a bit fat' doesn't come anywhere close to experiencing the full horror of the condition that I know so well, and fear so much. It's like being haunted by a ghost which has never gone away. And since my running has abandoned me, I can see the ghost more clearly and more frequently. I can feel him breathing down the back of my neck, and whispering things into my ear. Cruel things. He's becoming stronger and louder, bolder and more convincing than ever.

And the realisation of this fact is one of the most frightening things for me to face.

I have been forced to recognise that body dysmorphia has been my silent companion for the past twenty years. According to the charity, The BDD Foundation, body dysmorphic disorder (or 'BDD'), describes a debilitating preoccupation with perceived defects or flaws in a person's appearance. It can affect both men and women, and makes sufferers excessively self-conscious. They tend to check their appearance repeatedly and try to camouflage or alter the defects they see, often undergoing needless cosmetic treatments. Onlookers are frequently perplexed, because they can see nothing out of the ordinary, but BDD causes devastating distress and interferes substantially with the ability to function socially.

This has been my reality, and over the years, it has ebbed and flowed. At times, BDD has crippled me completely to the extent that I have struggled to leave the house. Perhaps the worst episode was during the late 90s whilst I studied for a Law degree at the University of Hull. My weight plummeted, leaving me with sagging, asymmetrical breasts. And although that was thankfully soon rectified by breast reduction surgery, I believe it was the trigger for a far greater problem: one where all I could see about myself were flaws.

During 'the Prozac years' of my twenties, the symptoms of BDD abated to the point where I was no longer crippled with the condition. I was always acutely aware of my physical imperfections and misgivings, but no longer a prisoner in my own home. In retrospect, it's my belief that being prescribed Prozac for my *other* mental health issue – bipolar disorder –

helped me to manage the condition with some success, rather like a happy coincidence. SSRI medication (of which Prozac is one type) is widely regarded as being one of the most successful treatments for BDD, and in managing the crippling symptoms.

I haven't been taking Prozac medication for some eight years, and I am the Queen of Denial. Look how successful I've been in denying my body doesn't want to run! Being particularly gifted in this way has helped me to ignore all the flashing neon warning signs that this ghost is coming back to haunt me but I can't run away from it forever.

I am standing facing the large mirror which hangs proudly over the fireplace in our living room. I've been here for a good while now, running my wide-toothed comb through my long hair and going over the same small sections with my hair straighteners. It was poker-straight a good while ago, but I go over and over it again, just in case. It now feels like I'm ironing straw rather than hair, and I'm frustrated because of all the static I'm creating, but holding out for perfection.

'Do I look OK, Tills? Does my hair look OK?'

My daughter is playing with her Sylvanian Families camper van at my feet, and my tiresome questions are interrupting the pizza delivery which Mr Hedgehog is about to make to the Rabbit family on his moped. The words come out of my mouth and I immediately wish that I could stuff them back in and swallow them, pushing them deep down into the pit of my stomach. I feel ashamed that this compulsive questioning is simply too powerful for me to resist.

'Yes, Mum, it is. Why do you keep asking me that?'

'Sorry, Tills. I – erm – I'm sorry.' There's a brief silence filled only with my shame. I hate myself once again for allowing the words to spill out, but it's too late now. Seconds pass, and it happens again.

'But are you sure? It's just that I'm wondering if the hair-dresser has got my hair colour right, this time. Is it too dark? Do you think the colour is too dark?'

'MUM! STOP! I won't answer you if you ask me that again.'

She is simply tired of my futile, pointless questions, and her instinct is absolutely right: she knows that she is not helping me in any way by responding to my desperate need for constant reassurance. And it's been happening a lot more recently.

I finally switch off my now seriously overworked hair straighteners and give myself one last glance in the mirror. And then another ... but I'm not altogether sure what I'm looking at any more, just the outline of a person in a frame. I trudge through to the kitchen, where my Other Half looks up from the table and gives me a pitiful look. He has heard me quizzing Tilly about the shade/colour/cut/straightness/static of my hair, and he doesn't need to say anything at all; it's written all over his face. As I shuffle around the kitchen unpacking the dishwasher in silence, and pointlessly rearranging mugs in a cupboard, I desperately want to ask him if my hair looks all right, but I manage to hold it in as though I'm stifling a sneezing fit. I'm not thinking about my shame any more. It's like being Dory the fish. Because, other than Dory, when does anyone ask the same question, to the same person, within moments of receiving an answer?

When they're in the vice-like grip of body dysmorphia. That's when.

Later that evening, once Mini Me is tucked up under her pink unicorn duvet, my Other Half broaches the subject. 'You need to stop asking Tilly how you look, Rach,' he says kindly, offering me his open bag of Revels to ease the blow (I always end up with the coffee ones). 'It will damage her. You have to find a way to stop it.'

My first instinct is to cry, run upstairs and throw a huge tantrum, because I DO NOT WANT – OR NEED – TO BE TOLD THAT I AM POTENTIALLY 'DAMAGING MY DAUGHTER'. I'm a good mum … I'm the best mum I can possibly be … I have spent the past seven years bringing my daughter up to believe that she can do anything! All kinds of things. Take junior parkrun, for example. I have taught her that she can be brave enough to stand on the start line, and try her very best to make it to the finish.

Instead, I sit and squirm on the sofa, forcing myself to stay there and not dart upstairs like a stroppy teenager who's just been grounded. Because I know that he is right. This ghost has come back to haunt me, and I need to exorcise him once and for all – if not for myself, then for my daughter. So, I won't run away from this conversation, I will sit and listen, as hard as that is. You see, I've known this monster has been growing in strength and ferocity since my loss of running, and although it may have been lying dormant for some time, it never really went away.

I've been aware that the condition 'body dysmorphia' exists for a long time now, but there wasn't an epiphany as such. There was no 'A-ha!' moment, no single point in time when everything miraculously made sense to me: when I suddenly saw my self-loathing and perfection-seeking as anything other than just unfortunate 'quirks' in my wiring – just a part of who I am. It took me a long while to join up the dots. I would read magazines and books, and watch TV. Problem pages, talk shows, 'real life stories'. This drip-feed of awareness happened over a long period of time, far longer than I can even recall. Eventually the penny dropped.

I sit on my bed, google searching 'BODY DYSMORPHIA TREATMENT', because I know that I can't deal with this by myself. As I scroll through page after page of information, I focus on one particular search: getting help with BDD.

I read all about the two main treatments offered for the condition: Cognitive Behavioural Therapy (CBT) and/or medication – usually in the form of SSRI antidepressants, which I know so intimately already. In amongst all the information, support and advice I read about online, I come across a website advising of a research study being undertaken by a psychologist at the Karolinska Institutet, Sweden's largest centre of medical academic research. This study is designed to establish the feasibility of successfully treating BDD using Cognitive Behavioural Therapy via an online treatment model. *YES, THIS IS IT! THIS IS WHAT I NEED!* Soon, I find myself fully absorbed in the process of filling out endless extensive psychological evaluation and assessment questionnaires. I'm trying to be as brutally honest as I can possibly be, because I so desperately want to be accepted onto this treatment programme. It feels like I'm being thrown a lifeline.

An hour or so later, I click ' SUBMIT', knowing I've done all I can.

Two days later, I receive an email:

Thank you so much for expressing interest in being a participant in our research study at Karolinska Institutet. We will contact you shortly about scheduling a time for the next stage of the screening process.

YES, YES, YESSS!!!! It feels like I'm inching ever closer to receiving some help. I'm *desperate* to avoid making the return visit to my GP and have him prescribe my old friend Fluoxetine (Prozac) after this long period of abstinence. Of course, if there was absolutely no way of taming this beast without taking Prozac, then sure – I'd consider going back onto medication – but I really want to look at all other options available to me, first.

I do some more research on Cognitive Behavioural Therapy:

'CBT is based on a structured programme of self-help so that a person can learn to change the way they think and act'.

Hmm … I like the sound of that.

'CBT starts with building a good understanding of the problem and what is keeping it going in terms of how your mind works. One way of thinking about BDD is that it is a problem of "not being able to see the wood for the trees" – that you can no longer make an objective assessment of your appearance because you have become so distressed and preoccupied.'

Yep. That's me.

'During therapy, you are likely to learn to re-focus your attention away from yourself and re-engage with activities that will improve your mood and your life.'

YES, I WANT THAT!

'To fight back against BDD, you will be asked to resist comparing your appearance, to stop ruminating, test out your fears without camouflage and to stop rituals such as mirror-checking and excessive grooming.'

Oh shit! That sounds scary. No more asking a million times a day if my hair looks OK? Gulp.

'Many people find it helpful to think of CBT for BDD as training in how to stop being bullied by their BDD and to re-direct themselves into all the other aspects of living that are important to them.'

GOOD! I need to tame this beast once and for all.

'The main side effects of the treatment are the feelings of increased anxiety that occur in the short term. However, challenging one's fears becomes easier, and the anxiety gradually subsides.'

I simply have no option other than to believe that it does.

Some days later, I receive another email from the research programme's Project Manager, Dr G. He invites me to undertake a comprehensive video assessment interview so that he can establish my suitability for the research programme and for the CBT treatment. I have never been formally diagnosed as having body dysmorphia before, having only been treated for bipolar disorder, but ever since I discovered such a condition exists, I knew instantly that I have lived with BDD for a very long time.

It was in the years just before I sought help for my increasingly depressive episodes when body dysmorphia had its strongest hold on me. I was only nineteen years old when BDD eroded my life to the extent that it consisted of me staring into a small, round mirror, propped up on a tatty windowsill in a student bedroom. Of course, I knew then that my mental health was wavering and I was perilously hanging off a cliff over the deepest abyss, but I had no idea of the condition I was suffering from along with my bipolar, depressive states.

Like then, life feels to have fallen into a dark, helpless place. I'm not able to run, and I don't yet have a plan for managing the demons rampaging through my mind. I simply go from day to day in a fog of confusion, desperately wondering when my 'normality' will return. And what's worse is that the small, round mirror which sat and bewitched me on my windowsill in my teens has now magically transformed into a large, fancy Farrow & Ball one which lives above the fireplace in my front room. It has come back to reacquaint itself with me, and I'm completely devastated that it has.

* * *

I've been told to make sure that I'm in a 'quiet, safe space' and to 'allow anything up to two hours' for my chat with the psychologist from the Karolinska Institutet. I've made sure that I will have the house to myself – I've tidied up the attic bedroom and told my Other Half in no uncertain terms that I must not be disturbed between the hours of 1 and 3 p.m. I've washed – and excessively straightened – my hair, and given myself every opportunity to maximise this chance:

the chance to finally get help in dealing with the monster under my skin.

I feel anxious, as though I'm about to put myself in front of a NASA space flight panel selection interview. I'm pacing around the house. I've been to the toilet as many times as I possibly can, and I've walked up and down three flights of stairs at least fifteen times – no doubt against my physio-therapist's advice – to check on my overly-straightened hair before my scheduled video assessment call with the unknown Dr G.

A man's face suddenly appears on my screen: he has dark hair and warm, intelligent eyes. I can feel my heart beating fast in my chest as Dr G introduces himself to me. The first thing I notice is that he looks much younger than I expected, and he has a strong American accent. Today is only an assessment, but I feel distracted. There is a small screen in the corner of my MacBook in which I can see myself.

FUCKING HELL, THIS IS THE WORST POSSIBLE START!

I'm too acutely aware of how I may look to him somewhere in the highfalutin medical research centre over in Sweden.

Surely this is proof enough that I'm consumed by this bastard thing?

I can't even have a Skype video call without being haunted by my own image staring back at me from the corner of a screen. But things move on at a rapid pace. First, Dr G needs to establish whether I suffer from BDD as I claim, and – if I do – then he needs to assess the severity. His questions begin in swift succession.

Q: 'Do you compare aspects of your appearance with others? Please select from the following: not at all; a little; often; a lot; all the time.'

A: 'Yes. A lot.'

Q: 'Do you check your appearance in mirrors and other reflective surfaces? Please select: not at all; a little; often; a lot; all the time.'

A: 'Yes. A lot.'

Q: 'Do you avoid mirrors and other reflective surfaces, or looking at photos and/or videos of yourself? Not at all; a little; often; a lot; all the time.'

I'm becoming confused. The questions seem to contradict each other. Yes, I check in the mirror far too often, but there are also times when I will actively avoid looking at myself in photos or videos for fear of what I may see. I have a mini flashback to some advocacy training I was required to do as part of my legal qualification. I suffered a panic attack over being filmed for the final assessment, and refused to watch the video back, almost failing the module as a result.

The questions continue, I get more confused, and my mind is becoming tired with the rapid-fire interrogation, and the complex questions I am answering over and over again. I'm no longer thinking fully about my answers – I don't have any time to work my way through the confusion. Monosyllabic, instinctive words come out of my mouth in response to Dr G's relentless probing, and I scan desperately around the room to see if I have a glass of water somewhere, because I have a banging headache and my mouth is dry.

'Thanks so much, Rachel. That's the assessment complete.'

I glance at the clock and realise that I've been under the prying, assessing eyes of Dr G for almost exactly two hours, now. It feels like I've been put through a fast-spin cycle in the tumble drier but at least I've stopped focusing on the small square in the corner of the screen with my own face in it, tying myself in knots at my many dubious facial expressions. I no longer have the energy to care – maybe this is all part of the therapy.

We end the call and I'm honestly too tired to even mind whether I get accepted onto the programme or not. And I wonder: *Is this what the therapy will feel like?*

6

THE CACKY-BROWN CYCLING SHORTS

2009

Maggie is standing at our front door. She looks every bit the keen cyclist, dressed head-to-toe in colour-coordinated high-vis Endura cycling gear, along with her Merry Band of Mountain-Biking Women, who are gathered, chatting away, with their fancy bikes flashing like Christmas trees on our driveway. I, meanwhile, am wearing an ancient pair of Chris's oversized cacky-brown cycling shorts, the crotch swinging loosely somewhere around my knees, and a dodgy old Regatta raincoat. His helmet feels (and looks) like a colander on my head.

'OK, Rach, you ready to go?' Maggie asks, before I've even had a chance to explain to her that I DON'T HAVE A BIKE OF MY OWN; I'VE

BORROWED CHRIS'S BIKE ... AND I DON'T KNOW HOW TO RIDE IT. 'Just one thing,' she says before turning to join the rest of her Lycra-clad girly gang. 'Do you have anything hi-vis you can put on? It can get a bit dodgy on the climb up to Stoodley Pike, and you'd be best wearing something bright to make sure you can be seen.'

Chris suddenly dives into a plastic bag which is hanging behind the front door and hands me a couple of snap-on illuminous yellow arm bands. I snap them onto each arm, and then I know with absolute certainty that I now look like a person who has never been on a bike before, and possibly one who will never go on one again. But I don't care about aesthetics, just now. On hearing the words 'Stoodley Pike', everything else stops. You see, I know exactly what that is. It's a famous local monument which dominates the Calder Valley skyline. It also happens to be placed on top of a 1,300-foot mountain, which – it would appear – I'm expected to be cycling up tonight with my newfound group of girlie cycling friends. Worse still, I'm fully aware that the route to the summit of Stoodley Pike is not tarmacked. Not at all. It's a rough, unsurfaced, rocky, lumpy track scattered with boulders, potholes, tree roots and a million other obstacles which I know with absolute certainty

I have NO CHANCE of cycling up/over/around or across ... least of all IN THE FUCKING DARK!

Just as I feel myself about to fill my borrowed oversized cacky-brown cycling shorts, the offensively coordinated Girly Cycling Clique are making a move. Everyone, and every bike, suddenly begins to flash and then move. I quickly hop on board my loaned Specialized man-sized mountain bike, and instinctively start to pedal. I'm immediately aware that my handlebars feel to be so wide that I now have a virtual wingspan.

We haven't cycled further than a few steady 'chatty' miles through the local village and onto a main road before we turn off and into the climb. My heart begins to race, and I feel my eyes widen like a field mouse on sudden alert of a sky filled with circling, impending doom. Do I have special night vision? I wonder. I have never noticed how sharp my vision is before. That said, Chris's centrally-mounted expensive LED light is bright enough to replace all the bulbs in the freezer aisle at Sainsbury's. Oh well, I may be completely out of my depth on this ride, but at least I can see!

With one blessing, however, comes a curse: I can see ... absolutely everything. We are now climbing up an off-road, loose, gnarly track. All the ladies in the Girly Cycling Clique are ahead of me, and they're chatting away up in front. I vaguely tune into some diatribe relating to a recent dinner party which required a change of location for each of the five courses. 'We made pea and goat's cheese risotto for starters,' Kathy chirps from somewhere in the distance, 'but I was disappointed with it, to be honest.' I drift in and out of the conversation as my new Night Vision eyes seem only able to fixate on the largest boulders in my path ahead. When I stare at the most gargantuan obstacle in my way, without fail it guarantees my front wheel then seeks out that very thing. I wrestle my wheel from collision with a large rock, and the bike skids to a halt. My big toe mercifully touches the ground before my knees do, but the Girly Cycling Clique haven't noticed.

'... But how AMAZING was your salmon en croute, Penny?' Kathy shouts across to her friend, who appears to be riding over entirely smooth terrain, and not the endless, wretched obstacle course I'm faced with on every revolution of the wheels. 'You MUST give me the recipe. Me and Pete were totally pissed after that bottle of fizz! God only knows how we even made it across for Maggie's crème brûlée!'

Meanwhile, I'm now off my bike. All I can see ahead of me are lumps, bumps and boulders.

The others are cycling along, still chatting. My arms and shoulders ache from holding them in the permanent wingspan position, and my arse is beginning to feel sore from sitting on Chris's saddle, which is actually a blade. Every time I think about jumping back onto it, I see another boulder or tree root in the near distance, and my confidence nose-dives once more.

And then it goes completely dark: the battery in my Sainsbury's freezer-aisle LED light has died. Chris has (wrongly) assumed that there would be enough charge left in it for a short 'girly' ride, but this isn't one of those. It's a prolonged, off-road, technically challenging night ride with a bunch of women who are completely oblivious to the fact that I'm struggling to ride with them whilst they natter on about how pissed they were for the cheese course of last weekend's Come Dine with Me-inspired supper crawl. Personally, I cannot think of anything worse than trudging from one house to another feeling increasingly nauseous as the risotto churns with salmon, which in turn collides with the crème brûlée and is all washed down with a gallon of Zinfandel and overpriced, fizzy pink stuff, left over from a badly attended Christmas party. Least of all whilst I'm struggling to remain upright on a bike.

'MAGGIE! KRISTIE!' I call out to the illuminous flashing lights bobbing up and down some way ahead of me, and gradually disappearing into the distance. They all come to a sudden stop.

'Rachel? Are you OK? What's going on?' Maggie calls down from her position as leader of the Girly Cycling Clique peloton.

'It's my light. The battery's gone, and I can't see where I'm riding!' I holler back up to her. I hear a few muffled words, and then one of the girls calls down to me: 'Come and ride with me. Stay close, and you can follow my light.'

So that's what I do. I stay close to Kristie – or at least I try to – but once again I seem to attract every bastard tree root and pothole on the track, and Kristie can barely keep moving forwards twenty feet before she must stop and wait for me to wiggle and wobble my way over more loose rocks.

'Try to stop looking at the boulders,' she says, on the fortieth pause she has had to make in the space of five minutes. 'If you focus on the obstacles, then you'll gravitate towards them – that's what's happening!' she continues, beginning to sound a little exasperated that she is the one having to literally guide me up the rocky track on a dark night, with one shared light between us. She has definitely pulled the short straw. 'Trust your bike to roll over the ground, Rach, and look a little way ahead of you, not down to your wheels.'

So I take her advice literally, and it works. I feel slightly more confident looking ahead rather than down, and I'm not so panicked by every single loose rock I now refuse to set my eyes on. But I also feel frustrated and humiliated. Frustrated because I couldn't just hop onto Chris's mountain bike and ride with the Girly Cycling Clique as I'd hoped. I have no idea what made me imagine that I could ride with them without any kind of skill, knowledge or mountain biking experience whatsoever, but I had put that pressure on myself. And I've failed to live up to my own ridiculously high expectations. Worse still, I feel humiliated – like I've been set up to fail. Rightly or wrongly, the Girly Cycling Clique seem to have presumed that I have a level of biking knowledge and ability which I simply don't possess. I have misjudged everything about the ride, and I arrive home in a state of semi-shock that I've just experienced the Bike Ride from Hell, with a group of other women who seemed to find it a doddle.

'Bloody hell, Rach!' Chris says, standing in the porch with the front door wide open as I finally return home. 'You look – erm – are you OK?'

It's nearing 10 p.m. on a cold, dark Wednesday night in mid-November. And I'm not OK.

'The lights failed,' I whimper back, but I simply can't go into any further detail about the horror I've just experienced. 'The batteries died.'

'Oh God! I had no idea you'd be out for that long. I wondered what had happened to you. Where the hell did you go?' He looks genuinely concerned.

'No matter. I'm back now,' I say, trudging up the stairs to bed. 'I won't be needing to borrow your bike again, either.'

My final thoughts before falling into the deepest sleep: I fucking hate cycling, and I will never cycle again.

I'm too tired to notice or care that I'm still wearing Chris's cacky-brown cycling shorts.

7

DENIAL

Desperate for some inspiration, I've been fixated on reading world champion obstacle racer Amelia Boone's recent blogs about her recovery from no less than TWO fractures to her femur (the thigh bone, and the strongest bone in the body) whilst at the very peak of her elite obstacle racing career. For the unenlightened, 'Tough Mudders' are ten- to twelve-mile muddy obstacle course races, where participants overcome various unpleasantries such as submerging themselves into pools of icy water, climbing up fifteen-foot rope ladders, jumping into clay pits and scrambling up impossibly muddy banking on the other side.

In my own mini, pathetic soap opera of a personal disaster, it's helping me to know that someone like Amelia has been hit a hundred times harder, has fallen from a far greater height, and has somehow managed to pick up the pieces from a broken heart of shattered racing dreams.

HALLELUJAH! It is possible!

And here I am, with a niggle to my left calf from which I am – at times – seemingly inconsolable. What does that say about my so-called 'inner strength', my ability to handle even mild adversity, and the state of my already question-able mental health? I feel mentally weak right now, but I'm encouraged by her story and so I focus on the possibility that I can come back from this sad place.

My BIG goal for today is to run: I will try to run two measly, painfully slow miles. Just like a heat-seeking missile, that is my only aim.

Once Mini Me and her last few remaining chicken pox scabs are collected from school, I plan to drive down to Copley village. I will park next to the canal and, surreptitiously, get changed under a winter coat whilst squirming around in the driver's seat, trying hard not to sit on and therefore release the handbrake. I will then head off running – one mile out along the canal – and then one mile back to the car. Even writing it down sounds so ridiculously easy.

I park up and a few well-timed contortions later, I'm changed and ready to run. My nerves are building as I ask myself, '*Am I ready for this? Is my leg ready to run yet?*'

Sadly, I already know the answer, but denial is a cruel and powerful thing.

Ignoring everything happening around me, I set off running. But every step is laboured, and the pain in my left calf is now precisely that – there is no confusion with tightness.

'Are you all right, love?' a kindly dog-walker asks as I hobble along the canal, tears streaming down my face.

'Yes, thank you,' I manage to squeak in response before arriving back to the safety of my car, where I sit at the steering wheel and sob uncontrollably because I know for certain that this isn't just about the running, it's about so much more than that. This is about my ability to manage the Bastard Chimp who is now rampaging through my mind, and is actively setting out to destroy all the progress I have made over the last seven Prozac-free years. In fact, this is now making me question whether I've progressed at all.

'I think my running is over!' I send my Other Half a WhatsApp message as I sit, devastated, at the wheel of my car, which is strewn with clothing, and feels to be a messy, chaotic mirror of my flailing mind.

'Don't be silly, Rach. You're catastrophising! Your leg just needs more time to recover, you know that,' his message back to me reads.

I appreciate that he's being as rational as he possibly can be without being offensive, because I know that in my current highly distressed state, I'm very easy to offend. I also realise that I'm being melodramatic, extremely emotional, and I'm lacking any sense of logical reasoning whatsoever. But in this moment, that's precisely how I feel: I've lost a part of myself, and I can't even imagine getting it back.

Later that evening, my Other Half decides to give me his Valentine's Day gift. He desperately wants to cheer me up following my earlier disappointment down by the canal. I know that he's planned something special, and he waits to give me his gift when I'm not otherwise occupied reading bedtime stories to a scabby young child. Still fragile and fatigued from today's emotional roller coaster, I have absolutely no idea what is coming.

I sit down on the sofa and he grins, handing me a large brown envelope. Inside it is – predictably – an enormous Valentine's Day card. I look at the card, and I feel my tears welling up, because it's plastered with our gormless running selfies from recent years.

'This photograph was taken at that hilly half-marathon race in Wales …' I splutter. 'And do you remember this one? Running along the seafront in Barcelona.' Suddenly, I feel a wave of fury as his special Valentine's Day card taunts me that I can't do the very thing that I – and we – love to do the most. RUNNING. RUNNING IS HAUNTING ME!

Fucking hell, pull yourself together, Rachel.

'It's beautiful, thank you,' I manage through my heartbreak.

Behind the card is another, smaller envelope. I open it and unfold a typed letter, which I read out loud: an hour's consultation with an international elite athlete, who – the booking confirmation says – 'can advise me of any tweaks in my training for the upcoming London Marathon …'

Training? I can't train! I can't even run, not a single mile!

I sob again as running seems to have usurped the sweetest and most thoughtful Valentine's gift and kiboshed it PRECISELY at the time when I least of all need another emotional kicking.

My head's just about to explode when I find a smidgen of inner strength: *Fuck it! I'm not going to let this bloody injury rob me of this. NO WAY! I can speak to this professional sportswoman about some of the times when she's perhaps struggled with injuries. And she's an elite athlete, so what the hell must THAT pressure be like?*

Almost instantly, my tears dry up and I begin to feel mildly excited. That aside, today is also the day that I threw my running trainers in the bin in a fit of rage after the canal meltdown. My Other Half took them out again, but I've got a serious grudge with them, so they quickly went back in and were subsequently buried under a large quantity of cold baked beans.

* * *

I feel slightly less burdened – maybe all the melodrama of yesterday has wiped the emotional slate clean? I'm having difficulty coming to terms with my *new normal*: my mind is struggling to adapt whilst my body takes some convincing that it will ever want to run again. This is what my *new normal* looks like:

- 6:45 a.m. – I complete my first set of physio rehab exercises on our bedroom floor in the semi-darkness. *I notice all the bits of fluff and long blonde hairs on my bedroom carpet, and I now have a perfect view of the various minuscule life forms under our bed. I desperately need to vacuum down here* ... CHECK!
- 8:30 a.m. – We battle through the usual chaotic paraphernalia of our morning school routine, orchestrating one small person into clean pants and a thermal vest. *JESUS, HOW HARD CAN IT BE? THERE IS ONLY ONE OF HER, FFS!* CHECK!
- 8.45 a.m. – I drop one small person at school ... and spend twenty minutes completing and signing some legal waiver

forms so that she can be given 5ml of Piriton to prevent her having to wear a scratch-averting collar like dogs do when they come out of the vets. CHECK!

- 9:15 a.m. – I arrive at work and have already downed copious amounts of coffee before 9:18 a.m. ... CHECK!
- 12:05 p.m. – I complete my first set of questionable physio rehabilitation exercises on the disgusting mats in the gym at work ... *eugh!* CHECK!
- 12:08 p.m. – I briefly pause to wonder if my physio rehab exercises should have taken me longer than three minutes, but even that felt like an hour. MOVE ON, CHECK!
- 12:09 p.m. I begin my *upright** bike pyramid cardio session. My training consists of a ten-minute easy warm-up, followed by one-, two-, three- and four-minute sets of hard effort, with a minute's recovery (easy pace) in between sets. It's a tough workout, and I can smell the evidence of my effort on myself by the end of the session ... CHECK!
- 1:04 p.m. – I'm back at my desk, having quickly sprayed my armpits and got changed in the thirty-five seconds I have between hopping off the *upright* bike and needing to respond to my pending emails. *Phew!* CHECK!
- THE REST OF THE AFTERNOON – I'm feeling reasonably happy with my efforts on the *upright* bike, and I treat

---

* This may not seem like a big deal to you, but up to now I have only used the recumbent gym bike, so this is exciting news in my world (although both are about as much fun as licking the inside of a bus window!).

myself to a bag of chocolate peanuts kindly donated by a bemused colleague as I burst back in through the office door, still panting. CHECK!

BUT ... But today, I *think* my left leg feels a tiny bit better. I'm *sure* it's not as painful as it has been, and I'm now able to walk and move more freely on it. Granted, I haven't had any more delusions of running pain-free along the canal, but I'm *convinced* that it's beginning to turn the corner, and it feels less acutely painful than it has done for the past couple of weeks. *Jesus! Has it only been a few weeks? It seems like an eternity.*

Does this mean that I may be heading in the right direction? Maybe not all is lost ...

* * *

I feel so buoyed that I decide to go for another test run, knowing my left leg isn't ready for running yet, but denial is – still – a strange and wonderful thing, and I seem to be stuck in this particular phase of the Kubler-Ross Change Curve. That is, my innate ability to convince myself of an untruth is frightening.

I set off running from work, and it all feels wrong. *Wrong, wrong, wrong!* I limp along, pushing through the discomfort and I MAKE myself run, once again. I FORCE myself to keep going, even though every ounce of me knows that I'm in the wrong.

Everything around me feels to be spinning, and I can't stop the panic rising in my chest.

I arrive back at my desk, and I feel empty – like the bottom has just fallen out of my world. *HOW CAN I BE ALL RIGHT WITHOUT RUNNING?* I'm too afraid of the answer. The expression on my face tells my colleagues all they needed to know: this hasn't gone well. One of them tries making polite conversation with me. He attempts to crack a joke, but my usual jovial response is entirely absent. It has gone. He and another chatty workmate try again, but my head won't let me join in. Nothing feels light-hearted. I don't want to communicate. Not to anyone. Not at all.

* * *

I sit outside the physiotherapy practice in my car, watching the clock until a reasonable time appears on the dashboard: arriving fifteen minutes too early for a half-hour appointment is just about acceptable, thirty minutes too early is not. *Tick, tock, tick, tock.* Eventually, I head inside. One of Magician Dave's younger trainees politely asks me how I am, and I respond with my honest, if heavy answer: 'Not good.'

'Well, if anyone can sort you out, then Dave can!' he assures me, brightly.

I sincerely hope he's right.

Inside the treatment room, Dave puts me through the usual mobility tests: 'Can you bend this way, and that? Can you reach across, in front, high above and down below?' The answer is always 'Yes.' And then, as I lay face down like a flattened kipper on the physio couch, Magician Dave perches on the corner of the table in front of me.

'I think a lot of this is a stress response, Rach.' I prop my chin up on my hands and listen as he gives me his prognosis. 'I honestly think that this is your body responding to intense, prolonged stress. It's how you deal with it mentally that's going to be the key to unlocking all this.'

I know that he's right: I *have* been ridiculously stressed, as if permanently on high alert for impending doom. It's been stealthily creeping up on me for a long time, with self-imposed pressure to live up to a version of myself that I can't honestly achieve, let alone maintain. And running was becoming a bigger and bigger part of that, with a diary full of races, an iPhone addiction to Strava (a social fitness app commonly used by runners, which tracks running and cycling via GPS and can be used to connect – and compare – routes, distances, courses, races and times with others), where I would monitor my weekly/daily/hourly mileage next to *A N Other* runner. And I realise in this moment that running has slowly warped into something it was never meant to be for me: a big old shitty stick with which to beat myself. 'The Power of Yet' has morphed into 'The Curse of Enough'.

I'm heartbroken.

And now, my body has had enough. It doesn't want to be beaten up any more. It's done with the self-flagellation and the unnecessary pressure. 'Enjoy the journey,' I've heard wiser people say, and I'm beginning to understand what that means. Or, more honestly, I'm identifying with how it feels to simply *NOT* enjoy the journey at all.

I sit with my elbows propped up on the physio-turned-psychotherapist's couch, listening to wise old Magician Dave, and every ounce of my being knows that he's spot on. He advises me to treat the single, most important – and most-vulnerable – part of myself: my head.

I leave my appointment feeling a kind of relief that this inexplicable inability to run has been identified as being a stress-related physical response, and although I go through waves of frustration that a straightforward 'strain' or 'tear' would be so much easier to handle, I've essentially been given the all clear to treat the one crucial factor here: my mental state, and learning how to handle my fears.

Maybe it's the biggest breakthrough in all of this.

But then, I'm stuck on the Kubler-Ross Change Curve.

Later that day, I head off for another predictably doomed 'test run'. *How many more of these am I going to torture myself with?* It's only a matter of hours since I sat and listened to Magician Dave inform me that my head is the key to all of this. But something hasn't sunk in yet.

DENY ... DENY ... DENY ...

My leg hurts; it screams. It feels like I've deliberately gone and slapped myself in the face with another futile attempt to run when it's the last thing my body – or my mind – wants to do.

And what the hell is wrong with me? It was only this morning when Magician Dave told me what the problem is.

Why can't my head process the fact that my body doesn't want to run?

My mental health is wavering, and I simply don't know how to be OK without my regular running fix. That's the truth, although I won't admit it. Not yet.

* * *

It is the day of my Valentine's treat, but yet another abandoned run later with my Other Half and I'm in tears.

DENY … DENY … DENY …

'Maybe I need to go back on Prozac,' I blurt out, as I wonder desperately how my mind can cope with my body's refusal to run. 'I don't know if I can be OK with all the chaos running riot in my mind without being able to run,' I plead, almost confirming my conclusion that this is surely the most obvious step towards me finding a mentally safe place again.

So, I do what I hoped I wouldn't have to: I book an appointment with my doctor, but am told that the next available appointment is in a month's time.

NOOOOOO! I CAN'T WAIT THAT LONG!

'It's just that – well – I'm in a bit of a bad place,' I say to the receptionist, gulping hard as tears stream down my face, 'and I really need to see the doctor.' Already I can hear my voice crumbling as I sit opposite him in his treatment room, declaring, 'I'm not fixed, Dr Taylor (sob). I honestly thought that I was (sob), but quite clearly, I'm not.'

I'm hurtling towards a mental health black hole. I'm really, seriously struggling to cope.

Back in the car, I sit quietly in the passenger seat as my OH focuses on getting me to my Valentine's Day 'treat'.

'Are you nervous?' he asks, no doubt misinterpreting my silence for apprehension.

'No, not at all,' I reply, flatly. That's how I feel. Flat. Lacking in any emotion. I'm not excited, or nervous, or pondering over what I'll say, or what she will ask – I simply feel nothing.

I'm a nauseating cocktail of anxious, sad, confused and vulnerable as I sit down on the couch opposite the athlete. I try to calm down and appear 'normal', but I know it's not working. Instead, I sound like Spud from *Trainspotting*, only I haven't taken any speed.

Running Guru seems rather nonchalant and gives the impression of being a steely-eyed, no-nonsense elite training machine, although I wonder if that's just a reflection of my current dark mood. Regardless, I try hard to sound chirpier and more positive than I feel, and to counter any 'negative vibes' I may be emitting in her general direction.

She speaks matter-of-factly about possible training sessions whilst I'm unable to run, but her heart isn't in it. She doesn't know that I could literally burst into tears at any given moment, or that I feel dead inside. Finally, our torturous hour is up and, in fairness, she's done her job. I've taken the following from our exchange:

- It is quite possible to have a 'Training Plan B' for when it's unfeasible for me to run. THIS IS A VERY GOOD THING. I decide to take this as an opportunity to try out new activities, and to train in a new way. But it sounds so fucking logical and sensible, and I know that I'm neither of those things;
- She suggests that I try aqua jogging. WTAF?! I never imagined in my wildest dreams that I might be sitting here contemplating buying a buoyancy belt and underwater trainers with a view to jogging on the spot in the deep end of Sowerby Bridge swimming pool, but it's happening;

- That there is a practical, non-emotive way around my current predicament. Maybe the fact that she was so poker-faced about it all was good for me. Perhaps she inadvertently pulled me back from needing a virtual teary cuddle to thinking more practically about what I can do in my current circumstances.

8

HELP ARRIVES

I feel like I'm no longer an active or relevant part of the community who are likely to understand me the most. I'm standing on the sidelines of the running community, looking in on a world of marathon training progression, post-race selfies, mini 'yay!' moments and personal victories.

That used to be me.

I feel isolated, and like I've lost a part of my identity: possibly the biggest part. But strangely enough, it is here – on the Internet – where I'm also looking for answers.

I scroll through Twitter and actively ignore any hashtag relating to the 2017 Virgin London Marathon, choosing not to torture myself. Instead, I'm interested in the 'other' stories. I want to hear about recovery from this place, and I want to know that it is possible. My legal training kicks in, and suddenly I'm on a mission to gather evidence that I can – *that I will* – make my way back from here. It simply *must* be possible.

Then I see it: an email about the BDD study I applied to take part in just a few days ago.

I am emailing to inform you that, having discussed your case at some length with the team, we have decided to accept you onto the BDD therapy study.

I am completely stunned. I have absolutely no idea what just happened, or what lies ahead. But this is big news. It is big news for two reasons: first, it means that I have now – finally – been diagnosed with suffering from body dysmorphia. Possibly twenty years too late, but the confirmation comes as a relief of sorts. I'm given the results from my BDD video assessment and I'm told by Dr G that I have a score of 24 on what he describes as 'the Y-Box scale' but, when I Google-search it later, is actually called the 'Y-BOCS scale'. This, he says, is the gold standard for diagnosing and assessing the severity of body dysmorphia. The scale ranges from 0 (i.e. zero evidence of BDD) through to the most severe cases, which come out with a whopping 40. My score of 24 is categorised within the 'moderate-to-severe' range. I'm only grateful to not be blighted with a higher score than this: the horror of living with a significantly worse form of this exhausting and damaging mental health illness is difficult to imagine. But at least I know, now, that I *haven't* imagined all this, it *wasn't* some fanciful, cut-and-paste label I conveniently adopted to stick onto my insecurities: *BDD is real, it exists and I'm done with suffering from it. My self-diagnosis has been verified.*

Second, this is big news because it means that I now have the best opportunity I've ever had to receive treatment and finally get some help with taming this beast. This will be my first experience of undergoing Cognitive Behavioural Therapy (CBT) and I'm excited by the prospect that I *may* be able to deal with my mental health difficulties *without* the need for medication – or running.

* * *

It's the start of a brand-new week, and my twelve-week online BDD therapy programme begins.

I've a call scheduled with Dr G, during which he will talk me through the 'online platform' and how I will work through the various sections by myself over the coming months. I'm relieved that I won't have regular video calls (because they are both exhausting and intense) although I understand that we will need to have intermittent reviews throughout the course of the programme, which I can just about cope with.

I'm once again ready for my video chat with Dr G. Just like before, I'm immediately put off by the sight of my own seemingly contorted face bobbing about in a small square on my MacBook screen.

FFS! How shiny is my chin?!

I am momentarily horrified, but for now, there are more pressing matters.

Dr G talks me through the eight modules that form the therapy programme.

'… And to the right, you'll find the worksheets for all the modules, together with your BDD diary,' he continues. 'These will be the basis of your practical tasks, and it is very important that you fill these out on a WEEKLY BASIS – sometimes, daily.'

Practical tasks? Worksheets? A BDD diary? And, finally, homework assignments? I can feel my sixteen-year-old petulant self re-emerge after years of lying dormant, happily undisturbed. *Shit! I will be accountable to someone!* My mind races, grappling with the reality of undergoing this treatment: *Dr G will be monitoring my progress. He will know my most embarrassing, awkward BDD thoughts, and I will have to face talking to him on my MacBook Pro with that knowledge!* I feel a tiny shudder of anxiety rumble across my body and I now have goosebumps on my arms. But what did I expect? Did I really think that this would be a 'read-only' exercise and that I could once again get away with being invisible?

I will be required to complete and submit weekly assessment questionnaires and, as I click through, I immediately recognise some of them from my initial video assessment with Dr G.

Oh no! Not these again!

'Please tick the box that best describes the way you have felt about a specific feature of your appearance over the past week, INCLUDING TODAY.'

Fucking hell!

'Do I compare aspects of myself … do I mirror-check … do I brood over past events … do I avoid certain situations … do I try to camouflage my flaw(s) … do I avoid reflective surfaces … do I attempt to hide certain parts of myself … do I question others about my appearance …'

I'm beginning to think twelve weeks sounds like a very long time.

9

PLAN B: AQUA JOGGING

Today has got TRAINING PLAN B, REHAB and RECOVERY written all over it. I have some brief respite from Mummy Duties within school hours – *woo hoo!* And so, following the advice of Running Guru, I have the following scheduled:

11–12 p.m. Yoga class
1–2 p.m. Physiotherapy session
4 p.m. My first ever attempt at … aqua jogging.

Remembering her definitive prescription for a 'TRAINING PLAN B', I have since put in place those things which – I'm told – should help me steer myself in the right direction over the coming weeks and – sob – possibly even months.

I could never conceivably go from running fifty miles per week to becoming a Pringle-eating couch potato – although my Bastard Chimp would have *loved* that as proof, if proof were needed, that I would one day return to my Mars bar-melting, sad, sedentary self. He would be *ecstatic* to finally be proved right – that all this running nonsense was never really 'me'. He's told me so many times: I would do well to remember who I am. But I won't give him the opportunity.

Running Guru also helpfully sent over some training suggestions, too:

Aqua run sessions

Aqua run pool: 10–12 min easy, 8 x 15 sec on/off, 3–4 min rest, 5 x 30 sec on/off, 3–4 min rest, 2 x 45 sec max w/2–3 min rest, 8 x 15 sec on/off

Aqua run pool: 10 x 45 sec on/15 off (tempo), 3 min rest, 8 x 30 sec on/30 off (VO2 max), 3 min rest, 2 x 20 sec anaerobic w/1:40 rest

Aqua run pool: 10 min warm-up 8 x 15 sec hard/ 15 sec rest, 3 min rest, 2 x (6 x 1 min hard/30 sec rest), 3 min between sets (VO2 max), 10 min warm-down

Static gym bike sessions

All below should include 10-minute warm-up & 10-minute cool-down *(does she not realise that I only have an hour for lunch?!)*

Bike: 4 x 30 sec sprint w/30 sec rest, 2 min rest,
3 x (3 x 4 min w/1 min rest), 3 min after set,
15 min warm-down

Bike tempo:
2 x 15 min tempo w/5 min recovery in between
(recovery should be about 20% slower than tempo effort)
Keep heart rate steady until last 3 min of each tempo,
then increase

Bike: 8 x 30 sec on/30 sec off, 2–3 min rest,
8 x 3 min VO2 effort w/45 sec rest, 5–6 min rest,
1 x 4 min max effort

After translating and fully digesting the content of Running Guru's suggestions, I think that I finally have something resembling a 'Training Plan B'. My head feels much happier with this as a concept, considering the enormous abyss which has been created from the loss of my beloved running. Just knowing there are things I can do – realising there are *many proactive steps I can take* to make sure that I stay as physically and mentally strong as I possibly can throughout this period – is helping me to manage the rising panic I feel on an almost hourly basis. Yes, it means I will have to plan ahead, and to think very differently about my training going forward, but that's a very small price to pay for my physical and mental health.

I've also started going back to my old yoga class, which I haven't really bothered with for years. And I don't know why I'm so surprised, but my regular Thursday morning class is proving to be unbelievably therapeutic. I chat to my lovely fellow yogi friend, Pam, who can see that a little piece of me is missing. It makes me feel ever so slightly less insular and self-absorbed, as earlier this morning it was a struggle to make myself get out of bed and to leave the house – I just wanted to crawl back under the covers and hide. I'm so pleased I didn't do that.

I'm going down to the local swimming pool shortly to try my hand at this 'zero impact' activity of aqua jogging for the first time. Part of me feels kind of pleased/mildly smug for being prepared to give it a go. I don't do swimming; I'm not a water baby. I find absolutely no joy in getting cold after ten minutes and lugging around carrier bags full of sodden towels, only to find them growing fungus in the boot of the car three weeks later. One of the reasons I love running is the simplicity – the lack of fuss. If you've got a pair of trainers, some shorts and a T-shirt to hand, then you can run. You can set off from EXACTLY where you are. Swimming? Not quite so straightforward. *When is the pool open? When is it 'Fun Time with Inflatables' madness for the kids? What about the serious, semi-pro lane swimmers? When should I avoid their wrath?*

I feel self-conscious and weird wearing my new aqua trainers (yes, these do exist), fearing the pool attendant will blow a whistle at me whilst I blatantly walk towards the water in footwear. I wonder if he knows these are AQUA

JOGGING, NON-SLIP SHOES? At the poolside, I wrap my enormous blue buoyancy belt around my waist and fasten it tight like a tourniquet on a severed limb, and I slip myself and all my clobber into the pool. I immediately try out a vaguely recognisable running action. My feet are still touching the floor as I 'jog' in what can only be described as a sub-aqua moonwalk (all I need to perfect this move is a single diamante glove). I soon get into my stride, and build up enough confidence to move up into the deep end.

Two young girls are splashing each other and laughing in the pool. They are about Tilly's age, perhaps a year or so older. One of them looks across at me, and smiles awkwardly. *Maybe she thinks I can't swim?* She glances back to her friend and they both giggle with embarrassment. When I try to 'jog' faster, I go absolutely nowhere in the water. I consider that I should perhaps be embarrassed at the thought that (a) I look utterly ridiculous; and (b) the young girls may think that I can't swim. But I honestly don't care what I look like. I give myself credit for being here, and for trying something new. I feel brave, and my body feels good for experiencing a surge of endorphins. Surely this is a mini-breakthrough moment for me: I can feel my heart beating hard in my chest, and I'm wrestling back control from the Bastard Chimp, who would have me hiding under the duvet, eating my body weight in Pringles. And that's all I'm bothered about. Both girls smile back. This feels like progress, because although I don't particularly take to the whole 'fake-running-in-the-shallow-end-of-the-pool' aqua-jogging vibe, it reminds me that it *is* possible for me to feel the joy of movement, of training and exercising in ways other than running. I doubt very much that this will become a regular thing for me, but right here, right now? I'll take it as a small step towards a happier place.

I finish my aqua jogging session and haul myself and all my sodden paraphernalia out of the pool. As I reflect on the high intensity/recovery intervals, I feel reasonably smug and smirk at my Bastard Chimp, who is now sulking in a corner. That's just before wringing out my 'Mr Happy' beach towel and deciding how best to manoeuvre my enormous, dripping buoyancy aid, wet trainers (or 'aqua shoes'), plus a travel bag full of other swimming essentials half a mile back to the car without wearing any pants and socks, which I dropped on the changing room floor into what – I hope – was water.

It's all helping me to be in a more peaceful place, without any way of knowing how long my running safety blanket will be absent. I'm doing everything I can to stay strong, and putting all these things in place is giving me back a sense of control over the helplessness I otherwise feel.

I may be turning a corner with this.

10

AND RELAX

'I honestly don't think I'm missing running very much,' I say to the pretty, curly-haired lady, who is sitting next to me on the windowsill, waiting for the yoga class. I say the words, but I know they are not the truth. 'Who needs running, anyway?' I fake laugh, not sounding even vaguely convincing.

'Yeah! I'm trying to mix my training up a bit more,' she replies, smiling. As she is talking, I wonder what her training consisted of, before. Did she – like me – have an addiction to Strava and a tireless compulsion for another endorphin 'fix' like some junkie waiting for his next hit? Was running almost permanently on her mind, with a diary full of races and grand plans to kick ass at this year's London Marathon? Did she wake up at nights pondering her last training run, going through the mile splits in her head, wondering how to make marginal improvements? Is she trying to avoid a fast-track-back-to-Prozac, like me?

Regardless, I feel happy that I'm in a more sociable mood this morning. *What has lifted my spirits? Would I feel like this if I'd been forcing myself to run, today?* I can't help but think not: I would most probably be feeling dejected, miserable and burdensome with running-related woes. Instead, I feel free and – well – kind of happy! And I don't know why that comes as such a surprise to me.

Another one of Lianne's regular ladies turns up and joins in our pre-class banter. She's a self-confessed fitness addict, and I know that she *completely* understands what running is to me.

'Did I hear somewhere that you're running a marathon in Tanzania?' she asks out of the blue. It takes me back a little.

I go on to tell her about my plans to take part in the very first Tanzanian marathon later in the year. That's if I'm even ABLE to run, by then,' I say, gulping hard as I struggle to comprehend my own statement.

During the yoga class, I feel strong. I *know* I feel strong. My body works hard, holding the various yoga poses. It straightens itself up and lengthens otherwise tight, shortened muscles whilst simultaneously challenging the limp, unused ones (mostly in my upper body, I discover). I'm getting used to the effort of controlled, focused breathing. I feel myself filling up with strength as I breathe in deeply, and I sigh with relief when I breathe back out again. Prior to this, when was the last time I gave any thought to my posture, my spindly arms or my core strength? I can see the makings of some muscle definition. Really, since *when* do I even HAVE any muscles in my arms? But I do, now. In some ways, I'm beginning to feel stronger than I was before. And I love the feeling.

The relaxation at the end of the yoga class comes like an ice-cold beer on a hot summer's day. It's soothing and peaceful, and it convinces me – if I needed it – that this yoga class is sent to touch the parts of my mental wellbeing that my myriad self-help books simply can't reach. I'm so thankful to be here – it feels like a gift.

'Thanks, Lianne,' I say, once I'm out of my relaxed, Zen-like state. I never leave the class without thanking her, but I'm not sure she understands quite how grateful I am.

11

THE BDD DIARY

I'm having to keep a diary of my body dysmorphic disorder (BDD) experiences. This makes me laugh out loud when, on Day 1, I already have enough examples to completely fill it ... by noon.

I'm asked to describe 'the situation', i.e. when and where I am when a BDD thought is triggered; 'my thoughts at the time' – I'm told that these should be specifically documented in the form of an *'if ... then'* statement; and, finally, 'what I did to reduce my discomfort, or avoid the situation' (otherwise known as 'safety behaviours' and – quite simply – 'avoidance'. These are terms I will come to know well). The very first morning of my BDD diary looks like this:

SITUATION 1: In bed, 6:45 a.m. Woken up after a disturbed night's sleep, and I'm worrying about having bags/dark circles under my (probably bloodshot) tired-looking eyes.

THOUGHTS: If I have bloodshot eyes and big dark bags/circles under my eyes, then I will look ugly and I will KNOW that I look ugly, which will make it hard for me to leave the house and look at people today, and especially difficult to face the school mums in the playground at drop-off, or go to work. And I have two meetings at work, so it's likely to affect those negatively. ACTIONS: I pick up the small mirror/make-up bag on my bedside table (it's still 6: 45 a.m.), and – turning the offensively big light on – I put concealer under my eyes to try and disguise the bags underneath them. I'm aware that I haven't even washed my face yet, and I still have sleep in my eyes (plus, they are barely open), but regardless, I can still practise putting on my concealer for later, to see if it will work.

I ask my Other Half if he can take Tilly to school on his way to work, making up some feeble excuse about having to make an important phone call for work, but really, it's just because I don't want to face the school mums and I don't want them to see me looking ugly, today. He says that he can do, so that's good, and I feel slightly better.

I look in my work diary and consider re-scheduling one of the meetings I have booked in for this afternoon. I wonder what will happen if I turn up to the meeting looking – and feeling – like this? Will I flunk everything and forget what I'm supposed to be talking about, too worried about how shit I look? One of the meetings I simply can't avoid, so I'll just have to get through that one as best I can (I'll sit quietly in the corner and just breathe, counting down the seconds until it's over) but the other one I could possibly move to another day?

I ask my Other Half if I look tired, and if he can see the big, dark circles under my eyes. He says no, he can't, but I think he's lying just to be kind to me, so I ask him again. I keep asking him until I think he's telling me the truth, but he doesn't: he just walks out of the bedroom, instead.

SITUATION 2: Arriving at work, 9:25 a.m.
THOUGHTS: I feel a huge wave of anxiety wash over me as I pull into the car park. I don't want to get out of my car, but I know that I must. I plan what I will do when I get into work: I will go straight to the toilets, where I can check on my eye bags/bad hair situation and assess the damage. Only then will I feel able to go to my desk and carry on with my day.
ACTIONS: I go straight to the toilets, as planned, and spend ten minutes looking at the dark circles

under my eyes and putting my hair in different styles to try and make myself look a bit better. I wish I could stay there for longer, but I may get into trouble for being late for work.

SITUATION 3: Getting to my desk at work, 9:40 a.m. (ish)

THOUGHTS: I've successfully managed to avoid speaking to anybody, or being seen, and I feel relieved about that. I'm still feeling agitated and like I want to go back to the mirror in the downstairs toilet so that I can assess for damage and be on guard for ugliness, but I will have to wait a little while longer before I do. The feeling is like a compulsion – I'm being pulled back by the mirror, because I need to know how bad I look. That thought whirls around in my head, and I struggle to switch it off.

ACTIONS: I look at the clock, and tell myself that in ten minutes' time I can go back down to the mirror in the toilets. I feel relieved that I don't have to wait very long, and I start counting down the seconds until I can leave my desk and go back down to the mirror – I don't know why I feel safer there.

I email the woman who I am supposed to be meeting with this afternoon. I say that I am very sorry, but I'm having to leave work early today because my daughter isn't feeling very well, and I will have to pick her up early from school. I feel bad for doing this, but I don't see that there is any other option. I also feel relieved that I've managed to avoid the stress of this meeting.

Ten minutes later, I go down to the toilets, and I repeat the mirror-checking and hairstyle-changing. I think it's ten minutes or so later when I return to my desk, but it may be slightly longer than that. A colleague asks me if I'm all right as I'm walking out of the toilet, and I say 'Yes, thanks,' but blush with embarrassment and hurry back to my desk.

SITUATION 4: Attending a meeting at work, 10:30 a.m.

THOUGHTS: I'm sitting in a semi-circle of chairs with five colleagues, one of whom is my boss. We are having a 'weekly update' managers' meeting, and take it in turns to tell everyone about the headlines/latest developments from the past week, and to update each other on our progress since the last meeting. I am panicking because I feel tired and ugly, and I think that I LOOK tired and ugly. I wonder if my colleagues are looking at me, thinking, 'What's wrong with Rachel today? She looks tired and ugly.'

My colleague is talking, talking, talking. I can barely concentrate on what he is saying – partly because his voice is so monotone, and he is updating us on seemingly everything, including what he had for breakfast. I honestly don't care. But mostly, I'm not concentrating because I'm trying to quell the panic I feel rising in my chest, and the sound of my incessant, rampaging Bastard Chimp as he taunts me that I 'look tired and ugly ... tired and ugly ... tired and ugly ...' I simply don't know how to silence him; I don't know how to stop listening to him as his chants become louder and louder.

ACTIONS: I decide to select only the essential updates for my colleagues, thereby minimising the time I am under the spotlight. There are a few things I know I probably should tell them about, but I reason these can wait until I produce my written monthly management report. Besides, I'd rather not drone on like my monotone colleague. Unfortunately, I haven't really been listening to him, and so I have absolutely no idea what any of his weekly headlines are, or what he had for lunch on Friday. My chimp was shouting too loudly in my ear.

It's now noon, and I have already filled in four pages of my online BDD diary. I read over the extracts before sending them across to Dr G, and I realise how much of my morning was consumed – yes, it was *consumed* – by this wretched thing. Granted, it was a particularly challenging morning, I tell myself. It was infinitely worse than normal because of a broken night's sleep, but still, it is difficult to read back my own words describing all the ways in which these crippling BDD thoughts have impacted on my day.

As I read the words I have written, I can place myself back in those exact situations, feeling the same thoughts as though I were standing in front of the living-room mirror, or sitting in the painful meeting at work. It affects me, deeply.

I feel so sad.

12

REST

Rest. That word … I can't – and I won't – rest. *I HATE IT.*
I have an aversion to the word itself which would rival most
nut allergies on the planet: my head feels woozy and begins to
throb, I start to sweat and my heart rate increases at the mere
thought of doing … nothing. I just can't do it, I've tried.*

With this in mind, I've been conducting a little experiment.

I want to find out how much 'rest' I really give myself.
How much 'recovery time' do my legs honestly get? I've
been upping my cross-training activities, including walking
(sounds innocent enough), aqua jogging (OK, I went once),
yoga classes and sessions on the static bike (a necessary evil).
So, this should *surely* be the recipe for a miraculous recovery,
resulting in me having legs so fresh that I could skip over stiles
with the effort of the nimblest spring lamb.

Has that happened? No, it hasn't.

Why?

---

* I'm also convinced my tongue swells up, but it turns out that's just when
my coffee is too hot.

This, dear readers, is what my experiment has been designed to try and find out.

THE ANSWER? *BECAUSE I CAN'T SIT DOWN.*

I bought a Fitbit Alta HR and I wore it for one week. Here's what a NON-Rest diary looks like for me:

MONDAY

I speed walk up to the supermarket from work in my lunch hour to pick up two variety packs of Magnum ice creams for my boss. It's a hot day, and so I also pick up a large bag of ice, so that said Magnums don't melt on the three-mile-round trek back to the office. My rucksack weighs a tonne (I'm now carrying 2kg of ice bricks), and I'm already on tired legs from hiking sixteen hard miles on tough terrain across the Pennines the day before. But how could I resist? It's sunny outside and the supermarket is only up the road, and it's a breath of fresh air, and a break from my desk, and ... well, it's only walking.

Total: 19,095 steps

TUESDAY

I decide to walk/jog back home from the school drop-off. But why go the most direct route home? It's *sooooo good* to be outside. It's beautiful on the moors, and what's the harm in adding a

couple of extra miles onto my journey home?
Hmmmm...
Total: 17,791 steps

WEDNESDAY
God knows how I manage it, but I somehow clock
up 16,309 steps for the day simply by traipsing
up and down the stairs at work from my desk to
the coffee machine and back ... 500 times.
Total: 16,309 steps

THURSDAY
I must have ants in my pants. Or ADHD. Or
neurosis (most likely).

I walk (the long way) back home from school
drop-off (again), and then decide to walk into
town. I could drive there in half the time, or even
get the bus, but why would I? I desperately need
to get outside. I need some fresh air, and I need
to move. I suddenly feel self-conscious as I'm
walking along the main road, but I'm not sure
why. My heart is beating faster, but I know it's
not because of the walking. I make a mental note
to remember this feeling of discomfort and to
write it down in my BDD diary. Just being able
to identify the panicky feeling, and to know that
it's there helps me to think logically and begin

to process it rather than become engulfed in a head-fog of anxiety.

I focus on my breathing to try to stem the panic threatening to rise inside my chest. Just when I feel like I've contained things, I'm wolf-whistled by a passing white van man, which makes me jump out of my skin. I feel embarrassed by my dramatic reaction, but when I've finally calmed down, I laugh to myself. The guy in the van would have had no idea that I was in the process of managing an impending panic attack when he decided to 'flatter' me.

I meet up with my mum in town and we bump into a frail old gentleman we've known from years gone by. He asks my mum, 'Is your daughter [pointing to me] at school, now?' I'm absolutely thrilled at the prospect of looking like Britney Spears from the '…Baby One More Time' video, and immediately dismiss any possibility of him suffering dementia, Alzheimer's or a sight-degenerative condition that may have caused him to be SO far off the mark.

Total: 16,972 steps

FRIDAY

Ahhh, at last I have an enforced rest day! I have a yoga class, which is inside a gym studio and

so doesn't require me to travel any distance, over any speed, and so – I surmise – this constitutes proper 'rest'. And I don't allow myself to walk/run/cycle or pogo-stick my way there, today. I drive there, like any other person of sane mind in my predicament would do. But I feel bad about this. I berate myself for taking the 'easy option', and I reprimand myself for being lazy. Why? I have no idea. The Bastard Chimp has taken hold once again, and he's beating me into submission.
Total: 9,790 steps

Since my unapologetically non-scientific experimental week, I've realised that honestly, and literally, I can't sit down: I hate rest, and I need to move. I'm compelled to feel my heart beating in my chest and my muscle fibres twitching, because the alternative – stillness – frightens me. It's an uncomfortable, eerie silence, a feeling of non-aliveness that I can remember so vividly from all those years ago when I didn't know how it felt to move, and when my daily step count was a return trudge to the fridge for yet another oversize portion of Viennetta, and then back to slump in front of my telly to guess the price of a 1994 top-of-the-range caravan and a fully refurbished kitchen (including white goods) in *The Price Is Right*.

I never knew how it felt, back then, to feel truly alive. But I do now, and I can't let that go. *Not ever.* It doesn't dawn on me that there might be a compromise to be made, or a 'healthy balance' to strike. It's difficult to process, having lived at both ends of the scale, and I need to believe that I can make my way tentatively back along to some middle ground, where I can still feel the joy of movement and of being alive, whilst allowing my body to rest and recover when it needs to. It feels like I'm being asked to walk along a very high tight-rope – it's easy standing at either end, but I feel frightened, wobbly and vulnerable in the middle.

Don't look down, Rach. Just don't look down!

13

AVOIDANCE

You are likely to have tried many things to get rid of your anxiety about your appearance. However, they have not helped. Seeking reassurances and avoiding situations are classic responses to BDD. The goal of this treatment is to help you reconsider why you are worried, and to help you respond differently to anxiety-provoking situations. By approaching fearful situations head-on rather than avoiding and trying to control them, you may notice that you are more able to manage your BDD...

Since beginning to fill out my BDD diary just a few weeks ago, it's clear to me that avoidance has become my default setting. In fact, I look at my first morning's diary extracts, and I can easily identify my behaviours, which were based on precisely this:

- I avoided taking my daughter to school;
- I re-scheduled a meeting at work;

- I even considered missing work altogether and phoning in sick, only just managing to pull myself together and resist turning my car around to drive straight back home.

I read through these entries again, and I'm just beginning to comprehend the enormity of these avoidance-based behaviours. I didn't take my little girl to school because I felt too ugly; I re-scheduled a meeting at work. Without any justifiable reason (other than my own mental health issues, that is), I messed up not only my own working day, but another person's schedule, because I felt too ugly. I almost pulled a sickie, because I felt too ugly to go to work and do my job. And I know I've done this many times before. Suddenly, the realisation of this and the destructive impact BDD is having on my life overwhelms me.

I COULD LOSE MY FUCKING JOB BECAUSE OF THIS!

It feels like I'm staring this beast squarely in the face for the very first time.

Along with avoidance behaviours, I scan down my diary entries for other examples of reassurance-seeking. I don't have to look very far:

- I'm transfixed by the mirror in our front room, as though only by staring into it will I be guarded against the real and imminent threat of ugliness. Although I can't *ask* the mirror for reassurance, it is still considered to be the same *short-term-fix-vs-long-term-damage* compulsive behaviour.

- I run the risk of missing the traffic lights changing colour on my journey to work, as I'm too engrossed in picking myself apart in my car's rear-view mirror.
- I'm bewitched by the mirrors in the ladies' toilets at work, only feeling safe when I'm within sight. I feel myself being constantly pulled back there like a homing pigeon who has strayed off his familiar flight path: *stay safe, Rach. Stay safe.*

But I'm now learning that seeking reassurances and avoiding certain circumstances is counter-intuitive in its effect on managing the symptoms of BDD: rather like a junkie who only needs *'a tiny bit of smack'*, it feels to be helping me, and reduces my discomfort in the short term, but this behaviour only increases my symptoms and reduces my quality of life in the long run – I can certainly vouch for that.

It sounds so ridiculously simple, but to me this feels like a breakthrough. Logically, it makes perfect sense: I can understand the analogy of the crack addict needing 'just one more fix'; I can relate to the feeling of short-term relief, and the sure knowledge that it won't last very long (usually a matter of seconds). And my thinking, logical brain can accept that I will somehow need to wean myself off this behaviour if I'm going to feel any benefit in the long-term management of my condition.

Hallelujah, the theory is making sense!

But this stuff needs to happen in practice, now, just like Dr G said. It's one thing knowing and understanding the theory behind it, but I know that I'll have to start putting my learning into action. And that thought terrifies me.

14

SOMETHING MISSING

A few months have passed, and I hate to admit it, but Running Guru's advice is helping. She may not be on my Christmas card list, but her suggestion for a 'Training Plan B' is proving to fill at least some of the gaping holes in my current non-running reality. Yoga is bringing me a sense of calm and strength, whilst trying new activities like aqua jogging reminds me that there are many 'alternative' (ahem!) ways to train, which I hadn't perhaps considered before. The cross-training sessions on the static gym bike are working well in the sense that I can replicate some of the cardio interval training and endurance sessions my body requires in order to produce the vast quantity of endorphins I clearly need to be OK.

But something is missing.

It's lunchtime, and I'm sitting on the static gym bike at work. I'm thankful for a five-minute recovery break after my first fifteen-minute tempo set, which was incredibly hard work. My bum still constantly threatens to slide off the plastic seat, but I've become used to that frustration, now. A woman walks into the gym and heads straight to pick up the remote control, after switching on the enormous wall-mounted television. My peace is immediately shattered by the noise of two Z-list celebrities who, I surmise, are visiting antiques fairs and having a competition to buy the most impressive piece of antiquated tat.

I look outside and the sky is a bright blue. The puffy clouds are cartoon-like and remind me of *The Simpsons*. And then I realise: *I want to be outside*. My static bike makes me work hard for another fifteen minutes, but I so desperately wish I was outside doing this instead of being stuck in here. I miss the rush of air and the feeling of freedom; the wind in my face and the view from the top of a hill. I miss the rolling fields and the patchy carpets of grass; how the cold makes my sweat evaporate before I've even noticed that I'm working hard. I miss the buzz of the passing traffic and the noise of life going on around me. I miss the peace of my own thoughts and the space I see wherever I look.

That's it. I've worked out what's missing: I just want to be outside.

I NEED to be outside.

But how can I possibly do this outside? It's been nearly ten years since I've ridden a bike, and I don't even know if I still can. My mind floods with conflicting thoughts, fears, possibilities and memories. It feels like I'm having a game of table tennis in my head: small white balls are being smashed around over a tiny net, and I can barely keep up with them.

Can you even ride a bike, Rachel?

Of course you can!

No, you can't!

Why on earth can't you? You've got a bike in the cellar.

You rode that, once. Remember?

Get it back out again!

But you'd probably kill yourself on it.

What are you frightened of?

You're frightened, aren't you? OMG, you're too scared to ride a bike!

That's right, isn't it, Rach? YOU'RE TOO SCARED TO RIDE A BIKE, AREN'T YOU?

PING, PONG, PING, PONG … the balls keep flying over the net, but one thought settles with me, and I can't shake it off: I'M TOO SCARED TO RIDE A BIKE. But why? How can I possibly be too afraid to get on a bike and ride it? Millions of people ride bikes *every single day*! What on earth is making me think that I can't be one of them?

15

BACK IN THE SADDLE

I'm balancing on the tightrope, again. 'The Power of Yet' is in a duel with my Bastard Chimp, who is now jumping up and down, desperate to remind me of some basic facts: YOU CANNOT RIDE A BIKE, RACHEL. REMEMBER THE HORROR OF THE GIRLY CYCLING CLIQUE? YOU COULDN'T RIDE A BIKE THEN, SO WHAT MAKES YOU THINK YOU'LL BE ABLE TO RIDE ONE NOW? YOU'LL MAKE A COMPLETE FOOL OF YOURSELF. WHY ARE YOU EVEN CONSIDERING DOING THIS?

I listen to his arguments, and it reminds me of the mooting competitions we held whilst I was a law student. I do my best to remain objective, as though weighing up the evidence and trying to sift out the hard facts from any rebuttable presumptions, those being assumptions that are taken to be true *unless someone comes forward to contest them and prove otherwise.* I think back to my conversation with Tilly about 'The Power of Yet' whilst walking home from the farm shop, eating her sausage roll. What would she say to rebut the Bastard Chimp in his assertions? Surely it would go something like this:

- YOU CANNOT RIDE A BIKE *YET*, MUM … but you *will* be able to at some point in the future.
- YOU DON'T FEEL VERY CONFIDENT ABOUT GETTING ON YOUR BIKE AGAIN, MUM … but you *will* feel more confident if you are brave and take little steps forward.
- YOU DON'T KNOW IF YOUR BIKE IS ROAD WORTHY *YET*, MUM … but you *can* find that out, if you really want to.

I picture her talking me through all the sensible, rational points in response to the case my Bastard Chimp has confidently put forward. He's pretty damn convincing, and I still shudder at the memory of the Stoodley Pike off-road mountain biking experience with the Girly Cycling Clique. But then I think back to when I was pedalling away on the static gym bike just a few days ago, longing to be outside under *The Simpsons* cartoon clouds and an eggshell blue sky. I so desperately wanted to be in the sunshine, and not stuck inside the godforsaken gym with the television blaring. *How badly do I want it?*

I consider the basis of my Bastard Chimp's arguments, and I conclude that – despite there being some truth to his protestations – all his points are based on one general presumption: *THAT I'M TOO FRIGHTENED TO RIDE A BIKE. I'M TOO SCARED TO TRY AGAIN.* His entire argument hinges on fear. On that basis, there is simply no contest. Tilly is armed with the far stronger weapon, and she settles this duel once and for all with one final swing of her mighty sword: 'The Power of Yet'.

'Could you pop down and help me get my bike out, please?' I shout up the stairs to my Other Half as I wade across plastic boxes and an old artificial Christmas tree in the cellar. 'I'm going to get it serviced so that I can ride it again.'

The duel is over. Terrified as I might be, thanks to Tilly, 'The Power of Yet' has emerged victorious: I will be riding my bike again at some point in the (very near) future.

* * *

I pull my old 2010 Trek mountain bike out of the cellar and heave it into my car. I'm taking it to Halfords for a service – and by this, I mean I need them to make sure that the wheels are still round (the back one is, I suspect, oval), to pump some air into the tyres which now resemble Scotch pancakes, and to ensure the brakes still work. As much as I'm no cycling connoisseur, the brand name 'Avid Juicy' has stuck in my memory. I heard Chris mention it some years ago, prior to the ill-fated Stoodley Pike night ride, and I recall that it has something to do with the brakes. I fear mine may well have run out of their vital 'avid' juice.

Once I've hauled my dusty old Trek up the stairs to Halfords' most inconveniently placed bike service checkout, I explain my requirements to the sloth-like bearded gentleman behind the counter. You see, I need to establish certain basic facts before I can allow myself to venture forth on my unfamiliar two-wheeled machine. I begin to reel off my list, as follows:

- Are both wheels round?
- Are the (hopefully circular) tyres pumped up?
- Are the 'Avid Juicy' brakes still working?
- Are the gears shifting?

I tell the man that they kept sticking when I last rode this thing, back in 2010. But I've forgotten how to use them, so it doesn't make a huge difference, anyway.

The bearded gentleman looks somewhat stunned by my safety checklist. He mumbles something about oiling the chain, and I look at him through eyes so perplexed that he quickly averts his embarrassed gaze back to the tatty piece of paper he is scribbling on, and tells me my bike will be ready for collection on Friday.

WHOOP, WHOOP! This is the start of a new era for me. My own personal plan to start off small, and to set myself some tiny, incremental, non-running – dare I say it, *cycling* – goals.

Memories come flooding back of my first experience of owning a bike. It's my eighth birthday, and – almost fit to burst with excitement – my dad holds my hand as I skip down to the garage for The Big Reveal. *Will my new bike be shiny and pink, with a big fancy ribbon tied around it? Or perhaps it will be sky blue with crisp, white 'go faster' stripes down the side, like my cousin Andrew's BMX?* I can't help but wonder. I've been thinking about it for days … *WEEKS!*

Finally, the wait is over. My dad grapples with the creaky old garage door, and there, standing behind it is … the rusty green relic. *Oh. Right.* Even as a young child I'm very aware of the value of things and certain social graces, so I'm keen to appear grateful despite my stinging disappointment. This bike isn't new. It's not shiny and sparkly, with a *NO CHILD HAS EVER RIDDEN ME BEFORE* kind of vibe. Not at all. Instead, it has a tired, roughly refurbished *nearly new* feel, which no child *ever* wants for a birthday present. My dreams of a shiny, pink bike wrapped in an offensively large bow are instantly dashed.

'The paintwork needs a bit of touching up,' Dad says without a hint of irony, and – even more incredulously – sounding absolutely thrilled with his bicycle choice. I notice a few flecks of green paint fall away as he rubs his rough, oil-stained hands over part of the frame. The metal is a burnt orange colour underneath. 'And the brakes need looking at, but other than that, it's just like new!' he beams.

I don't cry, because I know that would really upset my dad, who seems genuinely excited. But I'm momentarily stunned into silence.

The bike wasn't like new, and it didn't feel like it was mine. I have no fond memories of going out riding on the Rusty Green Relic ('RGR'). I have absolutely no recollection of being taken on any glorious, sunny bike rides on it. In fact, I don't think I ever ventured further than our overgrown back garden, where I was pushed around the relative safety of our un-mowed lawn a couple of times (Mum wouldn't let me ride the RGR on our cul-de-sac for fear of it collapsing without notice, or failing to stop, if required. Both of which were perfectly understandable and legitimate concerns.) Besides, with the best will in the world, I knew that refurbishing my *new* bike would come some way down on the list of other DIY disasters my dad had yet to remedy, including:

- The pile of red bricks sitting in one corner of the garden, which would at some stage purportedly end up resembling a barbeque;
- The DIY double-glazing, which was becoming more of a pressing issue since Mum rejected his earlier attempt at installing cling film to the inside of all the windows with the use of *my* hairdryer;
- The ginger Baxi Bermuda fireplace which – Dad had promised – would be miraculously transformed by 'a few coats of dark varnish'.

I think back to the God-awful, soul-destroying mountain-biking experience I endured back in 2009, when the Girly Cycling Clique hung me out to dry on their Wednesday night ride to Stoodley Pike, and I shudder at the memory.

It doesn't have to be like that, Rach, I tell myself. *You can start with baby steps – just tiny cycling challenges that you set for yourself – and nobody else even need know about them!*

I feel better for giving myself a mini pep-talk, and I feel the tiniest flutter of excitement at the prospect of my trusty Trek mountain bike being declared roadworthy, and collecting him on Friday with the certain knowledge that he is ready for action.

Phase One

Friday comes around, and I arrive back upstairs at Halfords' misplaced second-floor bike service desk. Bearded man isn't working today, but there's a monosyllabic teenager in his place.

'The brake disks needed changing,' he mumbles, 'And it looks like your chain hasn't been oiled in a long while.'

I look at him and smile gormlessly, safe in the knowledge that the chain has never been oiled. Not to my knowledge, anyway.

'OK, thanks,' I reply. 'Could you please show me how to raise my seat a little bit? Oh, and I think I also need a bell.'

I pay for my bike's first service in seven years (and my new bell, which inexplicably has a fluorescent yellow 'Acid House' face on it) and I'm slightly aggrieved the youth hasn't offered to help me carry my hefty-framed mountain bike down the stairs, and shoehorn it into my car boot. Regardless, I bounce the wheels down the staircase, gripping tightly onto the Avid Juicy brakes, trying hard not to fall arse-over-elbow in the process. With only the mildest hint of my own body odour, I then wrestle Trek into the boot of my car, having completed a Krypton Factor challenge of collapsing car seats and removing shelving to accommodate his chunky frame.

But I see this as a mini victory, and the completion of Phase One of my plan to discover the joys of cycling which have otherwise eluded me for an entire lifetime.

This is progress; this is progress, indeed.

Phase Two

Trek is finally home. He's received an Extreme Makeover, and now has freshly pumped tyres, a shiny, lubricated chain, and his Avid Juicy brakes are razor-sharp once again. Of course, this is progress, but now I need a plan. How will I get from 'I can't ride a bike ... YET' to a place where fear and self-doubt are replaced by confidence, and competence? What resources and experiences do I have to rely on, which can help me? I ponder on this for a short while, and it doesn't take long for my head to go back to a time when I was afraid to run – or to take part in pretty much any sporting activity, come to think of it, for fear of failing, of looking foolish, of not being good enough.

Do you remember when you were too scared to run, actively avoiding cross-country P.E. lessons at school because you were too frightened to take part? Of course I do – I remember it vividly. I can feel my back sliding down the cold brick wall near the vending machine at the local sports centre, and getting ready to dunk cheap white bread in some disgusting, chalky soup, whilst my peers were off somewhere else being active. How did I get here, from being there – in that place? I took many tiny steps forward, that's what I did. It didn't happen overnight, but as I inched my way from the proverbial vending machine towards virtual freedom, every step mattered. I didn't go from loathing cross-country at school to running marathons and – warning: YAY ME! moment coming up – even winning races in one leap, did I? Of course not.

So, with all this in mind, it's time to set myself some mini challenges – those incremental, fiery hoops of anxiety I'll be required to jump through to prove to myself – and to my Bastard Chimp – that I'm capable of this, that I CAN ride a bike, and that I WILL succeed at this.

It's time.

Phase Three
CYCLING CHALLENGE #1: CAN I RIDE A BIKE?
ANSWER #1: I'M NOT SURE, BUT I'LL GIVE IT A GO.

The first challenge I set myself is to cycle down to the local gym. This is a five-mile, mainly downhill route consisting of only two main roads – gulp, cold sweat – followed by a mercifully traffic-free section along the canal towpath but it's got bumpy, cobbled bits on it, and low bridges. Fuck!

I look closely at my Trek, and I wonder if he has any idea of the sheer ineptitude of his owner. He is a lovely-looking, if slightly ageing machine, but even I feel a sense of his humiliation as my daughter's neon pink fluffy unicorns drinking bottle complete with curly straw sits snugly in the bottle cage. He knows he's better than this – and he's right.

Suddenly, I feel incredibly anxious. I honestly don't know if I can brave the traffic, or stop at the traffic lights; I don't know if I can take one hand off the handlebars to indicate when I will be turning 'left' or 'right'. I have no idea how I will navigate any tricky road junctions when I will need to move over towards the middle of the road – in the face of oncoming vehicles – just to make a necessary turn. How will I deal with dogs running off their leads along the canal? What if they run across my path, and Trek and I end up bobbing about in the murky water? I've heard stories about cyclists falling into the canal, and I know that this is a real possibility for me. What if I misjudge the height of one of the narrow tunnels, and I end up colliding with the stonework?

How long will it take me to ride down to the gym, anyway? I have absolutely no idea. It's only five miles away from my home, but with all the above potential calamities, it could take me literally hours to drag us both out of the canal, or to push along a busted bike with buckled wheels resulting from an unfortunate tunnel collision.

I don't know why, but all these worries suddenly seem very real, and they overwhelm me. As I consider every possible disastrous eventuality I can feel my heart rate increase. And then my Bastard Chimp joins in the anxiety party: 'Ha ha! You? On a bike? Really? What the HELL are you thinking, Rach? You can't even ride a bike! You'll make a complete FOOL of yourself!'

I'm momentarily silenced. But I have heard all his cruel taunts many, many times before. *Remember when you felt like this before your first ever run?* I remind myself. *What did you do then? You went out and you did it anyway. And what if you DO fall off your bike, or collide with the inside of a tunnel? What will you do* then? I reject my immediate answer, which is that I'll crawl into a hole somewhere and never come out. You'll get back on your bike and you'll go again, Rach. That's what you'll do.

I have prepared some blackcurrant juice to go in my daughter's fluffy unicorn water bottle, and – inspired by this – I also think to take her bike lock along with me to the gym. It's the only bike lock I have (although it's bordering on comical to describe it as a 'lock' … and it's also candyfloss pink), but it will be better than nothing whilst I abandon my Trek for an hour or so.

I head off on my (thankfully, now confirmed) circular-wheeled Trek mountain bike, with nobbles on the tyres large enough to tackle the roughest Cambodian jungle terrain. The next five miles is littered with a million mini YAY ME! moments. First, I successfully ride my Trek bike out of our ever-so-slightly inclined driveway, and then I turn right onto the main road. YAY! I CAN RIDE A BIKE … ON A MAIN ROAD! I clunk my gears and suddenly find that I'm pedalling much faster, but I'm going nowhere. Shit, wrong way! I quickly reverse the move, using only my instincts, and thankfully, some resistance returns to my pedals. I can feel my feet pushing down on the pedals and making the wheels move once more. A lorry suddenly rushes past me. It's a narrow road, and the wind-tunnel effect shocks me momentarily as the heavy-tonner thunders by. SHIIIIITTTTT! My heart racing, I grip tighter onto the handle bars, hold my nerve, and just keep breathing as I continue pedalling forwards.

I make it safely onto the canal towpath, and I'm ready for my next big challenge: the unpredictable pedestrians (mostly with even less predictable dogs) and the task of riding across uneven, bumpy cobbles. Soon I become familiar with ringing my fluorescent Acid House bell, forewarning those ahead of my presence. My confidence is still shockingly low, with constant reminders from my Bastard Chimp that 'I'm no cyclist!' And so, I find myself sounding ridiculously British and self-effacing, apologising profusely to virtually every person – and canine – that I ride past. 'Sorry. Oops! Sorry ... Thanks ... Coming through! Sorry ... Cheers ... Thank you ...Sorry ...' I sound genuinely apologetic for having the audacity to get on a bike and ride it, excusing myself whilst cycling past complete strangers – and their dogs – along a canal towpath.

Arriving at my destination, I feel kind of smug, as though I've achieved something monumental. But, when I run through the series of disastrous 'what if' scenarios I've had to process – whilst accompanied by my faithful Bastard Chimp – then the simple fact that I have arrived here unscathed is no mean feat.

I take a large swig of juice from my fluffy unicorn drinking bottle, lock my bike up outside the gym with my flimsy £5 pink unicorn child's bike lock, and trot off to my yoga class. Surprisingly, Trek is still there when I come back out of the gym an hour later (a decent pair of kitchen scissors could cut through the bike lock), and so I cycle the five-mile route back home. But there's a challenging incline I must conquer en route. Fuck, fuck, FUCKKKKK! I manage to crank the gears down to make the effort seem easier, whilst my speed drops to something resembling a slug progressing steadily from the garden to a discarded bean tin in the recycling box. After stopping three times for a breather on the way to the top of the hill, I eventually make it home.

BOOM! VICTORY IS MINE! I've proven to myself that I can get on my bike and I can ride it, after eight years – and even then, I was shit!

I can navigate my way across main roads, through traffic, next to wanker lorry drivers, along bumpy canal cobbles, around clueless dog-walkers, avoiding piles of dog shit, under low bridges, via road crossings, and without colliding with pedestrians. If this challenge were a jigsaw puzzle, we'd be talking a straightforward six-piece affair targeted at age group two to three years. Most probably in a Peppa Pig design. Anyway, I've cracked it.

And as my Bastard Chimp sulks quietly by himself in the corner of my usually self-effacing, self-berating, anxious mind, I'm simply elated.

16

TRAPS

The C in CBT stands for 'cognitive', which simply means thinking in the form of words, ideas and images. Thoughts in CBT usually involve interpretations of oneself or one's external environment. They give meaning to what we see, hear, smell, taste and feel. These interpretations are subjective, meaning they are a result of our physiological perception, learned thoughts, past experiences, any biases or filters we have, and the context we're in at any given moment.

Sometimes we interpret situations correctly. However, sometimes our interpretations are exaggerated, or just false. During this therapy, you will learn how to challenge these thoughts, to stop them from controlling your life.

My head is full of them – these so-called 'interpretation traps'. I look in the mirror, and I don't even know which version of myself is staring back at me. *Chubby teenage geek, or blonde imposter? I can't tell. Runner or non-runner?*

It's hard to say. The only consistent thought I have about myself is one of confusion, because although running has given me confidence and a sense of self-belief, I don't know where that has gone, and I don't know where my quest ends. What I *do* know is that I'm not there, yet. I'm *never* there. *Faster, thinner, blonder, lighter, fitter, better* ... The words float around my head as I battle with a thousand different versions of myself from decades of self-doubt. Enough. When will I just be enough?

It feels like my head is in a constant battle between thinking logically versus illogically, between the rational and unbalanced. Intellectually, I can process all that I'm learning through the counselling therapy programme. It's making perfect sense to me. But logic doesn't always help. In fact, I've found that it can be utterly infuriating: to know that your own thoughts, behaviours and actions are fundamentally flawed and, at times, downright ludicrous, can be precious little comfort when suffering the effects of a mental health condition such as body dysmorphic disorder. *How can this be happening to me? Why can't I control my own thoughts? I know my behaviour is ridiculous, but I just can't seem to stop it. AAARRRGGGHHHH!*

At the peak of my running obsession, I was almost always too busy, too consumed with training, racing and performance, and well, just too damn tired to contemplate any of the messy head stuff.

The next module of the BDD therapy begins by confidently asserting, 'the first step to changing (my) thoughts and interpretations in a healthy way is to recognise what (my) current interpretations are'. I imagine my head suddenly being flooded with good-cop 'Thought Police', who are lowered from the military chopper into their mission HQ all SAS-style, under the cover of darkness. My Bastard Chimp runs for cover as the highly trained SWAT team takes over this desolate place, and makes it their primary mission to identify and destroy any INTERPRETATION TRAPS that might be lurking. My thoughts have never had this kind of military screening and protection before. They have never been questioned, only accepted as being the truth, but that's all about to change. I briefly consider how ludicrously simple it sounds – to be able to stop and question my own thoughts before they take firm hold, and become easy fodder for my Bastard Chimp to wrestle me to the ground. *Interpret and challenge my own thoughts?* It's the introduction of a new Stop & Search policy, whereby I'm at liberty to question any presumptions which my Thought Police have reasonable grounds to believe are about to lure me towards a trap.

My SWAT team is on high alert, and so I quickly begin to scan the list of possible interpretation traps, wondering what landmines I have blindly stumbled into over the past two decades without even realising it. *All-or-nothing thinking* ... Yes, I know all about that. Everything is either black or it's white, there is no in-between. If there is even a small flaw in my appearance, I am therefore ugly – there is simply no room for any middle ground. *Mind-reading* ... Yes, YES! I know all about this, too. When people look at me, I'm certain they're thinking something negative about my appearance. How many times have I been *so sure* of it? But I've never even considered investigating to see if any of my 'mind-reading' presumptions are true. *WHY?* I have no answers.

The SWAT team is now in full throttle. They will leave no stone unturned in their quest to eradicate any impending threat.

Fortune-telling, filtering, emotional interpreting, selective attention … The list of traps goes on and on. And EVERY time I'm forced to confront the fact that yes, this is the guerrilla warfare I've been subjected to by my Bastard Chimp. These are the weapons with which he has successfully managed to sabotage my mental health, over and over again for two decades. The realisation fills me with horror: that something as simple as my own thoughts being left unchecked – and unchallenged – could cause such chaos and destruction in my mind. But the troops have arrived just in time. I hope and pray that my SWAT team hang around long enough for me to learn how to protect myself from now on. That's the next stage of my learning against this beast: the art of self-defence.

17

FURTHER AFIELD

CYCLING CHALLENGE #2: CAN I VENTURE
FURTHER AFIELD? WHAT ABOUT RIDING
TO MY MUM'S HOUSE AND BACK?

ANSWER #2: I'M NOT SURE,
BUT I'LL GIVE IT A GO.

Quite frankly, the simple task of cycling *somewhere else ... on another route ... to another place* is a significant enough variable to extend my already bulging comfort zone from a six-piece Peppa Pig jigsaw puzzle to the next stage: a twenty-four-piece Paw Patrol one, target age group five to six years. There are more roads to navigate on the route to my mum's house, and therefore increased exposure to wanker white-van drivers and other non-cycling-friendly imbeciles on the move. However, there will only be a small section of riding along the canal towpath required, so fewer bumpy cobbles to traverse and hopefully not so many dog-walkers with mile-long extendable leads and accompanying piles of sloppy excrement for me to dodge. All things considered, this is variation – and it is therefore progression.

I'm taking things a little more seriously for this ride, though. I decide to ditch my daughter's pink fluffy unicorns water bottle and instead, I replace it with an Orange* Mountain Bike one I've found in the cupboard. I know that these are merely aesthetic, insignificant matters, but they are incremental to my morphing into a 'proper cyclist' and not somebody who has hijacked a child's bike, and also made off with their water bottle and bike lock.

Cycling on the roads is still a real panic for me. I have absolutely no confidence riding amongst traffic, and I try to telepathically communicate my intentions to the other road users rather than venturing to take one hand off the handlebars to indicate a change of direction. I particularly struggle when approaching a certain busy T-junction at the bottom of the hill, when I am required to *BRAKE WHILST CHANGING GEARS AND INDICATING!* I've absolutely no idea how doing all three things together is possible, and so I opt for doing just one of them – the most important one. I decide to BRAKE. Nobody knows that I intend turning right when the traffic lights change to green, and equally, nobody knows that I'm in the most ridiculously high gear, and that I won't even be able to pedal my bike when the lights do eventually change. Myself included.

---

* Orange are a well-known mountain biking manufacturer based in my home town of Halifax. They make *real* mountain bikes for *real* mountain bikers, and I can only apologise to them for any association with myself on two wheels.

I can feel my heart rate increasing as the seconds tick by, waiting anxiously for the red light to change to amber … to change to green. I need to be ahead of the game, here: lives are at stake! On this occasion, the drivers around me are forgiving. They hang back and allow me to miss my pedals. I crank my gears to the point where the bike jerks suddenly, and I can hear the chain being jolted roughly from one cog to another, and then another. Thankfully, I recover and I manage to half-raise an apologetic hand to the drivers around me, who have opted not to run me over on this occasion.

'Well done, love,' says Mum, sounding both surprised and relieved that I've arrived. As I sit drinking coffee on her sofa, I'm buzzing slightly, and feeling disproportionately chuffed with my little self, whilst my Trek bike waits patiently for me on the ground floor of her apartment block. I'm not sure if it's the sudden shot of caffeine, the mini boost of endorphins now swimming around my body, or the aftershock of adrenalin I'm experiencing on realising that I have arrived at my mum's house unscathed, and my bike is still in one piece. No doubt it's a combination of all these things, together with a generous dose of YAY ME! Kick-ass, 'This Girl Can', sticking-two-fingers-up-to-my-Bastard-Chimp kind of vibe.

I finish my coffee and the pair of us (myself and Trek) cycle home exactly the same way we've come. I'm still terrified on approaching the dreaded T-junction, only this time, I don't make the mistake of leaving myself in the highest possible gear: I think ahead and gently change down the gears without any offensive jerking movements before coming to a complete stop. I even manage to set off with the flow of traffic when the lights change to green, and I just about manage to raise my hand an inch above the handlebars to indicate that I will be turning left.

I'm still entirely focused on continuing my journey safely and navigating my way back home, but inside my head I can already feel the celebrations commencing at the prospect of successfully completing this, the second mini challenge I have set myself on my trusty bike. I can also feel the early onset of my Bastard Chimp sulking in a corner, as he will have to once again remain in his sad little box, having been unable to convince me that I'm indeed too shit to even try riding a bike. Oh, and I only stop *twice* to catch my breath whilst cycling up Slug Trail hill. Result!

My phone bings. It's a text message from Mum: *Have you arrived back home yet, Rach? I was watching you from my window. You didn't look overly confident on the roads, love. Let me know when you're back safely. Ma x*

My confidence is dented ever so slightly. I may have looked like I could cycle straight up the back end of a Skoda or have a close shave with a Corsa at any given moment, but I made it home. It's another mini victory in the small-fry book of minor achievements in my life – job done!

18

THE HILL

CYCLING CHALLENGE #3: CAN I CYCLE UP
A THREE-MILE HILL CLIMB?

ANSWER #3: I'M NOT SURE,
BUT I'LL GIVE IT A GO.

There's a bastard of a hill close to where we live. A little over three miles in length, it's just found itself on my radar of 'incremental arse-kicking mini cycling challenges' in the continuum of progression I'm now on. What's more, I feel to be on a roll, albeit a very small one.

I'm on rather a steep learning curve – we're talking just over a week, thus far. But already I can feel that my confidence is on the up. I can tell that in facing my Bastard Chimp head-on, with his permanent goading and his incessant quest to belittle me and to destroy my self-worth, that I have discovered some new weaponry. I'm keen to continue challenging myself and to keep putting mini obstacles in my own way, because I know for certain that in doing so, I'm giving myself every possible chance of wrestling my self-esteem back from the unforgiving grip of my Bastard Chimp. He has – sadly – been able to take a firm hold of it since the recent loss of my running, but this is another way I'm discovering that I can slowly begin to regain control. And it feels good.

This challenge is simple enough: I can either cycle three miles up a very steep hill, or I can't. *What's the worst that can happen? I'll have to get off my bike and push it. And if I do, so fucking what?* I decide to give it a whirl.

I look outside and the weather gods are not on my side, today. Thick, persistent rain is coming down in waves as I gaze out onto the sodden fields outside our kitchen window, and the branches of the trees look to be swaying heavily under the weight. It would be so easy to change my plans and to reschedule my ride to another, sunnier day. I haven't had the experience of cycling in horrendous weather conditions yet, so this could make my third mini challenge even more dubious. *How will the rain affect my control of the bike?* I wonder. *Will the roads be slippery? Will I lose control of the wheels and skid helplessly into the back end of a Calderdale Council recycling truck? Will I even be able to see where I'm riding, or will the rain obscure my vision, resulting in me unwittingly cycling into a ditch?* I remind myself that the worst-case-possible-canal-submersion-scenario never happened on my bike ride to the gym, so perhaps my mind is once again getting ahead of itself with these outlandish 'what ifs'. Thankfully, it helps to reduce the impact of this fearful 'Bastard Chimp' way of thinking.

Mercifully, I have some very basic waterproof kit to wear, courtesy of my very brief flirtation with cycling, back in 2010.

I purchased my trusty Trek mountain bike during the winter months and so invested in a Gore-Tex windstopper jacket and some waterproof trousers at the same time. They smell slightly musty as I dig them out of the box in the damp cellar, and they're a good two sizes too big for me now, but they'll do.

Within seconds of leaving the house, I'm completely saturated. My Gore-Tex jacket is sodden, and I can feel large droplets of icy rain trickling down the back of my neck. Regardless, I head off in the direction of my goal for today: the hill. A ten-tonne truck thunders past me on the country lane by our house, but this time, I don't panic like I did before. I feel undeniable palpitations as spray from the road whips up and around my face, but I hold my nerve and keep pedalling: my focus is already on today's hill challenge.

Mentally, I prepare myself as I approach the hill. I settle in, pushing steadily and consistently in as high a gear as I can manage, enabling me to still have sufficient 'torque', this being *the force* I am applying through the pedals, whilst maintaining my 'cadence', the speed at which I turn the pedals. (*See, who is this absolute cycling wanker I have become?*) Digging my off-road trainers into my pedals, I push down hard. I breathe deeply as I continue to push, push, push down on them. I'm working harder now, and the wheels are turning slowly, but they're still turning, nonetheless.

There are two blokes on skinny, light-framed road bikes just ahead of me on the hill. As I approach them, I'm suddenly aware that I don't look like a *real* cyclist at all, but here I am, gate-crashing their party – and without wearing cleats (special cycling shoes that clip into the pedals). Embarrassingly, I overtake them. I don't know whether to apologise as I grind my way past on my heavy Trek mountain bike, pushing down on the plastic pedals with my off-road trainers whilst wearing rather out-dated, and now completely saturated, waterproofs.

Once I've reached the top of the climb, I stand up on my pedals and lift my bum high in the air for the most incredible downhill section, and I feel a kind of elation that I haven't experienced in a long time. *YAYYYYYYY! I CAN FUCKING DO THIS!* I shout to myself as the wind blows rain and snot sideways across my face. Such is the increase in my confidence, I even take one hand off the handle bars and wipe the snot from my top lip/chin area, which has been dangling there for approximately fifteen minutes.

Back at home, I strip out of my sodden clothing in the kitchen and I make myself a cup of hot, sweet tea before taking a moment to reflect on my mini *YAY!* moments from today:

- Successfully riding my bike in the pissing rain;
- Achieving my main goal and managing to ride my heavy Trek mountain bike up a three-mile hill climb;
- Unexpectedly overtaking two road cyclists on the afore-mentioned hill climb;
- Standing up on my pedals for the downhill section;
- Managing to take one hand off my handle bars (albeit briefly) to wipe snot from my face;
- Almost – *almost* – beginning to feel like a real cyclist.

This, my friends, is a breakthrough.

19

DISCOMFORT

During this part of the treatment, you will begin to practise a change in behaviour that will result in less anxiety and a better quality of life in the long term. This is the practical application of the CBT model, and this is where you will spend the most time and energy during treatment.

Working through the BDD recovery programme is about to become significantly more challenging. I'm now entering the practical phase of treatment, where I will start to put into practice all that I've learned so far. Understanding the theory behind this model of treating body dysmorphia has been easy enough up to this point: I can grasp the general concepts, and I have faced up to the many thoughts and beliefs which may have led me to this place, thinking back to my sedentary teenage self, and the 'me' I came face-to-face with in the mirror every single day, with my delinquent unfit-for-purpose young body. Contrasting her with the Rachel I morphed myself into whilst at university – blonder and a few stone lighter, but with asymmetrical breasts and the paranoia of being judged and labelled as FLAWED. The breast reduction surgery remedied one problem, but did it inadvertently create another? I never stopped to consider my quest for perfection had to end somewhere. Ironically, I always said – and I still believe – that breast surgery was the best decision for me to make at the time. I could wear a fitted T-shirt and a normal bra without fear of anxiety taking over my vulnerable nineteen-year-old mind, but perhaps it opened the floodgates to an endless search for perfection which I would never be able to attain.

I don't know the answer.

Perhaps more damaging for me back then was the difference I felt my change in appearance made in my everyday life. From being all but invisible as a slightly overweight teen, my relatively modest physical transformation seemed to result in a disproportionately large shift in the way people responded to me. In hindsight, this is likely to have been more my own perception than reality, but the messages flooded my mind that to be accepted, I needed to be something far away from my invisible, physically flawed seventeen-year-old self. I believe this is where my futile quest began – I simply had no idea that I would end up here.

So, I now understand where body dysmorphia may have come from, and – more importantly – I know with absolute certainty that my handling of BDD up to this point has not helped me. In fact, I've only made the condition worse. I didn't realise how my avoidance and reassurance-seeking behaviours became so deeply entrenched, and how counter-intuitive they were. Rather than helping me, these behaviours only deepened the grooves of body dysmorphia in my mind, prolonging my misery in the long term. Discovering that running was one of my most successful avoidance techniques was akin to the early Greek philosophers, who worked out that the earth was round – fanciful and incredulous, but somehow entirely believable.*

I remember hearing the phrase 'Exposure Therapy' during my very first video chat with Dr G, after I'd been accepted onto the programme. Hearing the words sent a shudder down my spine, as there was no doubt in my mind what this meant. According to the dictionary definition, the word 'exposure' means 'the state of having no protection from something harmful'. A suggested synonym for the word is 'vulnerability'. Becoming vulnerable. That's what I will be required to do as part of this therapy: I will have to make myself become vulnerable, which goes against our innate human instinct. So, this is where I'm at – I'm about to *purposefully* make myself *EVEN MORE* vulnerable.

I'm filling out my BDD diary as normal, only I'm now having to write about my selected 'exposure therapy' challenges. *Where was I? What specific exposure therapy did I choose to confront? What happened? How did I feel?* But I feel ridiculous. These things I'm about to 'expose myself' to *are* ridiculous – or they would be to most people. I fill out my diary and I feel ashamed and embarrassed, but I know that I must do it. It's the only thing I have left to try and tackle this beast. My online 'exposure therapy' (or 'ET') diary looks like this:

---

* It wasn't actually Christopher Columbus who discovered this, I Googled it.

ET situation 1: 6:45 a.m. – I wake up after a disturbed night's sleep, and I'm worrying about having bags/dark circles under my (probably bloodshot) eyes, and looking tired (we've been here before, haven't we?).

Exposure therapy: I <u>won't</u> reach for the mirror on my bedside table, or practise caking multiple layers of concealer underneath my eyes before I've even woken up properly. Instead, I lie still and I breathe, imagining the Good Cop SWAT team are busy at work, identifying interpretation traps, whilst I'm here doing my job: starving my Bastard Chimp of oxygen, and refusing to play his futile games. I breathe in slowly, and then back out again. In, and out – that's as much as I can do.

ET situation 2: 7:05 a.m. – I get up and head downstairs, but I don't go straight into the bathroom, like normal. I'm going to take Tilly to school this morning WITHOUT having a shower and WITHOUT washing my hair. I feel awkward, uncomfortable and unclean, but it's a biggie, and I know that Dr G will be pleased with me if I can do this. I comb my hair, making a parting down the middle, which I then turn into two French plaits. I'm convinced that I can feel a layer of grease on my hair that would rival any respectable chip-shop fryer, and my skin feels kind of crawly. I can only face going out of the house with my hair tied back, and then wearing a baseball cap, which I realise could be interpreted as an attempt to disguise my 'flaw', but hey, it's a start!

ET situation 3: 8:45 a.m. – Me and Tills walk out of our front door and past my neighbour, who is standing in her dressing gown and slippers on the doorstep. 'Morning!' my chirpy neighbour says as she picks up her red-topped bottle of milk. 'Morning, Nora!' we say back. I wonder if she can tell that I haven't had a shower OR washed my hair today. Does she think I'm completely gross? Oh Jesus, how embarrassing! Maybe she thinks I'm unwell? Should I go back and explain why I look like this, so she won't worry about me?

BUT WAIT! My Good Cop SWAT team are on guard and they release a flare, warning me of an imminent threat: INTERPRETATION TRAP! I realise that I'm MIND-READING, and I have absolutely no grounds for presuming Nora is thinking either of those things. Perhaps she's thinking about making herself a cup of tea with her fresh pint of milk from the doorstep, and possibly having some cornflakes? Or maybe she isn't thinking about anything at all? I breathe a sigh of relief, and we head off to school in the car.

ET situation 4: 8:54 a.m. – We park up outside Tilly's school and I'm momentarily consumed with anxiety. 'Can we get out of the car, Mum?' Tilly asks, as we've been pulled up with the engine turned off for more than sixty seconds, but it feels much longer than that. 'Oh, er, yeah, sure ... Hey, this is your favourite song, Tills. Shall we wait until it's finished?' I say, desperately trying to delay facing the playground mums for as long as I possibly can.

BUT WAIT! I'm supposed to be FACING these things, not doing everything I possibly can to avoid staring these ridiculous scenarios squarely in the face. 'The bell's about to go, Tills, so let's head out now,' I say, forcing the words out of my mouth. I hold Tilly's hand as she skips across the road and in through the school gates. Two of the Glamorous Blonde Mums are standing by the wall, chatting and laughing as I walk in. Are they laughing at me? I panic. Are they finding it completely hilarious that I'm here, clearly not having showered or washed my hair, whilst they are looking all cool and sophisticated, dressed in their effortlessly glamorous 'playground chic'?

STOP! A flare launches, and I'm faced with my SWAT team's warning that this may be a trap. Could I be FILTERING what I'm seeing here, to seek out only those things which will reinforce the negative image I have of myself? What if the Glamorous Blondes are laughing at something ENTIRELY unrelated to me? What if the Cockapoo puppy did a whoopsie in one of their husbands' best brogues this morning, and it made him late for work? It's a possibility. I look over and one of them smiles at me. Suddenly, I feel a huge rush of relief – and joy – that I have just intercepted what would undoubtedly have been an interpretation trap and I have neutralised it, making it safe again. I smile to myself, and I wonder what Dr G will say when I tell him the exciting news: that this is ... working!!

20

A CYCLIST YET?

After my recent flurry of incremental cycling YAY ME! moments, I have my sights firmly set on a new one. I've even bought myself a new lid, some jazzy new cycling gloves, and I've dug out a pair of padded shorts and one of Chris's old cycling jerseys, which he handed down to me, back in the day.

This is happening, Rach. You know what you need to do.

CYCLING CHALLENGE #4: CAN I CYCLE A FIFTEEN-MILE LOOP – INCORPORATING THREE OF THE BIGGEST LOCAL CLIMBS – AND BE BACK HOME BEFORE 10 A.M. TO START WORK?

ANSWER #4: I'M NOT SURE,
BUT I'LL GIVE IT A GO.

I picture the route in my head, and – just like the three-mile hill climb I conquered only a few days ago – I visualise myself grinding up the first hill, which weaves steadily upwards to Norland Moor. I'll then stand up on my pedals for the long descent down to the far side of Rishworth valley, following the country lanes I know so well from miles of running around the area. Rehearsing it in my mind helps, as does reminding myself of all the mini victories I have already accomplished on this journey, so far. Mentally, I have some helpful tools available at my disposal. I recall the imaginary sparring contest between my Bastard Chimp with all his fearmongering, and Tilly, with her 'Power of Yet'. All those things I was so afraid of; all the things I believed I couldn't do; all of the 'extreme worse-case scenarios' that yes, I was right to consider, but in reality, never happened.

I run through all the tiny steps that I have already taken and the mini personal achievements I have amassed, which make me believe that I can keep going with my plan, and I can continue building my confidence – and my skills – on the bike. And the body of evidence is beginning to stack up. I'm no longer relying on the flimsiest threads as proof that my Bastard Chimp is so far off the mark with his 'YOU CAN'T DO THIS' unsubstantiated rhetoric. I can now rifle through a 'YAY ME!' index card box in my head, each card containing *ONE* single step I have taken, one specific thing I have conquered whilst progressing along 'The Power of Yet' tight-rope that I'm now balancing on. I can even take the index cards out and shuffle them around so they're in a completely random order. Pulling three cards out of my virtual pack, I take a look:

- I can ride my Trek mountain bike up big old scary hills (and even overtake road cyclists!);

- I can stand up on my seat with my bum high in the air for fast downhill sections, and feel confident that I'm in control, whilst I allow the bike to flow;
- I'm brave enough to try out new routes, with unknown variables, and I can handle them all.

Just a few weeks ago, these would all have appeared on my list of 'things I can't do YET, but WILL be able to do at some time in the future'. We're now at the other side of that place, beyond some unspecified 'time in the future', and all I need to do is to keep on going with this, because every 'YAY ME!' index card I write makes my Bastard Chimp shrink and recoil to some smaller, lesser place in my mind, where his shouting and goading can't be heard; a place where his exasperated sulks are far less effective in beating me into submission, and far easier for me to manage.

I head off on my way, and I try to pace myself mentally for today's challenge. The first thing I notice is that what just a few days ago were mini 'YAY ME!' moments for my index card box are now unremarkable – they're just a part of my ride. Yes, I'm still very cautious on the roads, especially at the busy junction at the bottom of our hill, but I'm riding on a road – *so what?* This shift in my perspective is interesting, because what had at one time seemed incomprehensible is now an assumed 'CAN DO'. Because of this new challenge, and the distance and time I know I will be out riding, my brain automatically selects more 'significant' mini victories for me to celebrate. As I ride up and around a stunning reservoir on the route past the first of today's climbs, I smile to myself, realising that just a matter of days ago, this in itself would be worthy of its very own index card. But I can perhaps be a little more selective, now.

Approximately fifty minutes into the ride, I make my first stop and pull over to take a selfie outside the door of my favourite pub. I send this through to my Other Half as evidence of my current location. I type the words, '*Look where I am!*' underneath my elated, gormless grin, together with an excited-looking emoji. I'm wearing sunglasses and appear to have more than a passing resemblance to Stevie Wonder, but I don't care.

I can't stop for too long – there's still a very long way to go and plenty of unhelpful 'You can't do this!' fodder for my Bastard Chimp to get his hands on. So I set off on my way again, only enjoying a mile or so of easy flat/downhill cycling before I reach the second climb. But it's tougher than I had expected, and involves more prolonged, steep sections than I remember from when I last ran the same route.

Bloody hell, Rach! my self-doubting chimp begins to chunter. *You've got absolutely no chance of doing this!*

I must stop him in his tracks, and not allow his negative chatter to fester in the dark corners, where he lurks.

'*So, you're finding it tough,*' I say to myself, now firmly in 'Managing Bastard Chimp' mode. '*but you're still going, aren't you? Just pedal a little slower and we can stop shortly for a break and a snack, but you can do this. No – you ARE doing this, Rach! Be proud, because you're doing this!*'

The self-coaching mantra works. I pull over for a quick breather (and to inhale an emergency Peperami) and I keep focused on making the bicycle wheels move forward – from one bend in the road to another; around one corner, and on to the next. That's all I need to do: focus on small, manageable sections, and deal with those one at a time. *One bend dealt with? Great! Move on to the next.* It helps me to cut down the seemingly enormous task ahead into more manageable chunks, and prevents my Bastard Chimp from being able to convince me that this is entirely beyond my – as yet – admittedly limited cycling capabilities.

Eventually, I make it to the top of another gnarly climb, where I briefly enjoy a panoramic view of the reservoir glistening in the valley below me, and I prepare for the fun part: I stand up on my non-clip-in pedals, take firm grip of my Avid Juicy brakes, and fly down the two-mile descent, which seems to flash by in just a matter of seconds. The joy of this section of the ride cannot be overstated: it is fast and thrilling, just enough to scare me, but still within my control. I let my bike wheels roll faster and faster down the hill, gathering speed on the open sections, whilst reeling it in a little for the blind bends and sharp corners. Wind whips the strands of hair around my face, and I can feel that a few clumps have been stuck together with snot. But I don't care. The cold air rushes at my skin and I inhale deep gulps through my mouth, as it is moving too fast for my body to catch it with normal breaths. The flow of my bike on this countryside road is like heaven: there are no clueless dog-walkers, or any horrible T-junctions to interrupt the rolling of my wheels. Steering is smooth, and I'm barely required to do anything other than stand on my pedals, catching breaths when I can.

And all I can feel is joy; the rush of the air, and freedom. *That's it!* I realise this is what I've been missing: a sense of freedom. But here – on this day, on this ride – I can feel it again. At times, I feel like I'm flying. And just like the joy I have known when running up and down these very same country lanes, I can feel that joy again, now. It's a revelation. Of all the 'YAY ME!' index cards I have now collected, this is by far the biggest. It feels like a secret door has been unlocked, and in working my way through those first baby steps such as getting my old bike serviced, riding along a busy road for the first time, cycling to my mum's house … all these were necessary to allow me access to a new place: a place of pure joy. Without them, I wouldn't be here, experiencing this. The realisation comes as a shock – I honestly hadn't ever imagined that I might feel like this about anything other than running. But I know this is only the calm before the unholy shit-storm of my third and final climb of the day: Ripponden Bank.

Now then, kids, this next part won't be easy. Then again, it wouldn't be easy on a skinny-framed, Malteser-light, carbon-framed road bike, or any wheels of any description (although an 'e-bike' may be the only exception – this being an electric bike, which is basically a motor-assisted ride. For the most part, they're a combination of a conventional bike with a battery and a motor, which takes most of the effort out of pedalling. Or, in simpler terms, it's a CHEAT!). My third and final climb of the morning will involve cycling up one of the infamous Tour de France Stage 2 routes, climbing past the Fleece Inn and over the tops, eventually dropping down into Barkisland village – and finally, back home.

My steel-framed Trek cranks and groans as I pull the gears back as far as they will go until the wheels are just about still moving forwards in granny-gear, and at slug-trail speed. With my cleat-free, non-cycling shoes, I push down hard on the plastic pedals. I inch my way slowly up the first part of the climb, unsure whether my bike is even moving forwards at all. As I approach a blind bend, I momentarily worry about what further incline I might see once I get a glimpse around the corner. The truth is, I'd rather not look. A car approaches from behind and slows down, because it isn't safe for him to overtake me. I can hear the engine struggling in second – possibly first gear, and I can sense his frustration at being stuck behind me and Trek as we continue to grind our way up the offensive hill. My quads are burning as I try even harder to move a little bit faster, but still the wheels feel to be struggling as if they are sinking into quicksand. 'Thanks, and I'm sorry!' I gesture to the car driver once he can overtake me safely a little further up the hill. I hope he wasn't in a rush, or the other five cars forced to snake behind him like the safety car on a Grand Prix racing circuit. And fucking hell, it feels tough, but I make it to the top!

I now dare to look up and all I can see around me are rolling hills, carpets of fields, tiny matchbox houses, and Meccano toy cars silently weaving along the roads, which look to be just a few inches wide. As the road begins to tip downwards, only gradually at first, I assume my standing position. Lifting my bum high from the seat feels like a relief, and as I lower my shoulders forward, dropping my chest closer to the handlebars, I can feel the muscles down the back of my legs lengthen – the stretch feels so good.

I remember back to the first running route I ever ran from my mum's front door: the country lane which had an incline like a warped, bendy spoon, followed by a mile or so of downhill, where I could *pretend* to be a 'real runner' for a short while. This feels like that on two wheels. As I stand on my pedals, my hamstrings sing with relief and I just about feel like a 'real cyclist'. I'm becoming a little more confident on the downhill sections, leaving it slightly longer each time before applying any pressure to my brakes.

The effort of grinding my way up not just one, but THREE significant local hill climbs (yeah, I know, it's hardly the Alps, but still …) and free-wheeling the final few miles back down the other side, I could almost burst with joy. *I'VE DONE IT! YESSSS! I'VE FUCKING CRACKED IT!* But this feels like so much more than another 'YAY ME!' index card for my box. Perhaps for the first time in one of these mini cycling challenges, my Bastard Chimp had some serious moments where he could have taken a firm hold, and convinced me that he was right: this was beyond me. But I intercepted him and stopped him in his tracks. And so, the elation I feel whilst flying down the last of the three downhill sections isn't purely a buzz from the rush of the cold air or the feeling of freedom, it's the cocktail of emotions I'm experiencing at having set myself a challenge which has pushed me way outside my comfort zone, and – despite encountering some wobbles and self-doubt along the way – the sense of accomplishment I feel at successfully completing my task.

You see, as my rides have increased in difficulty and complexity, so too has my confidence and my self-belief that

I can continue to take on new challenges and tackle them head-on. And I'm also learning that the challenges don't always need to be big and shiny with a fancy medal at the end. They don't have to be goals that other people even know about: they are *my* personal challenges, and I know what they mean to me. Thankfully, so does my Bastard Chimp, who has once again skulked off to brood in a corner whilst I'm busy doing a happy dance right in front of his face.

21

STALLING

It's been five weeks since I commenced with my online therapy counselling programme. I've fully immersed myself in learning the theory and putting it into practice. I've since confronted my very own exposure therapies of varying kinds: I've faced the playground mums with unwashed hair; I've even *been to work* without having a shower, having spent the entire day feeling like a chip-shop fryer. I've stood in front of the bewitching living-room mirror for no more than five minutes at a time whilst I plaited my hair, and then I've walked away – forcing myself not to return. I've swallowed back my desperate need to ask for reassurance on many occasions, often leaving the room when it becomes too much to stop the words spilling from my mouth. I'm making confident strides ahead in what I believe to be the right direction. But as with every journey, progress is never linear: there are bumps in the road, and I'm about to hit mine.

It's fast approaching, like a speeding train. Every time I look anywhere on social media, it's there – haunting me, taunting me. The London Marathon weekend is coming up, and I'm finding it increasingly difficult to process the fact that I won't be there. My mind drifts back to the devastating Valentine's Day 'treat' consultation with the international athlete-turned-coach who was *supposed* to advise me of top marathon training tips, but instead sat and informed me of the benefits of aqua-jogging and high-intensity interval sessions on a bike whilst my heart shattered into pieces. I think about the panicked phone call to my GP and my realisation that this isn't just about the loss of running: it's about my broken mind. My BDD therapy has given me a focus, together with my 'Training Plan B', which I've now integrated into my weekly routine, replacing my many futile attempts at a 'test run', which only served to further damage my legs – and my mind. But my knowledge of the impending London Marathon weekend hurts me deeply. We even have the train tickets and hotel booked, and … *I SHOULD BE THERE!*

'Why don't we still go down to London for the weekend?' my Other Half thoughtfully suggests as the April date creeps ever closer. I ponder on it and think that yes, perhaps that might be a good thing. Maybe we could have a stroll around the marathon Expo on the Saturday and then stand somewhere on London Bridge with a large cardboard sign saying, 'TOUCH HERE FOR SUPER POWERS! [arrow pointing down]' on race day. But that's before I stop to consider that it will break my heart to buy Tilly another London Marathon teddy bear and explain to her that, 'No, Tills, I didn't run this one. I, erm – I just went down to watch.' She has a small collection of London Marathon teddy bears which mean something significant to us both. They symbolise something about me – her mum – making it to the start line, and then all the way to the finish. And the prospect of me standing somewhere on London Bridge with a motivational kick-arse sign for runners whilst sobbing into my coat sleeve just doesn't have the right kind of vibe.

Mentally it's all too much, and it's steering me off course with my BDD therapy. I haven't filled out my diary for a couple of days now, and it's becoming harder to focus on my exposure therapy challenges.

I went to the hairdresser's and had my hair cut and coloured a few days ago, and it's unsettled me. I don't feel right: I feel anxious and uneasy, and I've become focused on – and consumed by – the prospect that my hair isn't 'right' (whatever that means). I can't seem to switch off the churning, whirling thoughts in my mind. And my Good Cop SWAT team are nowhere to be seen – they've gone AWOL. I don't know where they are, and I can't seem to identify any potential 'interpretation traps' – I just don't know where to look. Instead, my Bastard Chimp has rallied his troops and they are on the move, trampling over places which I thought had been liberated. But no, they're back, and I feel helpless as I stand by and watch them growing in strength, wondering why I can't stop them from destroying my recently discovered inner peace.

We're in Manchester city centre on our way to see *Grease! The Musical*. Tilly and her friend are excited as we spot increasing numbers of fake Pink Ladies milling about the theatre entrance. 'Look, it's Sandy!' Tilly shouts out as a pretty blonde lady with an uncanny resemblance to a young

Olivia Newton-John walks towards us with what is presumably her boyfriend – who, disappointingly, looks absolutely nothing like Danny. I'm suddenly overwhelmed with anxiety. I can feel it flooding my entire system, as though panic is being intravenously infused through an invisible drip. *What's wrong with me? What's happening to me?* My eyes dart around in terror. The wind is blowing my hair all over the place and I swipe horrible, straggly strands away from my face, but it keeps blowing back, sticking to my lips and making my eyes itch. I can't breathe. My throat is closing, and I can't breathe. Sandy has just glided past with her beautiful blonde hair in a sleek, long ponytail, and her immaculate red-painted, smiling lips. Meanwhile, I'm here struggling to breathe, as my flawed, ugly hair itches and wafts and irritates all around my face and my neck. I want to run; I want to run away. *Where can I run to?* I need a mirror. *I must find a mirror.* I must check my hair, and I need to comb it and straighten it and change it, somehow. *Where can I find a mirror? Where can I go?* I need to go. NOW!

'I don't feel right,' I say to my Other Half, who is busy rifling through multiple tickets as we approach the theatre doors. 'I can't breathe. I don't know what's happening to me, and I can't breathe.'

But I *do* know what's happening to me. I know *exactly* what's happening: I'm having a meltdown as my Bastard Chimp and his troops tear through my mind, bombarding me with cruel, hurtful thoughts. *You're UGLY. UGLY. UGLY. Look at you! You're a mess. You want to be pretty, don't you, Rachel? But you're not, you're ugly. Look around at all the pretty, beautiful people here. You want to be like them, don't you? But you're not. You won't ever be. Because you're UGLY.*

I try to focus on taking one deep breath in, and then back out again. Breathe in, and then out. In, and out. *WHERE'S MY GOOD COP SWAT TEAM? What about the interpretation traps? Where are they?* I can't find them. I feel exhausted and confused. What about my BDD exposure therapies? What about all that I've learned, all that I've done? Where has it gone? I can't even contemplate the prospect that my therapy is all for nothing, that it hasn't worked. I hadn't anticipated this: I am confused and devastated.

22

THE ROAD BIKE

I look at my newly padded arse in the mirror (I now own *two* pairs of Beyoncé-inspired cycling shorts!) and I don't know who I've become. I've taken to wearing cycling jerseys around the house. In fact, I'm currently sitting in my long-sleeved, zip-up cycling jersey and if I glance to my left, I can see two spare bike wheels sitting boldly underneath the lounge window, these having recently been changed over on my … NEW ROAD BIKE! Yes, *that*.

The road bike thing came about quickly, and entirely out of the blue. Like a blind date that ends up blurry-eyed in some Gretna Green B&B (or Las Vegas, if you're Britney Spears). *How? What happened? Did we really do this?* An innocent conversation with a work colleague that went something like this:

Him: *'I see you're getting into your mountain biking, Rach?'*

Me: *'Yeah! I'm beginning to really enjoy it. I can't believe I'm even saying that, but it's true.'*

Him: 'Ahh, you wait until you get out on a road bike!'

Me: 'Really? Why on earth would I want to do that? Those flimsy things terrify me. There's no WAY you'll catch me going out on one of those any time soon!'

Him: 'Speed, Rach – the need for speed. You won't believe the difference. I've got a 2012 Scott Foil aero I don't use any more. I don't have room for it and I was going to sell it to a friend, but that fell through. It's a beautiful machine – you're welcome to give it a go sometime, if you like.'

I hear mention of the word 'speed' and I'm already sold.

Me: 'OK … Are you free this evening?'

I don't hang about. I turn up at my colleague's house and he talks me through what's on offer: this beautiful, sexy, Scott Foil aero frame road bike comes complete with a Shimano Ultegra groupset (I've still no idea what this means!) and Planet X 'aero' wheels (I presume they're not made of bubbly milk chocolate), plus Shimano Ultegra rims (what?!). As he pointlessly talks me through the road bike's specifications, I'm mentally rifling through my very basic biking glossary, trying to decipher my *rims* from my *derailleurs*, and my *groupset* from my *seatpost*. It all sounds like double-dutch to me, but all I *do* know is that the road bike *has* to be mine.

'Why don't you take it for a ride home and see how you get on?' my generous, road-cycling colleague offers. I only live a couple of miles away and it's still light outside. Maybe I could give it a whirl? What have I got to lose?

And so, Challenge #5 – this time on a road bike – is born.

* * *

Challenge #5: Can I even ride this sleek, strange, drop-handlebar number, with the unfamiliar gears I don't know how to use for two-and-a-half miles back home *along one straight road* without causing any kind of calamity?

Admittedly, this bike is a beautiful thing: sleek and angular, with a slender crisp white frame. I lift it up and it feels like the biking equivalent of a Malteser – it's floaty light. *I've been cycling a fucking tank!* is my first thought (sorry, Trek), although it's a tank I've grown to know and love. I push 'Scott' (we're already on first name terms) a few yards up the hill, away from my colleague's front door to a flat stretch of road, and I tentatively climb aboard.

'Right, I'm off. Wish me luck!'

Trusting only my instincts and the basic premise of 'If in doubt, just pedal', I roll away and in the direction of home. This only requires me to navigate my way up ONE SINGLE MAIN ROAD with a reasonably steady incline, for just a couple of miles, with no discernible traffic issues, crossing only one major road junction, happening across minimal pedestrians, and equally, minimal opportunity to face-plant outside a local supermarket. The risks of this admittedly precarious new challenge are mitigated by these factors.

I can feel my heart pounding in my chest. Not because of the physical effort of the riding, or the gentle incline of the two-mile climb back home. My heart is thumping hard because I'm overriding my anxiety. I'm a baby bird jumping out of the nest, learning how to fly. *Will I fall? How far away is the ground?* I just hope and pray that my instinct kicks in, and my wings will save me.

Of course, Scott is still just a bike, with a frame and two wheels. I remind myself of this fact, and that I have proved that *I can ride a bike*, but everything feels so completely different. The seat is much narrower and placed further back on the frame; the handlebars drop down and my body feels as though it's falling forwards rather than sitting upright; the gears are freakishly located *on* the handlebars themselves, and I have no option but to experiment, frantically trying to figure out how this thing works. So I flick a lever inwards with my right hand, shifting the chain set down to one of the smaller cogs on the back wheel. I can feel how that affects my pedalling, as I'm suddenly having to push down harder, making it more difficult to climb. I flick another, smaller lever – confusingly still on my right handlebar – which this time cranks the chain set back up to the bigger cogs. The effort of pedalling eases again, and the incline becomes less of an issue.

Phew! OK, so that's how to shift the back gears. Now to try out the front ones.

I repeat my suck-it-and-see philosophy on the left, and again, I can sense how changing gears affects my riding. There's something about the fact that I am *feeling* how the bike is working which makes sense to me. I may not understand all the technical terms and the cycling lingo just yet, but I can *feel* how what I do affects how the bike works whilst I'm riding it.

Just a few experimental miles later, and I thankfully arrive back home in one piece. This is the first test for Scott and me, and we pass with flying colours.

Text message to my colleague: *Hi. I've made it back home and I'd like to buy Scott off you. I can transfer the money to you online tonight, if that's OK? Thanks! Rach (the soon-to-be road cyclist)*

Note to self: WHO THE ACTUAL F*CK HAVE I BECOME? Oh, and we need a bigger shed.

* * *

I'm on a roll with my new Malteser-framed, floaty-light road bike. Well, I made it home in one piece, and I'm prone to dramatisation. So, just like the first three mini challenges I set myself on Trek, my sturdy, slightly ageing and undeniably plump mountain bike, I decide to do the same with Scott: we will set off on a journey of discovery together, risking failure and face-planting in the process. Here's what we will do next:

CHALLENGE #6: CAN I RIDE FURTHER UP THE HILL, NAVIGATING MY WAY AROUND THE STEEP BEND, UP TO THE SMELLY FARM AND BACK HOME AGAIN? THIS WILL REQUIRE:

- more climbing;
- travelling on busier roads (and at a busier time of day);

- going up a steeper incline;
- handling a reasonable descent, where my metaphorical balls will be put to the test on my new speedy Malteser-framed, floaty-light bike. *Will it even hold my weight?* I have no idea.

Remembering my suck-it-and-see philosophy from Challenge #5, the ride home from my colleague's house, I try to re-acquaint myself with the unfamiliar gears. Referring to them only as 'the left one' and 'the right one' – and with no discernible knowledge as to which of the cogs, front or back, relate to either – we struggle to hit it off. Cycling along the two-mile road back home was one thing, and required very little mechanical manoeuvring, but we're on a sheer learning curve, and I must become familiar with the workings of this delicate machine I'm now relying upon. We're on our second date, and although we've eked out the painful getting-to-know-you first-date patter, the pair of us are slightly apprehensive about date number two.

I clumsily crank at 'the left one' and then jar unceremoniously at the right. As I cycle up and around the main road which veers steeply to the left, I can feel the incline noticeably increasing. Nothing feels smooth and nothing flows, like an awkward silence across a candle-lit dinner. Regardless, I continue making efforts to understand the mechanics. I'm busy flicking levers left and right: in and back out again, like a shy teenager fumbling about in the dark with his first girlfriend, when Scott suddenly buckaroos me off. He's turned into a racehorse who is fed up of accommodating such an incompetent, ignorant rider. *SHIT!* I manage to stay on my feet, at least.

Wait, that doesn't sound right. I try to roll Scott away, but I can hear a clunky, grinding metal sound and the wheels won't turn. The chain has come loose, and for a good while longer than a split-second I consider phoning home and calling for immediate rescue.

Is there a biking equivalent of the AA? If so, I want to join.

BUT I WILL NOT BE DEFEATED. I pick up my Malteser bike and carry him across to the safety of the pavement on the other side of the road, where I flip him upside down and confidently prop him up on his saddle and handlebars. With 'fake it til you make it' as my motivational mantra, I want to at least look like I know what I'm doing, so that any passing motorists will presume I've got this shit under control: *See that lady over there with the sleek-framed, white Scott road bike? Her chain's come off, but she clearly knows what she's doing.*

If only they knew.

Instinctively, I begin fiddling about with the greasy, oily chain – poking at cogs and turning them in (what I consider to be) the right direction. But oh, no, this is causing untold havoc to my recently acquired acrylic nails. *Bloody hell! Why is cycling so damn difficult?!* My shiny pillar-box red nails are now streaked with black, oily smears, and one of them has broken completely. Eventually, I manage to make the chain slot back into place, with teeth sitting in their respective grooves. Meanwhile, my Bastard Chimp pulls up alongside me:

Oh, Rach, look at you! What have you gone and done now? What if you've just fucked up the gears? There's every chance you'll get back onto Scott and fall straight off him again. You're riding along a steep main road. Everyone will see you if you set off in the wrong – and now broken – gear, and fall off. And you could even get flattened by a passing tractor. What if you've gone and wrecked Scott completely? FFS, Rachel, it's only your second ride out on him. What are you thinking? You should just give this up, now.

But I won't listen to him. Instead, I punch my Bastard Chimp in the face and I carry my featherweight friend back onto the road. I wait a long while until there's absolute silence, which I presume to mean there is no traffic within an approximate two-mile radius, and I tentatively hop on board, hoping and praying that I have placed the right chain on the right cog. *Is that a vehicle I can hear approaching half a mile behind me?* I'm not sure. With my heart in my mouth, I cycle off.

I change gear (left/right/front/back – who cares?) and I can hear them click smoothly into place. *YES! YES! FUCKING YES!* Mini victory celebrations commence to rival Prince Harry and Meghan Markle's royal wedding, and inside my head I'm popping champagne corks and dancing a victory jig at taking yet another incremental step towards being a slightly less incompetent cyclist. If we're painting by numbers, then I'd say I'm on to crayoning a mosaic picture with a subtle colour palette. I no longer need a chunky Crayola, and I'm (just about) staying within the lines.

It's quite simply a victory, people.

23

THE REVIEW

I've reached the halfway point of my therapy course, and Dr G has emailed me to arrange our review. He's not stupid, he knows I've been struggling.

It looks like it's been a little while since you logged in. Please try to do that when you get a chance so you can read my messages. Let me know how things have been going for you.

Shit, SHIT! I've been rumbled. Dr G knows that I haven't been completing my online BDD diary; he knows when I last logged on to go through my latest torturous module worksheets, and when I last completed one of my many 'assessment questionnaires'.

I prided myself on being a good student, with my recently appointed Good Cop SWAT team dutifully on hand to identify and eliminate any interpretation traps, and now I feel like I'm letting him down. I've started to regress, falling back into my old ways, and not even making the effort to pick up and use the new tools I've been given. I begin to catastrophise that Dr G will be disappointed in me, and will wish that he'd never accepted me onto the BDD therapy programme. *Shit, shit, shit! Plenty of other people could have benefited from this treatment, why has he wasted his time on me? Will he remove me from the course? Have I just blown my chance of ridding myself of this thing? Did I fail under pressure, simply because things got a bit much? How am I not even able to work my way through a twelve-week online therapy programme? Why have I stumbled now – at only the halfway point? And why am I here, wanting to quit when the going gets tough?*

My head is still spinning with the prospect of going down to London to NOT take part in the London Marathon, and as it stands, that's still the plan. But I can feel myself breaking down. Mentally, I feel vulnerable and, well, truly exposed.

I message him back my availability, which is later than he hoped due to my impending trip to London. I hope that Dr G will understand, and that he won't feel let down. I'm not sure he'll buy the whole 'snowed under with work' or 'sheer busyness' thing, but I'm kind of relieved that I won't have to face him (literally) and his endless assessment questionnaires this week. I feel like I've bought myself a little more time to get back on the wagon, and to claw myself back out of this dark hole which I've fallen into right when I was just beginning to see daylight breaking through.

You can get there again, Rach. You can climb out of here again.

And so, I begin. For the first time in what feels like weeks (it's actually days), I'm logged on:

'Please tick the box that best describes how often you have thought about your appearance or a specific feature over the past week, including today:

(a) not at all;
(b) a little;
(c) often;
(d) a lot;
(e) all the time.

Bloody hell, here we go again ...

* * *

'I'm really sorry,' I say to my Other Half as I heave myself and all my gym bags back in through the front door, 'but I don't want to go down to London tomorrow.' He understands why: he knows it was a long shot.

I've just been out for a walk. It was such a beautiful morning. As the sun rose majestically in the sky, bathing the fields in a golden hue, I looked out of the window and simply couldn't bring myself to get in a car. Instead, I walked through the grass, noticing where the sharpest rays of sunlight hit, making the dewdrops sparkle. A *hushhhhhh* settled over the woodland and I looked up at the trees. There they stood, magnificent and silent; unwavering. There was no wind at all. The only sounds I could hear were my own footsteps crunching gently through the long grass, and the occasional rustle of leaves where I imagined I might have disturbed a local inhabitant. A squirrel darted across my path and scurried up a tree. I could even hear his tiny claws as he scrambled at lightning speed to the top of the corrugated bark. I felt peaceful.

I'm tired now, as walking up and over the hills, attempting the bird and the pyramid yoga poses (amongst others), and climbing back up the hills in reverse was hard work. It's taken up most of my morning, but the walking has helped me to process my endless, whirring thoughts.

I want – and need – to refocus on my therapy. I don't need the distraction of going to London over Marathon weekend, or to risk my mental health wavering any further as I deliberately put myself in an even more vulnerable place. It's a kind of 'exposure therapy', I guess, but one that is most certainly *NOT* a part of my treatment.

I decide to focus all my energies back on my therapy programme, and away from any unhelpful distractions. The peace I felt wash over me during my woodland walk has helped me to choose simplicity and to steer myself back onto the path I was following, which felt to genuinely be helping me to identify, rationalise, process and manage my destructive body-dysmorphic thoughts from a place where I once had no power or control over them. I cannot regress any further, and so I begin to click through my routine rapid-fire questionnaires, as per the usual protocol:

Answer (d) a lot;
Answer (e) all the time …

24

EXPLORING

I wake up and I'm feeling brave: brave and adventurous. So much so that I don't even have a plan – I just want to get out on my bike and explore. I want to see where the road takes me, with no end destination in mind.

So, I plonk my padded backside onto my Malteser-framed bike, and we head off on our next adventure. I turn right onto the road outside my house, which carves straight through woodland and is densely packed with ancient, deciduous trees. They arch over the road almost meeting in the middle, giving it an enclosed, tunnel-like feel. Within moments, a 10-tonne truck comes thundering along on one of its frequent trips to and from the nearby recycling plant. I remember the first time I felt the very same wind-tunnel effect and the drag on my bike as the truck whooshed past me, pushing the air out of the way like a swimmer doing breaststroke. It still feels unnerving, especially on my skeletal, floaty-light road bike, but I know what to expect from riding Trek along the very same stretch of road.

Just hold on tight and keep pedalling, Rach! I tell myself, waiting for the resistance in the temporary wind tunnel to abate.

I turn left onto the same main road which climbs sharply as it bends, and where I was unceremoniously buckaroo'd off by Scott just days before. I still have some greasy black smears on my remaining fingernails as evidence of my emergency handiwork, but this time around, I've thought ahead and packed some disposable latex gloves I found stuffed in a box underneath the sink. At least I know how to put the chain back onto the cogs if it comes loose again, and I can minimise any further damage to my nails in the process. *RESULT!* But surely – as far as odds go – then it would be *HIGHLY IMPROBABLE* for the same thing to happen twice?

I continue cycling up the hill, and soon I'm approaching the steep bend. The incline is making it harder to maintain my cadence and so I crank roughly with the gears, but I've left it too late. Scott bolts, and the chain comes off in exactly the same place as it did before. *Fucking hell! How is that even possible?* But this time, I know what to do and I've come prepared. I lift my skeletal cycling companion up and unceremoniously flip him over. Unzipping the pocket of my rucksack, I don my disposable gloves. *Fuck you, oily chain, if you think you're going to wreck my nails again!* I fiddle about with the chain, shifting a few cogs here and there, and – just as before – harmony is restored.

I get back on the saddle, and we begin to roll away. A smile spreads across my face as I can feel myself increasing in speed, efficiency and confidence with every revolution of the wheels.

We soon ride past the same smelly farm I cycled to on Challenge #6, but I don't turn off here. Instead, I look ahead at the open road which beckons me further. *I've never been beyond that hill … I ponder. I wonder what's over there?* I cycle past my familiar junction and head out along the unfolding road ahead of me. It's all completely new. It feels exciting and I feel brave.

'*Ha ha ha! Get a grip, Rach,*' my Bastard Chimp chunters in my ear. '*You've only cycled half a mile further up the road! Hardly earth-shattering, is it?*'

Oh, fuck off, Chimp! It may be small progress, but these are all steps in the right direction. I give him the middle finger and quickly turn away.

I'm even beginning to have a breakthrough with mastering my gears. I continue to experiment, flicking smoothly to higher gears on the flatter sections and lowering them again on the climbs, and some small semblance of understanding begins to take place between us. *We're rolling, now!* I can feel the chain and cogs clicking into place, and I can sense when the gear change is forced and feels wrong: *Scott and I are beginning to converse and to understand each other.*

I look ahead and I'm immediately pulled back into anxiety management mode. *Fucking hell, that's the motorway bridge – I'm about to cycle across the M62!* A gust of air suddenly rushes at me sideways as my front wheel reaches the high motorway bridge. My grip on the handlebars tightens. This is an eerie, exposed place. I know that some people come up here only to jump over the side, onto the motorway carriage which is a long way below. I daren't look to my left or right, and I daren't allow myself to think about how someone might end their life in this way. Sadness is all around me. Samaritans posters run along the entire length of the bridge, and tiny coloured ribbons flap frantically on the railings, together with remnants of a sparse bunch of flowers which has been fastened securely so that the wind didn't destroy them within seconds. I want to get off the bridge: I just want to get away from here, and to the safety of the other side.

Scott feels vulnerable along here. He doesn't have Trek's chunky, robust frame and the wind whips around him in every direction, making him wobble frantically. I wrestle to control the front wheel and pedal as fast as I can to reach the other side.

I make it across the bridge and my quads are burning with the effort of the sudden increase in pace, whilst my heart thumps loudly in my chest. I can't honestly tell if it's due to the increased exertion, or the emotional weight of other peoples' pain that I have just cycled through: it's a reminder to me that we're all hurting in some way.

A mile further on, and I ride past a road sign saying, 'Welcome to Kirklees!' That's another metropolitan borough, and it makes me feel like I've broken through some invisible barrier, venturing further afield than I have ever done before. I have absolutely no idea where I'm going, so I just keep pedalling.

It feels increasingly remote, and I'm now surrounded by wild heathers and moorland. The wind is picking up, and I'm getting cold. Eventually, I approach a crossroads up ahead, where I can only turn left or right. *Phew!* I've been cycling uphill along this one, desolate countryside road for almost eight miles. I'm high up and it's a beautiful vantage point from here, so I decide to stop briefly in a parking area. Relieved to remove myself from Scott, I look ahead: I can see a reservoir which I never knew existed. Another road cyclist pulls up alongside me, and we stand side by side, gazing down at the water sparkling below.

'Excuse me. This may sound very strange, but do you have any idea where we are?' I ask, breaking the comfortable silence to risk sounding utterly ludicrous.

'Ha! Yeah, this is March Haigh Reservoir,' he says, sounding confused by the question. I've heard of it many times before, but I've never actually been there.

'Thanks. It's only my third ride out on this little number,' I reply, gesturing to Scott and trying to put into context the reason why I appear to be so entirely clueless as to my current whereabouts. 'I'm just out exploring.' I look down at my GPS watch, which confirms that I've just cycled eight miles up a hill.

'Wow! Not bad going, that. It's a hell of a climb up here,' he says. 'Nice machine you've got there, by the way.'

I smile at my beautiful Scott, now serenely propped up against a fence. I decide not to tell my new cycling friend that I'm still working out how to change gears properly, or that I've only just deciphered that the left gear works my front derailleur (the critical part of the bike responsible for shifting the gears, I have learned), and the right one the back.

'Thanks!' I reply, beaming. 'I only bought him a few weeks ago, and I already love him!'

I say goodbye to my new friend and head off on my downhill, white-knuckle ride back home. The wind whips across my face as I feel my speed increasing, mile after mile. I stand up on my pedals with my bum high in the air, snot blowing across my face. And there's a tune playing in my head:

Every stop I make, I make a new friend,
Can't stay for long, just turn around and I'm gone again.

I quickly identify it as the soundtrack to *The Littlest Hobo* with his love of adventure, and I can't help thinking to myself: *Who the actual fuck am I?*

I'm smiling, inside.

25

GETTING BACK
ON TRACK

Email from: Dr G
Subject: Checking in

Hi Rachel,

Thanks for your email, and honestly, it's OK. I understand how life can throw curve balls and that this can have an impact on therapy. I've put you in my schedule for next Tuesday for our mid-point review.

If you do have a spare moment, even just logging in briefly to look at the worksheets, or beginning to think about your first exposures and how they impacted on you is still better than nothing at all.

Good luck in these busy – and challenging – times. I will talk to you soon.

Dr G

As I read Dr G's kind response to my 'Sorry, Sir! The dog ate my homework' bail-out on our mid-point review, I breathe an audible sigh of relief. I feel relieved that I haven't burned my bridges and lost the opportunity to see how this course of therapy might work for me. And I do exactly as Dr G suggests: I log in and read over some of my diary entries. First, from the very early days of writing down my BDD experiences and identifying my damaging thoughts to possible 'interpretation traps' and the many exposure therapy challenges I set for myself. I remember it all so vividly; I can feel my throat closing as I sat panic-stricken outside my work, wondering how on earth I could step out of my car. I can also take myself straight back to that time – a time before I knew anything about 'interpretation traps' or the SWAT team whose job it is to bring them to my attention. I didn't know about any of that stuff, back then.

I continue reading through my diary, and I can still feel my heart pounding in the moments before I walked into the school playground with my unwashed hair for the very first time, feeling completely vulnerable as I faced my first 'exposure therapy' challenges. I can also recall the feeling of mild euphoria as I bounced back out of the playground, when it dawned on me that these were all lies I'd been telling myself. It seems such a long time ago, and I realise that a lot has changed in my mind, already.

I reply to Dr G and explain to him about my decision not to go down to London over the Marathon weekend, and the peace I needed to find instead. I tell him that I feel like I must stop and process everything, so that my stress levels don't develop into something darker and more sinister. And I let him know that I have done as he's suggested, and that it's already coming back to me: the challenges I've faced, the learning, and the progress I've made. I feel like I'm taking tiny steps forward again after my mini wobble.

* * *

It's time for my mid-point review with Dr G. Just as before, I've hoovered the carpet and picked up any discarded pants and socks from the bedroom floor. I've made a proverbial 'DO NOT DISTURB' sign for the other occupants of the house. I decide to go to my yoga class beforehand, because I know that it works wonders in resetting my head.

'You look well, Rach!' one of the regular ladies says as I'm walking through into the studio, carrying my yoga mat.

'Oh, thanks!' I reply, unsure what else to say. It takes me aback a little, because I haven't had a shower or washed my hair this morning. I make a mental note to discuss this with Dr G during our review this afternoon, because this has happened to me a few times, recently: not only have I continued placing myself in 'exposing' situations, but I've actually received compliments on how I look when I do! The irony makes me laugh to myself as I consider the lengths I would previously have gone to, making great efforts to ensure that I leave the house looking pristine, only to feel self-conscious and uncomfortable when I do. It's the last ten minutes of our yoga class. The teacher invites us to put on some warm clothing and to settle ourselves in a comfortable position. I wrap my bare feet in my hoodie and lie flat on my back, my arms splayed out to the sides, palms facing up.

'Where else can you let go?' the unfamiliar husky voice asks (it's not our usual teacher). 'It might be helpful to do a scan of your body, and to see where else you can soften.'

Taking her words literally, I begin to work my way down my body, making a conscious effort to ease my muscles, lose any tension, and to let go. I hadn't realised my forehead was crinkled with tension, or that my teeth were clenched. I switch off my facial muscles, loosen my jaw, and continue working my way down my body, un-shrugging my shoulders and allowing my belly to soften. It feels so good to allow my overthinking mind to switch off, and for my entire body to relax.

The sun is bursting through the skylight in the yoga studio and warmth floods my body. I begin to realise that my decision to come to the class without undertaking my previously onerous preening regime has freed me. It may have begun some weeks ago as an anxiety-inducing 'exposure therapy' challenge, but it has since allowed me to be present in a place without constant expectation, evaluation – and criticism. I've finally been liberated from my own relentless strive for perfection. The room is still, and I'm calm. I open my eyes and look up at the skylight, feeling my tummy rise as I breathe in deeply and sink into the floor as I breathe out again, and I feel grateful. I'm grateful for the exposure therapy challenges, and for Dr G; I'm grateful for learning about potential 'interpretation traps' and for the kind lady who complimented me as I walked into the class today.

And I can't believe that I'm perhaps most grateful for the loss of running, which ultimately led to me seeking help for this. I'm now convinced: I think the therapy might just be working ...

* * *

'So, how's it been going?' Dr G asks in his soothing American drawl. I realise that this is more of an ice-breaker than part of the review, but I'm keen to tell him about what happened at the yoga class today. I'm not sure how he can measure that, or whether it will be useful data (pronounced *dar-tar*) for his study, but I want to share it with him, anyway.

'Hey, that sounds great!' he says, once I've finished telling him about my unexpected compliment from Kind Lady At The Gym. His eyes are warm and smiling, as though he is genuinely happy to hear about my progress. He's launching into the mid-point review assessment questionnaire preamble when I realise something: *I haven't been distracted by seeing my own image floating about in a small square in the corner of my computer screen.* I remember the very first video assessment I had with Dr G, and feeling like my eyes were being permanently drawn back to assess myself for flaws. What's more, I haven't just spent an hour straightening my hair. Yes, I jumped in the shower when I got home after my yoga class, but I've left my hair to dry naturally, and I've scraped it into an unremarkable ponytail just to keep it off my face. I answer his rapid-fire questions with ease, responding to the usual 'How many times have you ...', 'To what extent do you ...' and 'Please select which of the following statements are true ...' as though it's second nature.

'Thanks, Rachel. That's the review complete,' Dr G informs me just as I'm getting into my stride. I can't help but feel a little disappointed. I have so many other mini victories to share with him, and so many other observations I have about the way my mind is starting to see things differently, and the changes I'm seeing – and feeling – as a result.

26

ONE STEP AT A TIME

Once I fully immerse myself in my *new* two-wheeled challenges, I eventually let go of the many futile attempts to force my body to run. Gone are the dreaded two-mile teary test runs along the canal, and my desperate efforts to run around the block from work (via the sandwich shop for my lazy boss). The London Marathon has long since been and gone. I am finally able to let running go, and to turn my attention to more positive, worthwhile goals, such as challenging myself to ride up some of the demanding local hills and exploring into unknown areas. The shift in focus helps me to recalibrate my head and to re-evaluate my goals. It feels like the shackles had been taken off and I've been liberated from the belief that running is the only possible answer for my mental health troubles.

But life has a funny way of keeping us on our toes and reminding us who's boss. The moment we allow ourselves to believe that we've finally got it all sussed, that's precisely when the game changes and we realise what we *think* we know isn't quite what it seems. So, it should have come as no surprise that when I'd fully immersed myself in my new cycling interests and goals – and of course, my BDD therapy – running would come creeping back to tap me on the shoulder and remind me that he's still here. As the wise old saying goes, 'If you stop looking for love, it will find you', and it looks like this might also be true for, well, pretty much *anything* – running included. *IF YOU STOP PINING FOR IT, THEN IT COMES KNOCKING ON YOUR DOOR.* Which is exactly what happens.

He came back.

But running had left me, once. He'd abandoned me at the altar, leaving me holding an unjustifiably expensive bunch of flowers and the prospect of paying for (and going on) a honeymoon by myself without any kind of explanation as to why he couldn't be with me any more. I'd been jilted; abandoned; devastated; and almost destroyed as a result. So, when he eventually turns up knocking again, I am cautious. I don't trust him, and I don't want him to think that he can just come striding back through the front door, all 'Hi honey, I'm home!' as though nothing has happened and expect me to be the same person that I was before. I'm not the same person. I've changed – I'm still changing. And I *like* changing! On this basis, I have a few ground rules that I need to establish before running can reclaim his sock drawer.

Me: 'There's something I need to tell you.'
Running: 'Right? What is it?' [trying to nuzzle my
               neck, but I push him away]
Me: 'There's someone else.'

Running: 'What? WHAT THE ACTUAL FUCK?'

Me: 'What are you talking about? YOU LEFT ME! And when you did, I met someone else. Someone I happen to like.'

Running: 'So, who is this "SPECIAL fucking SOMEONE" then?'

[A brief, awkward silence.]

Me: 'Cycling. I love cycling.'

[Running stomps out of the room, slamming the door on his way out.]

It's important that I have The Conversation with running, because everything *has* changed: running *isn't* my only love any more.

With this caveat in mind, running has returned slowly, but I have managed to keep him at arm's length. Gone are the days of waking up with only him on my mind, wondering when our next 'date' will be, and where we might go. And my legs are very helpful reminders of the damage that has been caused by taking a different approach. Yes, I'm running again, but it's an entirely alien feeling. My legs feel tentative and unsure. They do as I ask of them, but no more. At times, I'm preoccupied by the jelly-like sensation of my over-trained legs, and the occasional shooting pains, like electricity firing down both sets of hamstrings: almost a warning shot of the need for 'moderation', a word I had to Google translate.

We may run for a few steady, flat miles, but then I know that I can't – and mustn't – go any further. This isn't anything I have been instructed by a medical professional. Rather, it is me learning to listen to my body and to realise when it has had enough. The alternative – as I have discovered – is that my body simply won't run at all. At times, I wonder how it was ever possible for me to do some of the punishing training sessions I used to put myself through. *How did I wake up and run fourteen fast miles, bouncing out and back along the canal, just because I felt like it?* I can't imagine ever being in that place again. *What about the ten-mile back-to-back tempo runs? Ten hilly miles out, followed by ten equally hilly ones back home again.* How? I know for a fact that my legs simply wouldn't allow it to happen. Not now and, quite possibly, not ever again.

And running must also grapple for space in my recently modified training diary. It's a strange concept for us both, but a reality nonetheless: *Nope, I'm not running, today – I'm cycling to yoga, instead.*

Spring turns into summer, and my mind has expanded into a whole new world of adventure-seeking possibilities which are *NOT* exclusively running-related. This comes about firstly because I am still very aware of my own running limitations, and I know for a fact that my legs are simply not up to having any running demands being placed upon them, just yet. Remember our plans to take part in the inaugural Tanzanian Marathon in the autumn of 2017? I have come to accept that this will not be a reality for me, and I cannot have it looming over me like some deathly guillotine waiting to drop. But more than this, my mind is seeking out other, non-running adventures because I realise that ... *they exist! And it is possible for me to take part*! I can ride a bike, now. *Yes, I can do that!* And I have proven that I can learn how to challenge myself to improve and become more confident – and more competent – on two wheels.

'I think I want to enter into a race again,' I say across the breakfast table to my Other Half. 'It's time to get over the fear.' He doesn't seem too taken with the idea, possibly because he has seen the devastating impact running has had on me in recent times.

I choose the Ilkley Trail race on Bank Holiday Monday. It's not an obvious choice for a tentative first race since the debacle of the Dewsbury 10k back in February 2017, during which I'd been forced to make the Walk of Shame back to the start (before being picked up by the Unfortunate Bastards' Sweeper Bus). That was my last race.

Over the years I've experienced more than my fair share of race anxiety. I've been known to have sleepless nights before parkrun. *Yes, seriously!* That non-competitive, all-inclusive, everybody's-welcome-here event that is the weekly timed 5k more commonly known as 'parkrun'. I've woken up before sunrise on Saturday mornings with heart palpitations, in a fuzzy-headed, clammy sweat, cleaned the kitchen from top to bottom and *still* set off a good two hours before the lovely volunteer marshals have even pressed 'SNOOZE' on their Teasmade. And why? I have no answer. It doesn't really matter; none of it does. Nobody ultimately *cares* how I do – least of all at parkrun – or what time I drag my arse across the finish line. I used to think that it mattered, and that it proved something about who I am, and who I could be. But it doesn't. Successes are fleeting, like the perfectly white snow before it turns into a brown, disgusting sludge: enjoy it whilst you can.

A loss of form, however, separates the ego from the true self. It strips away the protective comfort of self-glorification and the pseudo mask of validation. Injury, illness, life events … Any one of them can suddenly derail even the most seemingly cocksure ego and have it tumble from the gilded perch on which it has merrily swung.

Q: What's left, then?

A: The shocking realisation and eventual acceptance that: IT'S NOT ALL ABOUT THE OUTCOME (CALL THE NEWSPAPERS: IT'S A REVELATION!)

I wake early on the Bank Holiday Monday, already processing my 'who am I, now?' crisp-white-snow-into-brown-sludge analogy. I've slept well. *PHEW!* This is a good start. No heart racing, no palpitations, and no reaching for the proverbial mushroom bag to help me calm my breathing down.

It's all under control, Rach.

Resting heart rate: 54.

Kit on, bags packed, I head out under a distinctly heavy sky in the direction of Ilkley. 'I don't feel nervous about today's race. Is that weird?' I say to my Other Half, who is acting as my Race Anxiety Support Crew, today.

'No, not a bit,' he replies, clearly still asleep.

'But I don't feel anything! No butterflies, no adrenalin, no tension. Just … nothing! I don't understand it. I slept like a baby and haven't taken to grinding my teeth or cleaning out the fridge at 6 a.m. It feels strange, that's all.' I continue, talking to myself as much as I am to him.

We are – true to form – a full hour too early on arrival at the Ilkley Lido. I slurp the remnants of cold coffee from my favourite Heisenberg travel mug with the heated seats on low, whilst my Other Half takes half-a-dozen attempts to pin a small square of paper onto the front of his vest without stabbing himself. The slate-grey heavens must have remembered that it's a national bank holiday and so they begin to spew relentless rain from the skies.

It feels like coming home.

Once my trainers have been replaced by my less-familiar trail running shoes, I step out into the shower which is now pouring from a monochrome sky, and I begin to jog – no, hobble – up the grassy banking towards the start of the race. I continue slowly up the offensive hill in a torturous pre-race dress rehearsal of what's about to come.

'I am fucked,' I pant, stopping my pathetic attempt at a warm-up jog only a quarter of the way up the hill, and stare blankly at my Other Half. 'And this is just the warm-up!'

Back down at the start line, we hang around at the rear like a pair of shy teenagers trying to smoke e-vapes behind the bike sheds.

'Start off slowly, Rach. And remember, it doesn't matter how you do, today. None of it matters. You're moving, and that's all that matters,' he tells me.

I know that he's right.

I set off slowly, towards the back of the pack. Thanks to the absence of any pressure, I relax a little and begin running up the inclining hillside, steadily inching past a decent number of runners, until I make it to the top. My legs have handled it: they are (just about) up to the job. The climb continues, and – unbelievably – my legs are still turning over, unbroken. A couple of miles in, and I've pulled ahead. But lack of racing fitness kicks in, and I take the opportunity to pull over and wait for my Other Half, who is sticking to his guns and approaching at a consistent, steady pace. I'm thankful for a breather.

The rest of the race is a battle of wills: I stop a bit, and I start again. I feel momentarily beaten, and then triumphant for fighting back and getting going again. The rain feels cold and cleansing, washing away any worries about my performance, personal bests or lack of form.

I'm here, and I'm back running. No, I'm back RACING!

Only it's racing in a very different way: I'm free from heaviness and from pressure; free from stress and worry. I'm racing on *my* terms, and I'm moving as well (or not) as my body can, on *this* day, today.

Crossing the finish line, I'm five minutes slower than the last time I tackled the very same race back in 2015, when – entirely without injury, illness, life event or force majeure – I was happily swinging away on my merry little running perch.

But I don't care. I'll happily roll around in the soft, white snow. Today, I'm grateful for the snow.

27

PROGRESS

The mid-programme review has gone well. In fact, it went *better* than well. Whilst talking through some of my body dysmorphic disorder exposure challenges with Dr G, I began to realise just how far I've come – despite the recent 'blip'. I flew through the million-and-one assessment evaluation questions at lightning speed, but it's virtually impossible to tell how my answers may have changed since the beginning of the treatment. That said, it's about far more than any 'improving treatment score' for me. Of course, it's vital that Dr G and his academic cronies can quantify the impact of their treatment, but for the likes of me – the *subjects* of their study – we simply want to be free of this wretched thing, and to live a normal life.

Email from: Dr G

I feel very positive about where we are going from here, Rachel. I have opened the next module for you, so you can start working on that when you get the chance. Please make sure to finish your exposure/

response prevention exercises, and the 'goals' work-sheets, in accordance with the plan we talked about.

Yes, yes, YES!!! I'm singing a happy song, and dancing a merry jig. HE IS PLEASED WITH MY PROGRESS! I'm officially not a 'time-waster', and I haven't taken up a valuable place on this treatment programme from A. N. Other *worthier* BDD sufferer.

Email from: Rachel

I can often fall foul of life's little curve balls knocking me off course and sending me spiralling into a negative place, but it appears that the early work we've done has been enough to help me challenge my unhelpful thoughts and has enabled me to intercept those early in the cycle.

I know I still have a way to go, but it is progress nonetheless.

Such is the reciprocal good feeling between myself and Dr G, I can't honestly tell if he's going to make it onto my Christmas Card list. What I *do* know is that this is working: the BDD treatment programme is having an impact on me, and I'm learning how to manage the guerrilla warfare tactics of my Bastard Chimp, which began in earnest some two decades previously.

I remember being nineteen years old. I had recently lost a noticeable amount of weight – mainly due to the one, three-mile running route I created from my mum's house, which I diligently stuck to over the summer break. I returned to university for the second year of my Law degree, and EVERYONE noticed the changes. But this flashback isn't one of me striding around the campus with my blonde hair bouncing in the sunshine, clearly oozing newfound body confidence. *Hell, no!* The picture I have in my mind is vivid. It comes to me so strongly, I wonder if this is it: is this the precise moment when it all began? Is this when body dysmorphia took a firm hold of me? Because it feels as though something big happened here. This is more than a memory; it's when something changed in my wiring.

I'm running on the treadmill at the university gym and I'm wearing the biggest, baggiest, dark blue Benetton T-shirt. I'm stick thin, and I'm disfigured. I'm running (well, hardly – it's more like an awkward trot) whilst hunching my shoulders and trying to keep my arms bent across my chest to disguise my glaring flaw. Three of the other girls I live with are also purportedly having a workout in the gym. They are laughing and chatting over on the other side of the cardio room: I can see them in the offensive, fully-mirrored wall in front of me. I'm convinced that they can see what I can feel: I can feel my left, saggy breast – or what is left of it – bounce with every foot strike on the treadmill, whilst my right breast (the smaller one) doesn't move. *Are they laughing at me?* I'm tortured by the prospect that they know my secret: *I AM DEFORMED. I AM UGLY AND DEFORMED.* This is the separation of me and them; of normal and abnormal; of fitting in, or not; of being accepted, or rejected. This is, quite possibly, where it all began.

Whether this was The Moment or not, I'm filled with a sense that now – for the first time since I stood hunched over with shame on the treadmill whilst barely out of my teenage years – I'm beginning to fully understand what body dysmorphia is, how it originated, and the thousands of 'interpretation traps' that have made it virtually impossible for me to escape its tireless grip, like being pulled into the tumult of a whirlpool. My mid-point review with Dr G has encouraged me to contemplate all that I have learned, and to acknowledge the enormous strides I have taken in freeing myself from the circling mass of water: I am finally coming up for air.

28

THE DUATHLON

Since relieving my somewhat shorter colleague of his Scott road bike,* I have revelled in some mini personal victories. Along with my series of progressive road biking challenges, I have also:

- Equipped myself with a bicycle pump and some other basic bike maintenance equipment, which I have absolutely no idea how to use (I now have enough Allen keys to make all the necessary adjustments to straighten the Eiffel Tower, yet raising my seat half an inch is still a bridge too far);
- Invested in a fancy bike carrier for my car – only because it will be necessary for me to transport Scott to the Oulton Park race track (we'll come back to this …);
- Affixed my fancy new bike carrier onto my non-fancy car. One entire Saturday afternoon is sacrificed as I wrestle

---

* This is relevant in so much as the bike is set up for a squat man of approximately 5'6" in height – I am a rather long-limbed 5'9" female. We will come back to this, later…

to marry my Nissan Juke with the various wires, arms, straps and contraptions contained within the neatly packaged Thule box. It drizzles mockingly as I stand in silence, watching instructional YouTube videos on repeat;

- Bought a pair of 'cleats' – these being shoes which will *fasten my feet onto the bike pedals* – a concept I still find utterly bemusing. Would it be simpler to just give me a hammer so I can break my own legs? Anyway, these are what *real cyclists* wear, so I'm told;

- *TRIED OUT* my fancy new cleat shoes on a short ride home from the bike shop. It didn't end well, as being unable to remove my feet from their technical bindings at a road junction resulted in a sideways Del-Boy-falling-through-the-bar face-plant manoeuvre.

I'm open to all kinds of possibilities now, with my mind focusing on goals of a more two-wheeled variety. I'm online, Google searching 'potentially interesting cycling challenges', sifting through the myriad ideas that have presented themselves. Local charity bike rides, cycling from London to Paris in a day, Prudential 'Ride London', Land's End to John O'Groats ... the options are endless. I do some more research, but nothing grabs me. Nothing feels 'right' and I don't want to force anything.

'Do you want a cup of tea?' I shout upstairs to my Other Half, who is soaking in the bath. I decide to leave Google alone for a little while (he's already steered me in many directions in my life to this point, including entering the New York, London and Dubai Marathons on a whim. I even ended up working on a game reserve in South Africa, all thanks to him) and I take a break from my cycling adventure research. I make myself a hot drink and close my MacBook down. I feel mildly frustrated, because I don't know what I'm looking for, but I'll know when I find it.

I begin to scroll mindlessly through Twitter on my phone. Someone has just posted, 'How many Jaffa Cakes is it acceptable to eat in one sitting?' I briefly consider maybe nine would be OK, possibly ten? I scroll down again, and there it is.

> *I've only gone and entered it! The short and long races are the same price, so I've entered the long one as it's better value for money. Oulton Park Autumn Duathlon in October… #runbikerun here I come!*

I don't know this person. I've no idea whether they are a professional triathlete or they spend more time posting stuff on Twitter than they do out running or riding a bike, but that doesn't matter. *Riding and running … running and riding. What could possibly be better than taking on a challenge where I CAN DO BOTH?* It feels kind of weird, like asking my partner for a threesome (my partner being running, who previously left me at the altar, remember?!), but I'm up for the challenge.

I'm ready to be a beginner again; I'm ready to risk falling off my bike, risk being the only person racing in non-clip-in shoes (I'm not brave enough to risk racing in these yet, after the face-plant incident), and risk coming last. I know that it will force me to face my fears, and to try something I've never done before. So, I decide to enter the Oulton Park

Autumn Duathlon. I do this on a whim (although I can't blame Google this time) when the realisation hasn't yet fully hit me that I'll have to at least *pretend* to know what I'm doing on a road bike.

How hard can it be?!

I choose to enter the longer-distance race. This will be a 9k run + 39k bike + 4.5k run. The alternative is a shorter Sprint distance (4.5k run + 21k bike + 4.5k run), but why bother with that? I'm not so fussed about the financial incentive with the cost of entering both distances being the same, but if we're talking money, then 'in for a penny, in for a pound' is my thinking behind choosing the longer-distanced race: if it's going to hurt for 21k on an uncomfortable, unfamiliar set of aero-framed skinny wheels and a blade for a saddle, then what difference is an additional 18k going to make?

I firmly believe that ignorance is bliss.

* * *

'I've decided I'm not going to wear my cleats for the race,' I declare to my Other Half as he stands in the kitchen, trying to work out how to gain access to the fridge, which is now entirely blocked by my upturned Scott road bike. 'It's not worth the risk, and surely I won't be the only person racing a road bike wearing running shoes?'

'No, of course not!' he replies, clearly distracted as he is still struggling to access the milk.

Once my Scott bike is sufficiently adhered to the boot of the car, the three of us – my daughter Tilly included – head off to Oulton Park race track. I spend the next two hours hearing Scott banging and rattling as I drive nervously along the motorway, utterly convinced with every second that passes that yet more layers of red paintwork are being abraded from my car.

'Are you sure we've fastened it on correctly?' I ask my Other Half, who is busy burying himself in Starburst sweet wrappers in the passenger seat. Occasionally, a small voice from the back seat asks, 'Can I have one, please?' The ratio of sweet apportionment is approximately 10:1 (adult: child).

* * *

We park up and a tall chap in a grey hoodie approaches me, smiling.

'You don't remember me, do you?' he says.

I look nonplussed at the approaching stranger, unable to disguise the fact that no, I have absolutely no idea who he is or where I'm supposed to have met him before.

'The Deer Park Dash!' he says, as if that will make it any easier.

Not a clue.

'Oh yeah, the Deer Park Dash! Of course!' I lie, as though repeating the race back to him were indeed confirmation that I have any kind of recollection of our exchange.

'I was the guy running with the pram!' he continues, as my vacant look hasn't gone unnoticed.

Lovely chap. Still no idea ...

We stand at the back of our car next to my bondaged Scott bike and the four of us – me, my Other Half, Friendly Hoodie Man and his wife – talk turkey about race tactics whilst Tilly messes about with my squashy energy gel sachets until one of them bursts.

'It's the last run that's a killer,' Friendly Hoodie Man says. 'Your legs are like jelly. You want to run, but your legs have turned to mush.'

I don't want to tell him that after our recent relationship struggles, the running sections are the parts of the duathlon that I'm looking forward to.

'Just maintain a good cadence on the bike and you can make up a lot of time with a decent cycling section,' he continues, helpfully.

'Great advice – thanks!' I say, wondering how much cadence I will be able to maintain whilst cycling in my running shoes on a road bike set up for a 5'6" sturdy male.

Oh, bollocks!

I look over at Scott, still gagged and bound to the back side of our car, and he suddenly feels like a complete alien to me. In that moment, I realise that I don't know him very well at all. I haven't worked out how he feels most comfortable, or what gears he prefers. I haven't taken the time to oil his chain or to lubricate his intricate parts. I haven't adjusted him to the correct seat height (I'm not a squat 5'6" male), and the metal pedals and I muddle along in some persistent misunderstanding which often results in chunks of flesh being removed from my shins. I bought an entire set of Allen keys, yet the seat still chafes parts of me only my partner knows. We are complete strangers.

What the fuck have I done? What the hell am I doing? I SHOULDN'T BE HERE! I suddenly panic, but it's too late for that, now.

Reluctantly, I wheel my alien – Scott – into the transition area (this being the place where the participants keep all their equipment when changing disciplines in a triathlon – swim / bike / run – or in this case, a duathlon – run / bike / run.)

'Could I safety check your bike please, madam?' a necessarily officious gentleman says as Scott and I approach him in our gormless state. 'Do you know that you've got an end bar missing?' he goes on, pointing to a part of Scott I've never noticed before. 'I'm going to have to tape it up, as I'd hate for you to impale yourself on the course if you have a collision.'

Oh. Right. Yep.

'And your tyres seem a bit low. In fact – crumbs – these won't last nine laps of the race track. Take it to the guy over there and he'll sort it out for you.'

I'm momentarily horrified. I didn't know what an 'end bar' was, or that I could potentially be impaled on one. And I was about to race in a duathlon around a racing track on a second-hand road bike with flat tyres. But I don't have time to panic. I trundle poor Scott over to another, younger gentleman, who winces when he feels the skinny rubber surrounding my wheels, like he's feeling the ribs of a starving dog.

'It's a good job you're here!' I joke, nervously.

He doesn't laugh. I wonder if he's in the biking equivalent of the RSPCA.

After standing in a pen for an informative safety briefing, we set off and I begin running confidently on my own two feet.

Yesss! I know how to do this!

I'm thrilled that running has reclaimed his sock drawer and that we're back together, again. I run past a number of professional-looking tri-suited competitors on the first of the two-lap running section. My pace is fast, and I feel good – I feel strong. No technical malfunctions are possible here, other than the obvious undone shoelaces or legs falling off (and I know how *that* feels). With thankfully no evidence of either, I arrive into the first transition area after just over 9k of running, entirely happy. But I know that this is where the fun *really* begins.

'Remember to put your helmet on *before* you take your bike off the rack,' I recall the wise words of Friendly Hoodie Man (who I still can't place) and so I stick my lid (sorry, cycling helmet) straight on my head before inhaling an energy gel and pushing Scott out into the traffic lane.

Shit! I've got to hop onto the bloody thing and ride it, now!

On the first of the nine laps, Scott tries to mould to me, whilst I squirm about on the impossibly narrow saddle and wonder if my relationship will survive another nine laps of potentially irreparable damage to my most sensitive female areas.

Fuck!

My foot slips and the wheels spin around at speed, making the non-cleated steel pedals hit me on both shins.

Fuck, fuck, FUCK!

I wrestle my Adidas Boost running trainers back onto the slippery metal pedals and grapple to get the handlebars back under control to avoid face-planting on the race track. When I look around me, no one else is cycling a road bike in Adidas Boosts.

NO ONE ELSE IS RACING A ROAD BIKE WEARING FUCKING RUNNING TRAINERS, RACHEL.

Wait! A girl over there is, and she looks as uncomfortable as I feel, too!

I feel like riding over and making friends with her, but she doesn't appear to be in the mood for chatting: maybe she's just hit her shins with the metal pedals for the hundredth time, too?

Lap three comes around and I feel sure my future is one of celibacy. I can see nothing through my entirely unnecessary Rudy Project racing sunglasses as the wind whips rain and snot across my face like a sad, sleeveless child. I look up and see my Other Half and Tilly watching me as I pass their weather-exposed stand for the fifth time.

'TAKE HER INSIDE, IT'S PISSING IT DOWN!' I shout across to my Other Half, who is looking perplexed at my unexpected instruction to find shelter whilst I attempt to 'maintain a good cadence' on my alien bike, in the rain.

There are hills on the course. I can't believe it. Just as I begin to think that I can manage to remain seated on my ill-fitting bike for what feels like an eternity, they throw two inclines on the track for good measure. And just as I'm attempting to lower my gear for the fifth time, I hear an emphatic 'Keep going, Rachel! Keep pushing!' coming up from behind. For a millisecond, I'm transported to the delivery room of Calderdale Royal Hospital in late September 2010, but a quick glance to my right, and Friendly Hoodie Man comes flying past, clearly making up time on his bicycle, just as he'd predicted.

Fucking hell!

The remaining cycle laps are a feat of a certain kind of physical endurance I've never experienced before. Like balancing on a thin, moving beam, praying for the moment when it will all end. Everyone else on the course looks to be more comfortable – and more proficient – on two wheels than I feel. I have impostor syndrome: that uncomfortable feeling of 'you shouldn't be here!' swims about in my head and I struggle to shake it off as infinitely better cyclists come whizzing past me, one after the other.

Why are they finding it so much easier than me?

I simply can't comprehend how some of the faster riders are handling the tight corners at such high speed. I don't know what I was expecting, but it wasn't this. My head had lulled me into a place of false security. This is a professional racing track. It has a smooth surface. There are no nasty potholes or cobbles, here.

Surely that should make it easier?

It doesn't. And I'm on a light-framed, skinny road bike. My chunky Trek bike would be laughed at, here! But I so wish I was riding him, now – I would be comfortable, at least. I don't know why my body is struggling to adjust to Scott's different dimensions. In theory, it should all be feeling easier than this.

WHY ISN'T IT?

I pray for the cycling section to end, vowing I'll do whatever necessary to avoid this ever happening again. I'll make sure that I'm professionally fitted on this bike: that the seat is at the right height, and – going back to basics – that I'm riding on a seat which is designed for my body size and shape. I can't help but be convinced that I'm not. (Since writing, I have subsequently discovered that the overall dimensions of the second-hand road bike were the cause of my severe discomfort. There are different bicycle frame sizes available *for good reason* – and it is well worth doing your research and selecting one appropriate for your size and height.)

I am finally – thankfully – approaching the second transition, but feel no fear about the second run.

Legs tired?

Of course they are!

A bit wobbly?

No shit!

Desperate to get off the fucking bike? *YES! YES, THAT!* I hop off Scott like a slightly drunken vagrant heading off to his last pub of the night.

OK, what now? Hang bike on rack? Check. Inhale a gel? Check. Right! Now, RUN, RUN, FUCKING RUN!

'Wait! You've still got your helmet on, Mum!' I hear Tilly shout from the barriers as I head towards the transition exit.

Oh, for the love of God!

I turn on my thoroughly knackered heels, thrust my no-frills non-aerodynamic Halfords 'lid' into the hands of a very helpful marshall, and run off, as far away from my Scott bike as is humanly possible. That's motivation enough for me.

'Great running!' one semi-limping guy says as I skip past him on my final lap of the track, feeling the thrill of my Adidas Boosts as they strike the ground. The last mile of running feels tough on the final climb up to the finish, but it's over soon enough. Besides, I'm now entirely numb from the waist down.

I'm approaching the finish line after a cold, wet, tiring and uncomfortable two hours and twenty-four minutes, and I can see my Other Half and Tilly – both perfectly dry and warm – cheering for me as I raise my thoroughly feeble arms in the air whilst attempting to look mildly victorious.

'WELL DONE, MUMMY!' Tilly says, pawing at my medal and blatantly eyeing up the CLIF peanut butter bar from my goody bag. 'You did REALLY well … But why were you so slow on the bike?'

Thanks, Tills! The adoption papers are currently being processed.

29

THE BIG REVEAL

Twelve weeks have been and gone. I've written page after page of BDD diary entries, documenting everything from my pre-treatment experiences to my exposure therapy challenges. I've played tug-of-war with my Bastard Chimp and his pathetic guerrilla warfare tactics. Sometimes, he's felt to gain a slight advantage over me, whilst other times I've been shocked by my own ability to completely immobilise him in the tightest stranglehold. But we've gone the distance, completing twelve gruelling rounds in the ring, and now it's time for the referee to pick a winner.

I'm in my corner, reflecting on how close I came to being knocked out. Almost losing the fight after such a strong start made me question how much I really wanted this. When it seemed so much easier to default into damaging old thought patterns rather than continue to stand and face the exposure challenges, or listen to my SWAT team as they plough me with intel on possible interpretation traps, and then leave it up to me how best to navigate my way through the carnage. I had a choice then, as I do now. Thankfully, I chose to stand firm and focus on the long-term positive impact of this treatment rather than the short-term pain. My Bastard Chimp may have knocked me down, but I stood back up again and carried on the fight.

And now, we are here. It feels like I've made it across the finish line, but I know that this is where my race really begins. I have a call lined up with Dr G this afternoon where he will feed back to me the outcome of my multiple online assessment questionnaires, plus the more in-depth reviews we've had throughout treatment. I haven't wanted to simplify any of this to just numbers on a scorecard or bars on a graph. Body dysmorphia is far too complex and devastating, and the impact is too great to reduce it to such simplistic terms. In truth, I don't *need* Dr G to inform me of the impact of this treatment. I felt it very early on when I first began to understand what was happening in my mind, and I learned that I had the power to intercept my thoughts and to challenge them – however difficult that was. It has helped me to understand how – and possibly why – I have been affected by this condition, and where it all began. Of course, these are only my own theories, but they make sense to me in the context of my heightened awareness of my physical misgivings, and my subsequent strive for perfection.

More than this, I can begin to understand the role that running has played, first in helping me to build some mental strength and resilience, creating a foundation of self-belief where previously there was none. And then second, in creating the best possible DIVERSION *away* from facing the reality of my body dysmorphic thoughts and the need to tackle them head-on. The duality of these two competing – and confusing

– impacts of running now finally seems to be making sense to me: in learning to run *towards* a place of strength and self-worth, I ended up taking a wrong turn somewhere along the way and began *running away* from myself, instead. Arguably, without the loss of running, I wouldn't have had the opportunity to make this discovery, and to tackle the Bastard Chimp and his Merry Men. They would have continued to reinforce their stronghold over me, and I would always have been subject to their mercy.

The face of Dr G fills up most of my screen once again. I'm relieved, knowing that this time there will be no multiple assessment questions for me to answer and no brain-melting, confusing statements for me to respond to within no time at all. That's all gone. It's been done, and Dr G now has a complete case study for his BDD online therapy treatment, namely that of 'Female "X"'.

'Hey, Rachel! How are you?' Dr G sounds slightly giddy, as though it's his birthday and he hasn't said anything, but is expecting a surprise party later today.

'Hi, Dr G!' I reply, smiling because I'm thinking about the possible birthday scenario and I'm imagining Dr G playing party games with a little paper hat on. The image I have of him tooting on a party blower is enough to make me laugh out loud, but I see a pair of my own dirty pants staring at me on the carpet over in the corner of the room, which stops me in my tracks. There was a time when I would have scoured the room, eliminating these frankly unacceptable items before a video call with Dr G. Now, I haven't washed my hair OR picked up my dirty pants from the bedroom floor.

Who the hell have I become?

'So, then, this is it!' he says, as though we're both about to witness the launching of a modern-day Royal Yacht *Britannia*. I can't honestly tell if Dr G is just excited because he won't have to trawl through any more diaries containing my daily body dysmorphic thoughts, or read about the small-fry challenges I have set myself to confront and rid myself of this thing: '… she's going down to the Co-op without her heavy-duty concealer on, today. Whoopy fucking do!' Hardly ground-breaking stuff, is it?

'How do you think it's gone, Rachel?' he asks, whilst I'm still busy contemplating whether it might *actually be* his birthday.

'Oh, erm … well! I think it's gone extremely well,' I say, aware of possibly sounding like a Miss World contestant who has just been asked her views on world peace. But it's true: as relieved as I am that the twelve weeks have now come to an end, I do feel I have learned such a lot. And I'm proud of myself for sticking with it, and for jumping through all the tiny fiery hoops of anxiety that were fundamental to my progress.

'So, I have some feedback for you following all the assessments that you completed throughout this programme,' Dr G manages to say through his seemingly fixed grin. 'You've made some significant progress, Rachel. I've seen it for myself from reading your worksheets and diaries, so it doesn't come as such a big surprise to me.'

What is it? What does he know that I don't? Of course, I feel to have benefited massively from the therapy, and I didn't want to get caught up in the expectation of achieving certain 'outcomes' because the positive impact of this treatment on my day-to-day life was always my sole motivation: the hours I will save myself by *not* being fixated on my own distorted image in the living-room mirror; the headspace I will free up by *not* being drawn back to the bewitching ladies' toilets at work; the freedom I will give my daughter by *not* constantly asking her whether my hair looks OK; the life I can live *without* dragging this heavy, burdensome load around with me, day after day …

'Oh! I see … Well, I guess all the quick-fire questions were for a reason, then!' I joke.

Thankfully, Dr G laughs.

'Of course they were! We have to establish your baseline BDD score, and then any variation to that throughout and at the end of the treatment,' he says. 'Do you remember your baseline score, on the Y-BOCS scale?'

The Y-BOCS Scale – or the Yale-Brown Obsessive Compulsive Scale, to give the full title – is designed to measure the severity and type of symptoms in people with Obsessive Compulsive Disorder (OCD). A version of the same scale has been developed for those suffering with body dysmorphia, who exhibit many of the same symptoms as OCD. The Y-BOCS Scale was validated by Goodman et al. (1989), who found that it significantly correlated with two independent measures of OCD. The same study also showed that the scale is sensitive to changes in OCD symptoms and that it has high internal consistency and reliability.*

---

* Ref taken from https://www.novopsych.com/y-bocs.html.

'Yeah, it was something in the mid-twenties, I think?' I reply, remembering that the YBOCS scoring went up to a maximum of 40, and wondering what it would be like living in that invisible, virtual prison.

'That's right. Your baseline score at the beginning of treatment was 24. That's a moderate-to-severe case of body dysmorphia.'

I know! I know that already!

But I don't want to rush him, especially not on his birthday (if indeed it is). He's been patient enough to deal with me for the past twelve weeks, so the least I can do is to allow him this moment of anticipation ahead of the Big Reveal.

'So, on to the results, then. Your Y-BOCS score at the end of this treatment is down to 9. Yes, 9! That's a massive improvement, Rachel. From a starting point of 24 down to a score of 9. This puts you in the pot with those lucky people exhibiting virtually no body dysmorphic symptoms. If your baseline score had been anywhere close to this on your initial assessment, then we would not have accepted you onto the programme.'

I take a moment to consider what Dr G has just said: my end-of-treatment Y-BOCS score has been reduced so significantly that I barely qualify as suffering from body dysmorphia. I'm officially no longer a person gripped by my Bastard Chimp and his gang of bullying wimps.

'Oh, WOW! Dr G, that's incredible!' I feel like throwing him a surprise party even if it *isn't* his birthday today.

Do I have any paper hats or party blowers to hand?

We chat some more about the reality that this is where the real work begins, and I'm momentarily side-tracked by the prospect that I may have to spend an eternity setting myself 'exposure therapy challenges'. Just the other day I witnessed a woman removing cardboard boxes from her car at the local recycling plant whilst wearing her towelling dressing gown and fluffy slippers.

Will this be me, soon? God forbid! Where will it end?

But for now, this is *more* than enough. And I know that the assessments don't lie. The questions are posed in a way that no one can possibly manipulate the answers. Like the game at our local trampoline park where random lights flash high on a wall, and you are required to jump and hit that light before the next one flashes up: flash, bounce, hit, flash, bounce, hit. There isn't time to think about where the next flashing light might appear; all you can do is bounce and hit.

Dr G explains that it's not *quite* over, just yet. There will be an end-of-treatment questionnaire for me to complete (but that's me scoring them, not the other way around) and I will have access to all my work, my diaries and my modules for a good few months whilst I continue to put into practice all that I've learned.

Finally, and only to be expected with Dr G and his exceptionally high standards, there will be a follow-up to the treatment in a month's time, when I can inform Dr G that yes, I did take a trip to the local recycling plant wearing my towelling dressing gown and fluffy slippers.

Will I officially have a ZERO score on the Y-BOCS scale, then? I wonder.

30

THE CHANGE OF PLAN

My body dysmorphic disorder (BDD) therapy is over and my cycling confidence is soaring! I'm cycling all over the place. I ride sixteen hilly miles to my yoga class and back home again; I cycle fifteen miles to the hairdresser's in the pouring rain, meaning any blow-drying and/or purported styling I've just paid for is completely futile. I'm *the only person* who sits in the waiting room of the trendy town-centre hair salon with dried snot trails smeared across her cheeks, wearing an adapted version of a sodden nappy. My hairdresser knows me well enough, and she doesn't bat an eyelid. But instead of the usual, 'Are you running home today, Rach?' she has adapted her hairdresser chit-chat to, 'You riding back to Halifax today, Rach?' It's the same when I cycle into town to have my nails done. Although modern 'gels' set like concrete, I've learned through experience to leave false acrylics alone – and my recently purchased cycling gloves certainly help.

Riding has slowly seeped into my pores, and I'm becoming as familiar with putting on my 'lid' as I am with digging out my running shoes. These subtle changes have taken effect over the past six months, rather like the old 'frog-in-a-pan' analogy. I stand in the school playground in my cycling shorts and a zip-up cycling jersey. I'm no longer Tilly's mum, the runner; I'm now Tilly's mum – *the rider*.

I'm so grateful to have cycling as a go-to place for my much-needed sanity fix. Knowing how much running broke me down mentally, when I took the wrong turn and looked to it as being the *only* place I could find any answers, I'm still very cautious of it. Thankfully, I'm no longer stuck there.

I'm also enjoying simple things like riding my bike alongside Tilly on hers. We enjoy cycling along the canal together, or taking a more challenging off-road route around a local reservoir. It becomes another thing we choose to do, sometimes as an alternative to the junior parkruns we've grown to love over the past five years. We are learning that we can enjoy *new* things – including hiking and biking – and so we find more ways to enjoy being active, together.

'Mummy, can I go out on my bike?'

I've just walked in through the front door. I have twenty-four bags slung over both shoulders, draped across my body, and the veins are popping out of the circulation-stopping grooves I've managed to indent into my hands by carrying too much stuff around in plastic bags. I've also completed an endless list of ball-aching chores, including getting cash out to pay for one of my daughter's various activity clubs/school trips. It might be something to do with a farm, or bowling, or it could just be protection money. I'll pay it anyway – I don't honestly care.

'Sure, Tills. Go and get changed and I'll fetch your bike up from the cellar. Give me ten minutes.'

I know with absolute certainty that this bike ride with Tilly will be the best and most enjoyable part of my day, and possibly hers, too. We both love the fresh air and the feeling of movement. Her little legs have become familiar with walking perhaps further than is *entirely* normal for a very small child ever since she was three years old, when I would collect her from pre-school, and we would then amble the mile and a half back down the hill, stopping on a bench halfway to eat a jam sandwich and read part of a story book. Now that she's a little bit older, we're enjoying time together on two wheels.

We're both ready to go. We push our bikes to the top of the drive – it's a bit too much to expect her to manage a hill start – and we turn right, onto the pavement. It's a quiet road, but I know that she's not quite ready for heavy recycling trucks thundering past her, just yet. We set off riding, and for the next mile and a half I have the concentration and focus of a lioness watching over her cub. I don't take my eyes off her for a second. I'm riding right by her side, hollering 'brake … BRAKE!' as she freewheels down the hill, grinning from ear to ear. She knows where we're going: we're off to play 'cycling bingo'.

'So, remember the rules,' I say, as she stands poised, ready to cycle off at speed to find the correct number in one of the old factory car parking spaces. 'And if you hear or see a car coming, you stop. If I shout to you, you stop immediately. Is that clear?'

'Yeah, Mum. I'm not stupid!'

We made this game up whilst out exploring on our bikes together. Realising that very little traffic ever turns into the derelict old factory car park, it's perfectly safe. I stand and shout out a number to Tilly, who then pedals off to find the correct square. She gets ten in a row and bingo! She has a 'full house'.

'Fifty-four!' I shout. Her eyes dart around the enormous numbered squares and then she's off, her plaits swinging frantically from side to side as her feet push down hard on the pedals.

'Got it!' she beams, waiting for me to call out the next number like a collie dog primed, ready for the whistle. I watch her laughing as she rides frantically around, giggling because she's ridden to number 63 instead of 36, and I know that she is filling up with joy. She is happy. Fresh air, movement and freedom ... This is the magic formula she is learning, along with her confidence and skills riding a bike. A few rounds of cycling bingo later, and I know what's coming.

'Can we push our bikes back up the hill, Mum? That was ace, but I'm tired now,' she smiles.

'Sure. So am I, Tills!' I reply.

I feel so happy, inside.

* * *

Before all this happened, my year was split into two distinct parts: spring and autumn. Why? Because – as any self-respecting marathon runner will know – these are the two main marathon racing seasons of the year. My spring marathon was London, and we all know what happened there: precisely nothing. What I failed to mention is that I had another plan in mind – this time for autumn. In October 2017, I was due to take part in the first ever Tanzanian Impact Marathon. The idea with the 'Impact Marathon' series is that these events take place in disadvantaged communities worldwide – and a focus is placed as much on contributing to the development within those communities as to running the marathon itself. I think that perhaps this was my attempt to put something in place to give myself the vague hope that I *might still* be able to run a marathon later in the year, once my body had been suitably admonished and decided to behave itself. In fact, it was a pipe dream; a pie-in-the-sky delusion that some invisible FACTORY RESET button could be pressed and everything would return to normal. But having lost running for pretty much the whole of 2017, I knew that I wasn't in any place to run a marathon. No such magic return-to-factory-settings option presented itself, and so the likelihood of my being able to take part in the Tanzanian Impact Marathon was disappointingly eradicated shortly after conception.

I email the race organisers and explain my reasons for having to withdraw. 'Ahhhh, what a shame! You must come back and run it with us next year,' the lovely lady replies. *Next year? NEXT YEAR?* But next year seems like such a long time off. What about *this year?* I panic. I need to do something now; I need to put something in the diary for *THIS YEAR.* I simply can't wait a full twelve months until a time when my body may decide it wants to run again, because what will my head do in the meantime? I don't know, but perhaps my new love affair with cycling might offer me a solution.

I have another motivation for setting myself a 'big' challenge. I know that I've come such a long way in managing my debilitating body dysmorphia, but ironically, I'm now having to adapt to my life becoming increasingly visible. I've completed my therapy treatment, and I'm about to put it to the test in possibly the biggest and scariest 'exposure therapy' challenge *EVER*. In just a few months' time I will be placing myself in the spotlight with the publication of my first book, *Running For My Life*. And as much as I've learned how to intercept and challenge my damaging thoughts, the paradox of having such mental health frailties whilst at the same time putting myself and all my flaws on the pages of a book for public consumption is simply unfathomable. *How can I do it?* I simply don't know. *How can I open myself up to be judged like this?* I have absolutely no idea how I can put myself through the comprehensive PR and media pantomime around the release of the book: a book about my life. I don't know how I will be able to appear on live television and radio programmes and talk about the very thing I have spent my entire life being fearful of other people's judgements about: myself. Call it diversion, deflection – possibly even smoke-and-mirrors – but my deep desire is to *do something so big and scary* which will take up so much of my headspace that I simply won't have the capacity to fear any of the fiery pits of anxiety I will soon be required to walk through. Enter stage left: CYCLING.

* * *

'I'd like to put something in the diary in place of the Tanzanian Impact Marathon,' I say to my Other Half, who is busy researching garden sheds online – we need somewhere other than our modestly proportioned kitchen to store our ever-expanding collection of bicycles. He understands why. And he is up for the challenge.

Meanwhile, I decide to reacquaint myself with my old friend Google and we are once again collaborating on forming a plan. *Cycling adventures; cycling tours; international cycle challenges; adventures on a bike; mountain biking challenges; the best cycling challenges; epic cycle rides of the world* ... The beloved search engine has never worked as hard in coming up with ideas. I research various possibilities – riding North America's Pacific Coast, cycling down the Danube, even exploring the foothills of the Indian Himalayas on two wheels.

Hmm ... let's see ... Riding from Seattle to San Francisco sounds incredible! But requiring the best part of three weeks to cycle 980 miles down the West Coast of America may be a problem. It's a long time to be away from my daughter, Tilly, and so I look for slightly less time-intensive options. *What about cycling down the Danube?* My research is proving to be highly educational, and informs me that the mighty Danube is Europe's longest river. I suddenly wish I'd listened to my uninspiring geography teacher instead of gazing out of the window wishing I was somewhere else. On this trip, we would ride through Germany, Austria, Hungary, Serbia and Romania. *Wowsers! Why cycle through one country when you can experience five?!* But hang on a minute ... my research goes on to suggest that the trip is best taken between

April and October (I'm looking for something in November and December) and it also points out that mosquitos are rife during the wet months – '... *And you're best to check in with the Austrian Tourist Board about possible flooding prior to departure.*' I decide to return to my searching.

Cycling in the foothills of the Indian Himalayas sounds both exotic and culturally intoxicating. My thirst for knowledge draws me towards an unlikely book I have sitting on my bookshelf. I don't even know where it came from, but I pick up Lonely Planet's *Epic Bike Rides of the World* and I read a feature written by avid cyclist Matt Swaine who has taken this incredible trip. He describes sitting cross-legged on the roof of a bus, and watching in disbelief as his bike becomes ensnared in low-slung power wires on the hair-raising journey into the Parvati Valley. *Hmm ... not quite the Beginner Cyclist's Epic Adventure I'm looking for.*

My research is filling me with ideas and excitement. I'm looking for an epic cycling adventure, whilst also being very aware that I'm a relative cycling novice. Yes, I can replace the chain if it comes loose, and I can also adjust the seat height with one of my myriad Allen keys, but I know my limits. Google eventually leads me to a place where I finally settle: a specialist cycling adventure company who take care of all the other aspects of the trip, so I can focus on the most important bit: the cycling. I see a brochure with the striking image of a red-eyed tree frog with his soft, round belly and tiny orange feet sitting atop a rainforest leaf. The words underneath the evocative image read: '*Pedal over 480km from the Pacific to the Caribbean!*' I'm sold.

'Costa Rica. Do you fancy cycling across Costa Rica in November?' I venture to my Other Half, who is hunting for a tape measure underneath the sink. I don't think he's heard me properly, but I take the ill-informed grunt to be a positive response. We will deal with the aftermath later...

A few emails later, and it's all sorted. Thankfully, I'm entirely naive about what lies ahead.

31

ANXIETY MANAGEMENT

I've really gone and done it this time, I think to myself as I sit cross-legged on my living-room floor and finally wade through the sizeable information pack we were sent some weeks ago relating to our forthcoming trip, mountain biking 480 kilometres across Costa Rica from the Pacific Ocean to the Caribbean. It still doesn't seem real. The large A4 envelope has sat unopened on the sideboard, tucked in amongst my seven-year-old daughter's scrawls purporting to be a Christmas list, and a printout of her school itinerary for the next sixteen weeks. I feel proud of myself for being ahead of the game until I notice on closer inspection that it dates from 2016.

Damn it.

How have I got here? It's only a matter of months since I set myself the sizeable task of retrieving my old Trek mountain bike from the cellar and then subsequently concocted a series of incremental cycling challenges designed to prove to myself that (a) I could ride a bike; and (b) I could become braver and more proficient on two wheels within a relatively short space of time. It's been a very interesting and – at times – quite frightening learning curve, but one which has enabled me to find some light in a sad, dark place. It has reminded me that there is more to my life – and more to my mental wellbeing – than just running. The discovery of this has been nothing short of colossal, and I have morphed into a stronger, braver and happier me.

But this latest cycling challenge is on a different scale. I read through the information pack we have been sent, and I'm terrified by what my slapdash 'Hell, why not?' attitude has gotten me into this time. It's one thing to learn how to ride a bike again – if I ever truly learned in the first place – but it's another thing entirely to commit to cycling 480 kilometres on a mountain bike across hilly terrain with a group of people who are *bound* to have infinitely more cycling proficiency, knowledge and experience than me. What's worse is that I was so enthralled by the cute-looking Costa Rican tree frog sitting on his tropical leaf that I failed to consider that this cycling adventure has been *graded*. Rather like ski resorts grade their ski runs: green for novices, red for intermediates, and black for … complete nutters, so the cycling adventure company have graded their trips. This one – I discover at too late a date – is the equivalent of a black run, and at this stage I could probably just about eke my way safely through a green one. I read the small print and am horrified to discover that '… *this cycle ride is regarded as one of our toughest overseas challenges* …' Gulp. My eyes are transfixed on reading more of the tiny words which are hidden far away from the image of the beautiful tree frog: '*… Remember that you will be cycling 480km, over seven consecutive days, and in very hot temperatures …*' Shit. Shit, SHIT! What on earth have I done?

'What's all this about needing a visa?' I ask aloud, suddenly perturbed by item number 2 on the suggested List of Essential Items, just one behind 'passport'. I swallow hard as the words YOU FUCKING IDIOT ring in my ears at this potential glaring omission (it was only last week I received confirmation that I don't have my tetanus vaccination, and it's now too late to get one).

'Don't worry about it,' my Other Half says, as I glance over and notice him Google searching WHERE IS COSTA RICA? on his iPhone. It's three days before we set off on a challenge which will blast us so far outside our comfort zones that we won't know our saddle-sore, padded arses from our grazed and bruised elbows. 'It'll be fine!' he assures me, as he scans down a Wikipedia page on Costa Rica, thinking I haven't noticed.

'And we still need to take the seat and pedals off my bike,' I remind him, as I sit staring at my once neatly piled selection of unworn padded cycling shorts, now unceremoniously strewn to one side by the arrival of the Sylvanian Families camper van.

My stress levels have been unusually high this past week. And it's not entirely – as you might expect – relating to the Herculean task of cycling 480 kilometres across all kinds of arduous terrain, possibly dodging volcanoes and avoiding sloths in the road (yes, they have those, apparently). In truth, I'm equally terrified by almost every other aspect of this trip – the mountain biking is merely the cherry on the anxiety management cake. The other panic-inducing aspects relate to a travel itinerary rivalled only by European Space Agency astronaut Tim Peake's Principia space mission in December 2015. This includes, in theory:

1. A two-hour drive to Manchester airport, plus half an hour navigating our way to the correct parking location (I have fallen foul of this before and had to call for emergency assistance at the barrier's intercom);

2. A forty-minute flight from Manchester to London Heathrow, which will likely take circa four hours, with an intravenous drip pumping Costa coffee into my blood-stream, before being stripped half-naked at check-in for a gentle frisking;

3. Once at Heathrow, finding the hotel which looks to be another forty-minute bus ride away (Heathrow is the size of our home town, Halifax, it would seem);

4. [the next morning] Boarding a shuttle bus from the hotel to London Heathrow Terminal 4 before 5:45 a.m., most probably whilst still asleep;

5. Another four-hour wait and a connecting flight from Heathrow to Amsterdam;

6. Hanging about for endless hours at Schiphol airport waiting for *another* connecting flight to San José, which I learn is the capital of Costa Rica (I had no idea);

7. An eleven-hour flight to San José;

8. Collapsing in a heap in a zero-starred hotel before a four-hour bus transfer to the start of our 'adventure' the following morning.

And then – she says without any hint of irony – the adventure begins. The above is what's *SUPPOSED* to happen. I don't know it yet, but it won't happen like this. Not at all …

It's a good job I don't know.

* * *

I'm at point number 2) on the Principia itinerary, standing in the queue to board a plane from Manchester to London Heathrow. I've already consumed my requisite three litres of airport Costa coffee and arsed about in WH Smith's. It's meant that we're now late in locating the correct gate, and so we rush to Gate A54, where a grim-looking snake of people has long since formed.

We are virtually last in the queue, and about to board the forty-minute flight to Heathrow. The only man and woman left standing behind us are smiling at me holding my pillow. But it's not a compact travel pillow: it's the big fluffy one from my king-size bed which I sleep on every night. The man observes, 'At least you'll be comfortable on the forty-minute flight!' He emphasises the 'forty minutes' and I laugh in acknowledgement of his summation that I'm not a seasoned traveller, and this clear evidence that I'm also fussy about my sleeping arrangements. Pillows are a tricky one to get right: too hard and it's like placing my head on a brick, too soft and I face sinking into a Scotch pancake. Mine is just right: fluffy and supportive. And it's coming to Costa Rica with me. Little do I know that my big, fluffy pillow will be my saviour over the next ten days.

Friendly Couple are on their way to Toronto to visit their teenage son who is apparently some young ice-hockey prodigy.

Aged just fifteen – they tell us – he reached the pinnacle of his potential over here in the UK and so it is that – still aged fifteen – he has flown the comfort and safety of his British nest to live in a new city, in a new country, knowing that he will see his parents just once every six months, if that. He doesn't know it, but he's my new hero. Aged sixteen, I was too busy melting Mars bars against my bedroom radiator whilst examining my latest hormonal outbreak in one of Mum's pressed powder compacts to concern myself with independent living or dream-chasing.

And I wonder about my own anxiety about this cycling trip. I'm thirty-nine years old, and I'm travelling in a group. I'm fretting about having a too-soft/too-hard pillow, a lack of mirrors, and the effect of mild sleep deprivation following a two-day journey to reach our destination. I'm worried about missing my little girl for the next ten days and my mum being home alone (although that's not exactly true – she's got a better social life than me!). But the story of Friendly Man's son has made me momentarily get a grip. I'm not sixteen. I'm not on my own. I'm not going away from my family and friends for two years to have the shit kicked out of me by young Canadian ice-hockey players. For all the above reasons, I'm sitting here, cuddling my oversized pillow the night before a long day of travel, and I'm thinking to myself – *I can fucking do this*!

I haven't even stopped to consider the *cycling* aspect of the trip, yet.

32

WHO ARE THESE PEOPLE?

We arrive at the airport early and meet the team. Julie is in her fifties. She separated from her husband five years ago, and has thrown herself into action-packed adventure holidays in the years since. 'I completed the Vietnam to Cambodia cycle trip with Women v Cancer last year,' she tells me whilst sipping on a large Pret latte. 'It was good, but there were too many princesses on the trip for my liking.'

I confidently reassure her that she has no cause for concern on this score, safe in the knowledge that I'm stripped bare of any luxuries such as hair straighteners or – more terrifyingly – disposable razors. I feel the onset of mild palpitations as I briefly wonder how long it will take for my legs to turn into strips of Velcro, and my hair to become matted and unkempt, and smell of chip shops.

I think back to my 'exposure therapy' challenges from earlier in the year, and the painful memories of wrenching myself away from the large living-room mirror. How far have

I come since then? What would Dr G make of all this? A trip which will eliminate almost every safety behaviour I came to rely on to give me the short-term fix I thought I needed. We will be 'roughing it' for the next ten days, sleeping on floors under the cover of a thin canvas tent; waking between 4:30–5:30 a.m. to ride on average fifty mountainous miles per day; most times having no access to shower facilities or hot running water, and almost certainly NO MIRRORS. I hadn't realised it at the time, but booking this epic adventure is going to be the biggest, baddest exposure challenge I could possibly imagine – and that's before I even stop to consider the cycling.

A group of fit-looking Scottish guys are amongst us. One is called Duncan. I only remember his name by thinking of Ant & Dec's pop aliases, PJ & Duncan. His is the only name I can retain in my head, which now spins with fatigue, social anxiety, and mono-syllabic name exchanges.

Sally is twenty-six with a perfect English rose complexion. She is a commercial property lawyer from Norwich, she tells us in her legally trained, articulate drawl. 'I used to row down the Henley Regatta, but it all got too much,' she says wistfully. 'So, I took a break from competing, and began to take on other challenges instead. I climbed Killy last year, and then cycled across Cambodia.' I pause briefly to consider what 'Killy' is before realising that she is referring to Mount Kilimanjaro. *Of course she is!* Suddenly, I feel utterly stupid. These people are on colloquial terms with Mount Kilimanjaro, and I don't even know it to speak to. This is like a game of Posh Traveller Top Trumps and Sally wins, hands down.

A pair of confident cockney boys swagger up to the tables we've now bunched together in Terminal 4's Pret A Manger. 'Are you up for the Costa Rica trip, then?' the bigger one asks. He is approximately the same shape and size as our recently purchased garden shed. All I can see are enormous white teeth as he grins whilst working his way around the tables, shaking hands and introducing himself. He's welcomed into the fold and takes his place amongst the discarded pastries and branded paper cups.

There are more of us, now – nineteen in total. My head still spins with names and confusion: *Who is Mark? Is there more than one? And Greg, which one is he?* PJ & Duncan's pop hit, 'Let's Get Ready to Rumble' begins to play on the jukebox inside my head. *Oh no, I've forgotten which one Duncan is!* Panic builds as I also wonder, *is one of the Scots actually called Scott? Or have I misheard him?* It suddenly seems absurd to have a Scot called Scott on the trip. Surely that can't be right?

An older couple in their early to mid-fifties approaches our tables, meaning that the female-to-male ratio has now increased to almost 1:4. He is small and serious-looking; she is wearing effortlessly glamorous, expensive sporting attire and looks fit for her age. I notice a small Ironman tattoo on his lower leg, and my heart sinks. It surely confirms that he has completed an Ironman event, this being a brutal long-distance triathlon consisting of a 2.4-mile swim, a 112-mile bike ride followed by a 26.2 mile run (that is a full marathon distance).

Oh, my God, he'll be doing this for fun!

Ironman's sporty-yet-glamorous partner is called Veronica and she is soon quizzed by matter-of-fact Julie on her reasons for wanting to take part in this cycling trip.

'I'd like to look around a sloth orphanage, if possible,' she responds in a high-pitched southern-counties voice with distinct echoes of the nineties Philadelphia adverts. I'm confused. Julie looks understandably perplexed and slightly troubled. She has misheard, and thinks that the blonde Bristolian has come along hoping to find a children's orphanage.

'The mummy sloths often get electrocuted on the overhead wires, leaving their babies to fend for themselves,' Veronica explains. 'It's so sad!'

Phew! She's talking about sloths – little furry animals which are native to the tropical rainforests of Central and South America. Julie has finally caught on and looks mildly relieved, yet at the same time entirely bemused by the conversation. And to be honest, so am I. What kind of a reason is *that* for undertaking a cycling challenge of this enormity?

And then it happens. PING! One of the monosyllabically-named Scots (not 'Scott') has just received a text message.

'Hey, have any of you seen this?' he asks the rest of the group. It's a very concise message informing him that our flight to Amsterdam has just been cancelled. Not delayed, or 'awaiting further information', but cancelled. Just that. There is a sudden flurry to check mobile phones, and yes, PJ (or Duncan) confirms that they've received it, too. In that moment, our flight schedule and Principia travel itinerary is shot to pieces and the following twelve hours will be spent trying to establish how the hell the group of us will get to Costa Rica. My head spins with anxiety, and it isn't yet 8 a.m.

It feels like the strangest icebreaker group bonding exercise.

Our bewildered adventure guide, Sam, is queueing up, trying to make sense of the madness, whilst attempting to put emergency plans together for the group of us.

Within the next two hours we are furnished with a handful of tickets, each worth £4.50. It doesn't quite cover the cost of a pint of Stella, but we've all stopped caring. Burgers, chicken wraps, a full English, a pot of mussels, and French onion soup are brought over to our collection of scattered tables and randomly strewn chairs, but I don't feel hungry. I'm still carrying the brown paper bag filled with a semi-squashed croissant and bruised fruit from this morning's take-out breakfast, which we collected at 5:35 a.m. My hair hasn't been washed, I feel greasy, and my mind is struggling to cope with the reality I now face. *Where is a mirror?* My anxiety levels are causing me to default into worrying BDD territory. *You look tired ... Your hair is greasy ... You need a shower ... Your face is shiny ... You look ugly, Rachel.* Where is my SWAT team, now? I desperately need them to identify the million interpretation traps I'm now being bombarded with.

'Right, I've got an update for you,' Sam, our poor solo adventure guide tells us. It's now 4 p.m., and we've been wedged in our Terminal 4 cheap seats for a total of nine hours. 'We've arranged an alternative flight for all but three of you,' he informs the group. 'You'll be flying to Columbia, leaving at 10 p.m. tonight, changing at Bogota.' I imagine the scene

– Pablo Escobar greeting us at the Columbian arrival lounge, surrounded by his guerrilla mafia drug-pusher henchmen. I may struggle with that: I can't even stomach Ibuprofen Plus (it has codeine in it). I look around the group, wondering which of us will be travelling to Bogota.

Where is a mirror??!

I'm so tired, and it's all such a mess.

The group of Scots are the unfortunate three: they will fly to Mexico, and on to Panama, before heading across to Costa Rica. We will *all* miss out on an entire night's sleep – and the ONE night of relative luxury in a zero-starred hotel before the real 'adventure' begins. And to think I was anxious about even that. My head is in an entirely different place now. This will be exposure therapy and sleep deprivation beyond anything I've ever experienced. And I wonder what on earth will happen – and how will I cope?

We sit and chat with the other people in the group. Time ticks by slowly … so fucking slowly. That's until we discover that Pasha, an unassuming and surprisingly adventurous member of our group, has just returned from weeks of survival training in the Amazon from ex-SAS. He tells of his expedition, which consisted of him trekking through a virtually uninhabitable jungle for two weeks armed with a traditional bow and arrow, and just a handful of peanut M&Ms as food to last him for the entire duration of his less-than-enviable stay. I simply can't for the life of me imagine anything worse.

'There was a hurricane the week before we arrived,' he tells us, 'and it meant that all the fish had swum around to the other side of the island, so there was nothing at all to catch in the water.' He smiles as he regales his experience. 'I was grateful for the M&Ms.'

WHO ARE THESE FUCKING PEOPLE? I begin to wonder. Who has climbed to Everest base camp and cycled across Cambodia? Who on earth has undergone advanced SAS survival training in the deepest Amazonian rainforests? And why – *WHY* – am I sitting here amongst them, in Pret A Manger at Heathrow airport's Terminal 4, thinking I can somehow pretend that I'm one of them?

How can I do this? What am I doing here? I can hardly even fucking ride a bike …

Panic has set in.

33

RIDING FOR MY LIFE

We finally arrive at Playas del Coco on the Pacific Coast for the start of our cycling adventure, after over forty-eight hours of travelling, with probably less than forty-eight minutes of sleep, via Manchester, Heathrow, San José and – of course – Bogota. Pablo Escobar *wasn't* waiting to greet us in the Columbian airport arrival lounge with his henchmen, and to be honest, I was so deliriously tired that I wouldn't have cared less even if he was.

I haven't had a shower, washed my hair or even changed my clothes for what feels like an eternity. The memory of my first real 'exposure therapy challenge' – plucking up the courage to walk into my daughter's school playground without having washed and conditioned my hair – makes me laugh out loud. It's been *days* since I felt clean. My hair now has the feel of a post-Sunday lunch roasting tin: there's a visible layer of grease which I would challenge even the brand leader Fairy Liquid to successfully tackle. The only mirrors I have at my disposal are those in the toilets of the various airport lounges we have languished in over the past two days. All have fluorescent lights which would make even Meghan Markle look like *Corrie*'s Vera Duckworth. I've stopped assessing the increasingly dark circles under my eyes: it's simply too hard to focus. My baseball cap has become my new BFF, and gives me some small comfort that I can hide myself in just a tiny way until this is all over.

Dr G, you would be *soooo* proud of me.

The whole travel itinerary has been shot to pieces. We missed out on our *one* night in a hotel. And, however basic that might have been, it was our only opportunity for relative comfort until we reach the Caribbean coast in ten days' time – which is 480 kilometres away from here. The group has had more than ample opportunity to bond, and we've established that these guys (and most of the group *are* guys), have trained hard for this cycling adventure.

'We've been going out doing forty-mile training rides most weekends, haven't we, Mark?' one of the non-Scots says, as though that's within my sphere of knowledge. I gulp, knowing the furthest I have *ever* ridden on a mountain bike in one go is circa twenty miles. Even then, I stopped midway for a prolonged lunch break and to give my nether regions a chance to recover – and just to cry.

'Well, I'm more of a runner than a rider, to be honest,' I reply, feeling like I need to firmly put down my anchor that I-AM-NOT-A-CYCLIST-AND-I-HAVEN'T-TRAINED-FOR-THIS. Non-Scot and Mark are best friends from back home, and most weekends they go out riding on their mountain bikes together. Their respective wives are familiar with this – the Boys' Annual Cycling Adventure (they did the 'Cycle India' challenge last year, I learn) – and I soon discover that this is true for many others in the group. It sounds like a grown-up version of a lads' holiday to me, with a few mountain bikes thrown in for good measure: the WAGS are back at home, happily choosing *not* to take part in this ridiculous challenge. I wonder if I'd do the same, given the option.

It causes me to take another look at the women on this trip, and I begin to see us all in a completely new light: there are only five of us in a group four times the size and as a collective, we hardly resemble a group of serious cycling enthusiasts. There is every possible age, size and body shape amongst us, with support bras, wobbly bits and all. And three out of the five women are *older*, by which I mean over the age of fifty. Sure, there's Sally, the confident young lawyer from Norwich who is on best terms with Mount Kilimanjaro, has rowed competitively down at the Henley Regatta, and who – enviably – has no need for either a reinforced sports bra or support-panelled pants. Then there's me – an undeniably long-limbed, thirty-nine-year-old half-decent runner with a fair number of marathons under my belt. But none of us look like we are even likely to put ourselves forward for a challenge like this. *Have we turned up to the wrong adventure, by mistake?* It's entirely conceivable that someone amongst us pressed 'ENTER' on their keypad at precisely the wrong moment, by which time they'd committed to something far removed from the more appropriate entry-level trekking adventure. Taking the 'appearances-can-be-deceptive' caveats aside, it's still a fact that two out of three of the women on this trip who are over fifty have already taken part in an epic cycling adventure of some description. Both Julie and Veronica (no doubt accompanied by her Ironman husband) have completed far-flung cycling expeditions abroad, and the classic London-to-Paris bike ride challenge back home. So, I must presume that they both have cycling knowledge, confidence and fitness that belies my rather naive first impressions. And as I said earlier, appearances can be deceptive.

Once I'm familiar with the depth and breadth of cycling experience of seemingly *every other* participant on this trip, I begin to shift my focus to the cycling challenge itself. And the reality is very simple: I haven't trained much for this trip at all. Sure enough, I've hopped aboard both my sturdy Trek and my lighter-framed Scott road bike many times since the embryonic emergence of Rach the Rider, but my twelve-mile rides to and from my mum's house, plus the more ambitious sixteen-mile journey across the local hills to my hairdresser's and back home again just doesn't come anywhere close to the kind of distances, time on the saddle, or terrain I should now be familiar with in preparation for this trip.

I remember the grading of the challenge: EXTREME. Would I don my skis and throw myself down a black run without undertaking any training, or building my experience on the gentler, safer green and red runs first? NO! So why then – WHY – have I leap-frogged the sensible, progressive stepping-stones, and gone straight for the toughest international cycling challenge this tour company offers? Once again, asking myself these questions is of little use. I am here now, and I must accept the fact that no amount of self-berating or name-calling will change any aspect of this trip. I must simply suck up the fact that I can't do anything about the training I haven't done: I just need to get on a bike and pedal ... and keep pedalling until I'm told to stop.

Finally, we get our first glimpse of the Trek mountain bikes we'll shortly be riding. They are all identical – a garish, light chameleon green colour – and they are stacked on top of the minibus, which will be our virtual mobile home for the coming ten days. Well, almost – except for our sleeping arrangements, for which we have various floor surfaces and tarpaulin covers available. This bus will be our lifeline. It will follow us along the *passable* sections of the route (which worries me greatly – because why on earth would any section be *im*passable?!), it will carry all our water, food, and any emergency supplies we will need; it will pick us up at the end of the day's riding (if we don't finish cycling at precisely the point where we will drop to the ground and fall asleep, that is), it will carry the weary and those who are simply unable to go on, if the riding becomes too much, or if someone becomes ill or otherwise incapacitated whilst on the trip. It will meet us at various points en route – roughly every fifteen to twenty kilometres – to provide us with much-needed water refills and snacks. The driver of the minibus is called Coco and will become our saviour over the coming days. We already love Coco, as we understand perfectly that he is now a key part of our survival.

Our guide Sam shouts out above the excitable cycling chatter as we're boarding the bus: 'We'll shortly be arriving at our camp for tonight. When we get there, you'll each need to find your bikes so we can make sure they're properly fitted. We've got an early start in the morning, so any problems will need sorting out tonight.'

An acknowledging murmur passes through the bus and a heady mix of travel fatigue and building excitement is making the group swing from long silences to sudden bursts of hysteria as the cockney boys joke about all the mishaps we've encountered thus far. Meanwhile, I ponder over Sam's instructions and wonder what 'our camp for tonight' might be. It isn't a hotel, we know that with absolute certainty. But what will it be like? I've heard of glamping, and I'm kind of hoping there will be some elements of relative luxury, such as hot, running water, perhaps even on-site hair straighteners? Also, I'm wondering about our 'early start' in the morning. We're already completely exhausted after what feels like an eternity of botched travel plans, so what time will we be roused? Six-thirty is my worse-case scenario guestimation. I'm not on my own wondering about this and one of the Scots asks Sam that very question.

'OK, guys, I know this comes as a bit of a shock, but we've got a long day of riding ahead of us tomorrow, because we've already missed a day,' Sam explains, laying the groundwork for managing our expectations. 'So, if we can be up for 4:30 a.m., get a quick breakfast, and be away for 5 a.m. at the latest, we should catch up on some of the mileage we've missed.'

Four-thirty in the morning? That's the middle of the night! WTAF?

The bus falls stony silent, which is only broken by the first mutters and grumblings in protest at this unwelcome news. Eyes meet each other in recognition of the reality we are now facing. As I sit and stare out of the bus window into the darkness, I can see little more than the outline of my own reflection – that is, a featureless face, two limp plaits and a baseball cap – but I don't care about that. I'm so tired. It feels like days since I had a shower, slept on a bed – or just slept at all. Night has long since fallen in Costa Rica, and we are now on the *final* leg of our journey to the *start* of our cycling adventure – an irony which isn't at all lost on me. *When did we leave home?* I'm already struggling to remember. It's pitch-black outside, and we are yet to arrive at our base for the night. We must then claim our bikes, have them fitted, locate a tent (which – we've been told as though it's any kind of luxury – have already been erected for us) and collapse into it, only to wake a few hours later.

Coco slows our minibus down. We turn a series of corners, and the streets become narrower until eventually we come to a stop. Floodlights illuminate a small, gated square of Astroturf on which are pitched eight or maybe nine two-man canvas tents. This IS NOT a campsite, I know that for a fact. And my dreams of a luxury glamping experience are suddenly shot to pieces.

'Lads, it's a five-a-side football pitch!' one of the cockney boys calls out in hysteria to the rest of the bus, just in case we couldn't see that for ourselves. I look out of the window and can't quite comprehend the scene as we pile out of the bus, and are told to go and claim one of the small tents on the fake grass. We stand around in awkward clumps pondering on this – the first night of our adventure – as Coco and his helpers begin to unload the bikes from the roof of the bus.

'This is it, then,' I say to my Other Half, who is trying to capture snapshots of the surreal scene on his iPhone. 'I guess this is what we'd better get used to for the next ten days.'

* * *

There's a steady hum of activity across the Astroturf pitch as people lug enormous bags – plus themselves – into two-man tents, inflate ineffective sleeping mats, and rustle around to locate dissected bicycle parts, which will all need fitting to our standard-issue chameleon-green Trek mountain bikes. Some have brought along special bar ends designed for increased comfort over long-duration rides (who knew?), whilst others have their well-worn seats and beloved clip-in pedals. I didn't end up dismantling my Trek bike in the end, figuring any slight tweaks to the 'no-frills' mountain bikes provided are unlikely to make a shit of a difference to either my riding ability or comfort levels on this trip – I chose to bring my fluffy pillow along, instead.

I locate my bike, and I warm to her immediately. She's a Trek, just like my 2010 model back home. It feels like a small blessing. I hear others grumbling about how 'basic' the bikes are, and how 'heavy' they feel, but I breathe a sigh of relief because at least she feels *familiar* to me. Whilst she may be a few pounds heavier and possibly slightly chunkier than I'd like – I'd rather that she felt vaguely *recognisable* to me, in a simplistic 'I-think-I-know-how-to-ride-you' kind of way. That's good enough for now.

I sit on her as we've been instructed to for the fitting, and the seat needs raising a little. I have a mini 'YAY ME!'

moment when I realise that (a) I know how to do that; and (b) I even have the correct Allen key to do the job myself. I dig around in the bottom of my awkwardly-shaped bright orange travel rucksack for my multi tool, and make the necessary adjustments.

I'm thrilled. Maybe I'm not such a gatecrasher at this party after all …

Our bikes have been fitted – or at the very least, my seat has been raised two inches – and I have successfully wobbled around two laps of the prickly Astroturf. And so, we begin the task of sorting out our tent for the night.

'There isn't room for both of us *and* our two enormous travel bags in here!' I plead helplessly to my Other Half, who is busy wrestling with himself inside his crumpled sleeping bag as though he were secured inside a straitjacket. Tiredness has overwhelmed me, and I simply can't process all the anxieties now convulsing in my head. It feels as though this trip is forcing me to come face-to-face with absolutely EVERY FEAR I could possibly imagine. If I were to sit down with a clear head (as opposed to the one I currently have: a travel-and-anxiety-induced fatigued one) and list them all, they may look something like this:

(1) SLEEP DEPRIVATION

Tiredness is something I struggle to cope with. It's for this reason that most nights I go to bed around 9:30 p.m. and I don't drink coffee after 2 p.m. I'm horrified when *MasterChef* is scheduled for 9 p.m. (which, BTW, is the watershed for my bedtime), although the modern-day concept of BBC iPlayer is a revelation for which somebody, somewhere, should be awarded a Nobel Prize.

Waking up after a bad night's sleep is a huge cause for concern, because tiredness seems to exacerbate all my mental health woes, rather like the effect of alcohol (I remember this from the days of combining my mental health medication with vast quantities of cheap white wine ...).

Extreme tiredness makes my body dysmorphic disorder symptoms more severe, whilst at the same time reducing my SWAT team's ability to identify interpretation traps and deal with any potentially damaging thoughts. Looking back at my early BDD diary entries, they are littered with concerns about my 'looking tired' and having 'dark circles under my eyes' – these being things which my warped, unruly Chimp would have me believe make me look 'ugly'. Tiredness also increases my levels of anxiety more generally. A small, niggling worry can quickly turn into a vast, sprawling panic as my mind is simply too fatigued to consider the possibility of perspective, and I can't muster the energy to offer a more reasoned, logical explanation.

My inability to handle a lack of sleep is also one of the main reasons why I have dragged my soft, fluffy pillow over 5,000 miles from the UK to Costa Rica. So, in summary, I need my sleep.

(2) SOCIAL ANXIETY

Meeting new people is hard work. Don't get me wrong, I *like* meeting new people and I can be – ironically – very sociable, but I'm also an introvert. I find that the effort I need to maintain my levels of interest in casual chit-chat and social interaction is disproportionate to that of those people at the more extroverted end of the personality scale. This comes as a surprise to some, who see me doing an extremely good job of disguising the fact. I'm genuinely interested in new people; I love to hear their stories, and to discover what we may – or may not – have in common, but I also find it exhausting. I can dip in and out of the social butterfly role with great success, but I'm not one to languish there. When social fatigue kicks in, I need to retreat and find my own space. I crave peace and stillness as a counterbalance to the small talk and banter I've been exposed to. Rather like radiation, too much of it can be harmful.

On this trip, there may not be a single moment when I can withdraw from the radioactive chatter, whether that is travelling on the minibus, refuelling at meal times, preparing our tents for the night, or even whilst riding the fucking bikes! Unlike running, riding is well known for being a more 'sociable' activity, in the sense that it is entirely possible – and even probable – for folk to chatter whilst riding along together, especially in a group such as this. But this worries me greatly, because I cannot imagine anything worse than a 5 a.m. breakfast filled with tales of 'When I cycled across India …' followed by four hours riding alongside someone quizzing me about various aspects of my personal life, including my recent cycling experiences, or lack thereof. My 'Yeah, I rode fifteen miles to my hairdresser's the other week' response may sound rather lame to someone who has frequently undertaken forty-five-mile training rides in the Peak District and is on first-name-terms with Mount Kilimanjaro.

(3) BDD 'EXPOSURE THERAPY' CHALLENGES TO RIVAL ALL OTHERS

'Is there a shower on site, Sam?' I ask our magnanimous guide, who now has the look of someone being beaten by life. He's had a far more stressful fifty-plus hours than even we have, and it shows. He replies saying that no, sadly, there isn't a shower here at the Costa Rican five-a-side football pitch. *Of course not!* Well, there is a small, dirty room the size of a broom cupboard around the back of the Astroturf pitch, where a dirty, wall-mounted pipe will dribble a steady flow of cold water, if that constitutes a shower – which I conclude it does, around here.

'Just make sure none of the water gets in your mouth!'

Sam follows up his immediate response with a health and safety warning.

Where are my home comforts? When will I next have a warm shower – or a bubble bath – and wash my hair? When will I be able to take steps to remove the chip-shop layer of filth from my entire body, which has now become a standard that I'm getting used to? If nothing else, it makes plaiting my hair a lot easier, as the strands are caked in a natural lubricant with absolutely no risk of 'flyaway' or static. I feel like a smack addict going cold turkey with the sudden and absolute removal of all basic grooming products, including a hair dryer and straighteners, or even a hair brush. Oh, and mirrors (at least ones I can see myself in – bus windows at dusk don't count). Come to think of it, has Dr G planned this trip for me as part of the follow-up assessment to his online BDD therapy treatment? I can't help but wonder …

(4) PLANS AND ITINERARIES BEING SHOT TO PIECES

I was nervous enough about this trip *before* everything went to shit and flights were cancelled, scattering the group far across the planet from Mexico and Panama to Bogota and – eventually – Costa Rica. It's funny how a sudden and unexpected change of plan can cause such a feeling of discomfort. Plans and itineraries, lists and schedules, all help me to mentally prepare myself for whatever lurks around the corner. I guess it's akin to pacing myself for a race: I wouldn't dream of running a marathon without mentally going through the steps of reaching miles 5, 10, 13, 19 and 26, first.

How will I feel at those points? What will my pacing be like? How can I expect to be handling things, physically and mentally? When am I likely to feel good? And not-so-good? What about nutrition? Where are the most critical, vulnerable sections going to be, and how can I prepare myself for those?

I *had* worked through this process ahead of this trip. In my mind, I had visualised the journey from my own front door, driving to Manchester airport and flying to Heathrow, waiting to fly across to Amsterdam, and then the long-haul reality of a journey thousands of miles to a country I didn't even realise was in Central America. I *had* contemplated what the more frustrating, tiring elements of that itinerary might be. I *had* worked through the inevitability of waiting in various airport lounges, and the discomfort of being incarcerated in a small airplane seats with little leg room for 'X' number of hours. I'd even come to terms with the absence of any home comforts, or mirrors, for that period. Accepting that I would be TRAVELLING ... A LONG WAY ... and that I would BECOME TIRED and possibly INCREASINGLY ANXIOUS was something I had processed with the itinerary printed out in black-and-white, and laid out in front of me. But this no longer exists. It hasn't existed since approximately 7:35 a.m. on the very first morning in Heathrow airport's Terminal 4, at which point it felt like reaching the start of a marathon only to be told that (a) the start time has changed; (b) the route is no longer as advertised; and (c) it isn't a marathon at all. In fact, the *precise* distance is yet to be confirmed, but it could be anything ranging from 26.2 miles to 56 ... and back again.

How am I supposed to prepare for that? How am I meant to pace myself, mentally or physically, for something which keeps changing and morphing into different versions of a challenge which scared me to death in the first place? It makes a complete mockery of Benjamin Franklin's well-worn adage, 'Failing to plan is planning to fail', because what happens when a plan fails?

(5) EXTREME CYCLING ... 480 KILOMETRES
ACROSS A FUCKING COUNTRY

How do you explain to someone what a black ski run is, who has no concept of either a green or a red one? How about explaining it to someone *who has only just picked up a pair of skis for the very first time*? This is a 'mountain biking challenge' and in literal terms, I can read about the *distance* we will be riding. I can refer to a map and get some idea of the *route* we will be taking (although this can be subject to change, many things depending, including an itinerary which has now been shot to pieces), but I have no clue how it *feels* to ride a mountain bike for forty-plus miles, day after day. I have no concept of the *kind* of riding – the different terrain, the severity of the inclines, the heat, the monsoon rains and the many other variables which could make ten miles of riding feel like a thousand; or could make forty miles feel like a walk in the park.

Also, I have no idea how my body will react to spending *seven consecutive days* on the saddle of my chameleon-green Costa Rican Trek bike. I don't know which areas will chafe (although I have a reasonably good idea), I don't know which muscles will fatigue first, or even how that fatigue might manifest itself. I doubt that I will 'hit the wall' as it's very possible to do whilst running a marathon, but does the tiredness creep up in a slower, stealthier way, and cause a different kind of discomfort, instead?

I'm about to undertake an extreme cycling challenge, and – in addition to all the other anxieties – I simply don't know what it will feel like to tackle this, the *cycling aspect* of this trip.

(6) THE UNKNOWN

Certainty gives me comfort, just like anybody else. I feel better knowing what the outcome will be, at times desperately searching for it, even when there's absolutely no way of finding out. It's part of human nature – if we know the outcome, we can mitigate the risks. But a huge part of my journey in life thus far has been to deliberately place myself in vulnerable situations where I can't comprehend what the outcome might be, and where anything – including failure – is a distinct possibility.

I had no way of knowing if I'd make it to the start – or the finish – line of the London Marathon, back in 2011, or through the six months of gruelling marathon training after giving birth to my daughter in September 2010. I had absolutely no reference point for guessing at an outcome, and part of my learning was to force myself to expand my comfort zone and become familiar with the anxiety of *not* knowing. So, from that perspective, I've been here before. It possibly explains why I could place myself on this cycling challenge at all – because over the years, I've become increasingly familiar with taking risks despite fearing the outcome. And so far, it's worked! But there are *so many* unknowns on this challenge. There are so many variables that frighten me, and they are threatening to force my ever-bulging comfort zone to bursting point. If I break it down into 'the unknowns' then I could list almost every aspect of the trip as falling into this category and therefore causing me anxiety: I don't know who will be on this trip; I don't know where or what we will eat from day to day; I don't know where we will sleep each night as we make our way across a strange country. I don't know where we will be cycling, or even how it feels to be on a bike of any description for more than a couple of hours at a time. I don't know how the group dynamics will develop as we become increasingly fatigued and irritable. Will Julie turn out to be intolerant of Veronica on her continuing quest to find a sloth orphanage? Will Veronica's Ironman husband become irritated because we simply can't ride fast enough to maintain his interest? Will my Other Half end up wishing he were anywhere else other than confined to a small two-person tent with me and my BFF, anxiety, for over ten days?

* * *

The alarm goes off, but I've been awake for ages. It's 4:30 a.m. and the floodlights around the Astroturf pitch are glaring offensively through our thin canvas tent. I can hear the rustling of bags, the unzipping of tents and general murmurings as my fellow cycling companions rouse themselves, ready for our first day of riding. We've been told that today will be a long day, and although mentally we can try to prepare for that, the truth is we have absolutely no idea what lies ahead.

I peer out of our tent and see that our minibus driver Coco and his helpers are already at the side of the pitch, laying out various breakfast options on a long wooden bench. I don't feel hungry, but I know that I need to eat.

Coffee. Where's the coffee?

I see some cheap plastic cups next to a large metal decanter, which is enough reason to wriggle myself out of the tent and head over to the pop-up breakfast bar. My Other Half is still in denial, his head hidden deep inside his straitjacket sleeping bag. My heightened anxiety is helping me, in a way: there is so much adrenalin now flooding my system, I'm on autopilot.

'Good morning, Sam!' I say to our lovely guide, who has been up for a good hour already, making final adjustments to various bikes and no doubt preparing for the other aspects of the trip that we need not concern ourselves with. He looks tired, but focused.

'Hey, Rach. You sleep well?' he asks.

WHAT? I realise this is polite, early-morning chatter, but I can't think of any suitable, honest answer. *NO. I DIDN'T SLEEP WELL. NOT AT ALL.* I consider the irony of my current predicament: there is nowhere for me to hide here. No place for me to go to escape my fears. I'm truly, and fully, exposed. The only small comfort is that I'm wearing my baseball cap, which feels like a luxury. A few of the guys had a shower late last night – we heard loud groans coming from cockney boy Luke as he stood cursing underneath the metal pipe with a steady flow of cold, dirty water. I decided to give it a miss, and continue to wear my filthy cap instead. I haven't taken the plaits out of my hair for days, and I wonder if it will ever be straight – or clean – again.

The black Costa Rican coffee goes down well. It doesn't taste anything like my regular coffee back home, but it's hot, and I trust that it contains some caffeine, which I will so desperately need when my adrenalin finally runs out. I pick at some strange white bread and take a slice of watermelon, but I can't face eating much. I've packed some peanut butter protein bars in my Camelbak, so I'll be able to have those if I get hungry later.

'Right, guys, we're planning to head off in ten minutes' time. That's TEN MINUTES, so finish up whatever you're doing. Meet by the bus when you're done!' Sam shouts above the bustle.

There's a sudden rush to swallow last dregs of coffee, and the Scots finish inhaling their Jenga stack of carbohydrates at the wooden bench. I'm done getting ready – my travel bag is loaded onto the bus, my bike is all set. I've filled my Camelbak with bottled water combined with a couple of electrolyte tablets, and the same with a plastic water bottle mounted on my bike. I still don't feel entirely comfortable drinking from my Camelback – I prefer using my plastic bottle, this being what I've gotten used to since looting my daughter's fluffy unicorn drinks bottle just a few months ago for my early biking challenges. And at this precise moment, familiarity is key. I need to remind myself of things I already know: I know what a mountain bike feels like, I understand the gears and I'm familiar with drinking from a plastic water bottle mounted to the bike frame. These things are important, and they give me a small feeling of comfort.

My double-shot black coffee has taken effect, and I'm ready. I've fastened my lid (I never tire of calling it this instead of 'helmet') and put my cycling gloves on. I'm standing over my bike, ready to go. One by one, the others in the group make their way over: it's now 5:10 a.m.

'Come on, guys! We're ready to leave!' Sam shouts with some sense of urgency, as Coco piles the last of the large travel bags onto the compartment underneath the bus. I can feel my adrenalin surge as I know that once we hop onto our bikes and begin pedalling, it will be many hours until we can get off them again.

* * *

I'm unsure of the collective noun for cyclists, but 'peloton' sounds far too competent and professional to describe the group of us. So, the *swarm* of us set off, away from our five-a-side football pitch campsite and our pop-up buffet bar of Costa Rican budget breakfast options. It's only Day 1 in the context of the cycling adventure, but we already feel as though we've been through a lot. Daunting as it is, it's also a huge relief to get on the bikes. Many of us in the group were wondering if we ever would. This thrill enables us to override our extreme tiredness and frustration from the days of travel mayhem we have endured and there's a buzz of excitement in the group as we finally roll away for the goal we have all come here to realise: to ride across the county from the Pacific to the Caribbean coast.

We head off cycling, awkwardly at first, unsure of our bikes and of each other. What is unfamiliar to one of us is equally so for us all, as we form a disorganised pack riding behind Sam. He's now been joined by the main Costa Rican cycle guide, helpfully named JC (I'm relieved that he isn't another 'Mark' or 'Scott'). JC is built like a brick shit house, and, looking at his bulging calves, I can fully imagine that he can power his way *through* mountains rather than cycle up and over them. His younger assistant is a slightly-built, quiet chap called Carlos. The three of them – Sam, JC and Carlos – will take it in turns to lead us on our way cycling across the country, whilst the other two sit back and manage the different ability levels within the group. They will rotate these roles, but JC is ultimately the one who will steer us along the right route, up and around the right volcanoes (yes, you read that correctly), and towards the end destination for each day.

I'm stuck behind one of the Marks, who is chatting away to Posh Sally. He's riding slowly beside her and I feel hemmed in. We're cycling through a small town square, and it's important to keep our wits about us until we are away from any traffic, although it's not yet 5:30 a.m. *Fucking hell!* I can feel my frustration building, as riding along the quiet main roads at a very pedestrian pace is already irritating me. *I thought this was an EXTREME cycling challenge*, I think to myself, as JC makes a sudden turn into a gravel lay-by and comes to a halt. We all follow suit. *What? We're stopping already?* I look down at my GPS watch and we haven't yet ridden 4km. *This is ridiculous!* My mind is now racing with *other* worries. This is going to be THE MOST FRUSTRATING DAY/TEN DAYS EVER if we're going to be stop/starting every 4km along a 480km ride. And there I was wondering if I'd be able to keep up! If anything is looking doubtful now, it's my ability to manage my frustration that this challenge is so pedestrian my non-cycling seventy-four-year-old mother wouldn't be out of her depth. *WTAF!*

'Guys, guys ...' JC shouts above the noisy chatter – some of which is borne out of similar exasperations to mine, and grumblings about stopping so soon. 'The reason we have stopped is because we will shortly be taking a sharp turn OFF the main road,' he tells us. I wonder if he will make us stop before we make *any* turns ... off *any* roads. '... and when we turn off the road, we will begin the first climb. This will be a long, tough section of approximately 15k. Coco will meet us with the bus at 20k, where you will have your first stop for drinks and a snack. Ride carefully, as the track is very bumpy. And take your time on the steep sections. OK? Right, let's go!'

We scramble back into some semblance of a pack and once again I struggle to manage the cocktail of adrenalin, caffeine and irritation flooding my system. I just want to get going! I need to feel like all this was worth it, and to chip away at the terrifying prospect of having to ride 70km before the day is out. Stopping and starting, then standing around chatting about our lives back home will *not* make any headway into our task ahead. And I didn't come here for this: I came here for a challenge, not some prolonged game of Patience.

Turning off the main road comes quickly, and it comes as a relief. There's a wide, sandy track ahead of us, and if I look up, I can see it snaking up and around blind corners. *This is more like it!* I think to myself, as the prospect of being stuck next to Chatty Mark whilst riding slowly along a noisy main road is no longer a possibility. *Yes! This is more like it!*

The group settles into a rhythm, and our characters are soon revealed. It's becoming clear who the group leaders are, and who wants to be at the front of the pack. It's easy to see those who want to push a fast, early pace, and those who are happy to sit at the back. Cockney boy Luke and his pal are strong riders. And so are the three Scots. Mark and his Non-Scot friend are slightly older and not quite as powerful as Luke and the three Scots, but they are still very good mountain bike riders, and push themselves to stay with those at the front. Veronica is being permanently safeguarded by her Ironman husband in the middle of the pack, whilst Julie and Karen – the two older women – are happy taking their time riding slowly at the back. Sally is naturally fit, and she is riding happily alongside one of the Marks, who is still chatting away. They look to be having a pleasant conversation, and she's not having any difficulty maintaining her pace whilst responding to Mark's plethora of questions.

Meanwhile, I'm struggling to know where I fit in. My high adrenalin levels and built-up anxiety means that my body naturally wants to go fast, and so I push on towards the front. Plus, I haven't moved for days! Being stuck in various airport lounges and then airplane – and bus – seats has been hell, and I just want to move. My Other Half is not wired in this way, and so he – sensibly – sits in the middle of the group, pacing himself for what is to come. I don't ride with him; I don't know why I can't – or won't – slow down. I ride along the wide, steadily inclining sandy track, and all I know is that movement makes my head feel clearer. I'm finding a rhythm, and I can feel my heart beating in my chest. I'm alone with my own thoughts, but I'm so focused on riding my bike that my chimp has been completely silenced. It's the magical combination of being outside, in a beautiful place, and feeling my body working, whilst my mind becomes quiet. It is the same joy I once experienced with running: it's the feeling of being alive.

It's still very early morning, and thankfully, the baking sun hasn't yet burned its way through the clouds, but it's already getting hot. I'm growing in confidence with my Costa Rican bike, and – as expected – I find that having a similar model back home helps me to feel more confident with changing gears and handling the nuances of the weaving track, which is like being on a roller-coaster ride. *Up, round, down … up, round, up … up, up, round … up, down, up …* Every possible combination of 'up', 'round' and 'down' means that there's not a single moment where I can switch off my concentration. We're climbing again now, and the dusty track is making it feel like hard work. The pale, sandy gravel is loose under my wheels, and I must push hard on my pedals to keep moving forwards. The short downhill sections require just as much focus. I stand up on my pedals and trust in my bike to roll safely down the loose, bumpy ground at speed, whilst turning sharp corners. I don't know how, but I'm trying – and managing – to keep up with the three Scots who are riding at the front. Besides, I still have Cockney Luke and his bulging calves within sight, so I know that I'm maintaining a decent pace.

'I see we've got a speedy one here!' one of the competitive Marks shouts as he suddenly increases his pace and rides up alongside me. We're approaching an *up, round, up* section again.

Bloody hell!

'Hardly!' I reply, wondering how much polite conversation I have in me, and, more worryingly, how many more variations of the *up, round, down* roller-coaster ride it's possible for this off-road track to present us with. This is vastly different to the first few frustratingly slow road kilometres that lulled me into a false sense of expectation, and a laughable worry that this challenge wouldn't be challenging enough. Those concerns are now long gone, as I continue to push onwards, around and upwards along this seemingly endless sandy track.

I can feel the sweat dripping down my back. We have fragmented into distinct sub-groups, and my early synopsis of the people and their personalities on this trip appears to have now been confirmed. Being neither a man mountain, nor built like a brick shit-house with calves like oversized breast implants, I'm continuing to work harder than I should be doing. Running is a different sport entirely, and it requires a different type of fitness and physique. Sure, I'd likely kick Cockney Luke's muscly ass over a 5km run, but on a bike, he has the benefit of power. Nevertheless, I am choosing to push myself.

Push, push, push …

My Other Half is nowhere to be seen. I haven't ridden anywhere near him for what feels like many miles. I wonder what he's thinking. Is he struggling somewhere at the back of the group? He's very fit, but – like me – riding isn't his thing. Over the past twenty years, he's crafted himself into a runner, not a rider. But I don't have time to worry about him just now. He's got to pace himself, and – like the rest of us – he'll have to get himself through every single mile en route to the Caribbean coast. I simply can't imagine what he's making of all this. Surely, it's not what he signed up for. No doubt I'll soon find out.

We've just finished climbing a gruelling *up, up* and *up* combination on the dusty roller coaster, and I'm beginning to feel light-headed.

Shit! Have I pushed myself too hard, too soon?

When I glance down at my GPS watch, I see that we've ridden almost 18km, and it's not yet 8 a.m. I hadn't noticed that the sun has now broken through the early morning cloud, and it hangs proudly like a gold medal in the sky. I can taste salt on my lips as though I have just licked the inside of a packet of Walker's salt & vinegar crisps, and my lower legs are now caked in a thick dusting of beige sand. I look ahead, and I can see the apparition of Coco's minibus in the distance. *Is it real?* What on earth was I thinking earlier this morning, when I was unduly concerned that I might become increasingly frustrated with multiple rest stops on this challenge? I'm now *desperate* to have a break. Seeing Coco and his bus gives me the boost I need, and so I dig deeper into my pedals, wanting to reach the point where I can have a rest and something to eat – I seriously need to eat.

Drenched in sweat, I carefully remove myself from my chameleon-green bike and prop it against the densely-packed vegetation lining the side of the track. I sense that Costa Rica is a place of extremes: the heat already feels oppressive and airless, whilst the lush, vibrant greens of the foliage are evidence of plentiful rainfall. We've been told to expect rain on this trip, and lots of it. When it arrives, it will come down in bucket loads. I wonder when that will be, and how many miles we will have cycled by then. Walking away from my bike feels a tad uncomfortable: I'd just started getting used to sitting in the riding position, but my nether regions are extremely grateful for the reprieve. I walk over to the bus, where Cockney Luke is grinning whilst inhaling packets of salty biscuits and some watermelon slices, which Coco has helpfully laid out on a small collapsible table. The watermelon tastes amazing and I could eat the entire plateful, but I must leave some for the others who haven't arrived yet.

'So, how are you finding it, Rach?' Sam asks, as he is refilling his Camelbak from a large plastic vat at the side of the bus. 'And what's all this nonsense about you "not being a rider"?' he adds, in a deliberately silly voice. 'You're kicking ass at the front!'

'HA! I think I just got a bit giddy, trying to keep up with the fast boys,' I say, feeling absolutely thrilled that I have successfully faked it as any kind of mountain biker, thus far. 'Don't worry, Sam, I won't be up at the front for long!'

I know it's very early days, and I've already pushed myself way outside my comfort zone. I feel much better after taking on some food – I eat one of my peanut butter protein bars, followed by some of Coco's salty biscuits, and refill my water bottle with electrolyte solution. There are certain benefits to riding at the front of the pack: we get first dibs on any drinks and snacks Coco has selected for us. There are still plenty of salty biscuits and watermelon left when I reach the bus, but not so much for those arriving later. We also have more chance to rest whilst we're waiting for the others to join us, and when they do reach the bus, they will need a decent recovery, too, so we have perhaps double the time off the saddle. Finally, there's the undeniable ego boost of being one of the 'fasties'. And, as history has proven, my fragile ego is a sucker for these mini thrills. I don't know it yet, but I will pay a price for my lack of self-control.

We are high up now, and far away from any roads, traffic or civilisation. The only sounds we can hear are the wildlife, which is hidden amidst the rich tropical vegetation, and general chatter amongst the group, which is growing in number. Those riding in the middle of the pack eventually cycle up to the bus, with the stragglers not far behind. I examine everyone as they ride up to Coco's 20km pop-up pit stop and assess them for vital signs: weariness, chatter (or lack thereof), smiles (or lack thereof), pallor, and general demeanour, and I reach the conclusion that we have all been shocked by the severity of the 15km climb, and suitably terrified by the prospect of what is yet to come.

It's not yet 9 a.m. We've been riding for over three hours, and we have the rest of the day looming over us like an IED. After refuelling, I perk up, and it dawns on me that there is something incredibly liberating about being here, drenched in sweat, with absolutely no concern for anything other than the task ahead. I'm not wondering how my hair looks or consumed with worry over having tired, baggy eyes. Instead, I resign myself to the reality that by the end of today, I may well be as sweaty, filthy and exhausted as I have ever been. But I simply don't care, because we are *all* in this together.

We will *all* be caked in thick layers of beige dust from the mountainous tracks; we will *all* have visible traces of salt on our faces and our clothes, and we will *all* smell like the contents of a teenage boy's bedroom. And, once I've got my head together, following an injection of pure carbohydrates, I allow myself a mini 'YAY ME!' celebration that I'm doing this, and I'm doing it ... *quite well!* Keeping up with the fast boys at the front of the group is seriously challenging me (and I'm successfully disguising how hard I'm working), but I'm managing it. 'Fake it till you make it' ... Seems the well-worn mantra is just as effective for riding.

You're doing this, Rach! You're bloody doing it!

My Other Half isn't having such a great time. Understandably stunned by the severity of the climbs on this roller coaster of rough terrain, he simply isn't used to any of this. He doesn't say very much, but he doesn't have to. He looks exhausted, and – quite possibly – he is in a state of mild shock. I can't help but feel bad, because this was my idea. We pose for photos next to a sign with a huge arrow pointing backwards to Liberia, the place we have just come from, and an oversized number 20 (km) printed alongside it. It feels like we're on our way – we're only 20km into a 480km ride, but we've made a start.

'Hey, guys! Come and have a look at this!' Cockney Luke has been wandering around our elevated pit stop, and he's spotted the first of our major landmarks of today: the Santa María volcano. I walk just a few hundred yards around the corner, and there it is: far in the distance, and separated from us by vast green fields and clumps of dark trees, which look like kale. The white, fluffy clouds are hovering in the sky just above the volcano's vent, making it look like a child's depiction of volcanic ash. I smile at the simplicity of the image, whilst contemplating how far away it looks to be. Suddenly, the enormity of the task ahead consumes me and I can't quite grasp how much further we still have to go.

'Right then, team!' Sam shouts over the lunchtime hullabaloo. We're another 25km further en route to the Caribbean, and closer to our destination for the night: a camp at the base of another volcano. The shock of the morning has finally worn off, and reality is sinking in. For the first time, I can feel my female undercarriage beginning to grumble following hours on a strange – and unyielding – bike seat, which is no doubt exacerbated by the bumpy, hilly terrain, combined with the intense heat. It feels incredibly uncomfortable, but I have limited options available. At break stops (there hasn't been another one since Coco's 20km pop-up pit stop) and at lunchtime, I head straight for the nearest restroom facility – which has proven so far to consist of a large bush and a small, dirty hole in the ground – and I smear myself and my sodden padded cycling shorts with anti-chafing cream. The greasy white gloop is now everywhere, stuck in my fingernails and daubed all over my black cycling shorts. It reminds me of those dreadful, sleep-deprived, middle-of-the-night nappy changes, when streaks of Sudocrem would appear on every surface in my tired desperation to spare my baby daughter from the horrors of nappy-rash.

'Listen up!' Sam continues, as constant chatter bounces around the cheap plastic tables we are gathered round. 'This afternoon's riding is pretty serious stuff,' he proclaims, immediately silencing the socialites amongst us. *What on earth does that mean?* My first instinct is sheer panic at the prospect that the riding so far is *not* considered to be 'pretty serious'. *WTAF?* I've only just managed to bluff my way through an entire morning of bulging comfort zones, cycling at the very edge of my confidence and ability. Not that I have a massive appetite for lunch anyway (I'm full-to-bursting with peanut butter protein bars, salty biscuits and watermelon), but any hint of hunger has now vanished completely.

'The bus won't be able to accompany us for ANY of the last 20km of this afternoon's ride,' Sam tells us. 'This particular section is completely impassable by vehicles. It means you WON'T have access to the bus, or anything on it. You will ONLY have what is in your own Camelbak – no drink refills, no food stops, no Coco – and it will be INCREDIBLY DIFFICULT for us to help you during this section. Please be aware that the riding on this part of the route is extremely challenging. The terrain is very technical, with boulders, loose rocks, and some very sheer climbs. JC has ridden this section recently, and he tells me some parts have been made even more difficult by the recent heavy rainfall, which has resulted in large grooves and potholes becoming even larger. Those of you who DON'T want to take on this part of the ride – after what has already been a challenging day – have the option to jump onto the bus and ride with Coco, where you will meet up with the rest of the group at the end. It's entirely your choice; you have fifteen minutes to decide.'

Murmurs circulate around the plastic tables as people ponder on their options, and the distinct personality types come into play once again. Cockney Luke and his fit cycling pals are relishing the prospect of this – some *real* mountain bike riding – the cycling equivalent of the offensively macho 1990s Yorkie bar slogan: 'Not for Girls'. The older Marks (I use the name 'Mark' generically, referencing those who are strong, experienced riders, and who are happy hanging onto Luke's coattails) are slightly apprehensive, but most certainly up for the challenge. Julie and Karen are both quiet – I assume they are, like me, seriously mooting their options.

The riding thus far has been significantly more challenging than myself or either of these two ordinary superwomen had anticipated, and we are at the very edge of our ability. Karen makes the sensible decision to quit whilst she's ahead and ride on the bus with Coco. She figures that this is only Day 1 of our cycling adventure and she must have enough left in reserve for whatever lies ahead on Days 2, 3, 4, and ... *shit! When will this thing end?* Julie, on the other hand, completely refuses to entertain the prospect of hitching a lift with Coco on the bus. 'What? No way am I getting on that bus!' she pronounces to Sam, incredulously, as he works his way around the group, asking each of us in turn for our decision.

I find myself once again in a comfort zone no man's land: I'm both terrified that this will be a bridge too far, and completely beyond anything I'm capable of tackling on two wheels, whilst at the same time aghast at the prospect of bailing out and sipping a can of Coke on board Coco's

Safety Bus, whilst the others scramble their way along 20km of hardball mountain biking terrain.

'Yeah, I'm riding,' I say to Sam, as his eyeballs meet mine.

Whatever happens, I can't duck out now – I must be brave enough to give it a try.

'Good girl!' Sam says, as though he hadn't even contemplated that I might furnish him with any other response.

Karen smiles and waves wildly from the window as Coco drives the touring support bus away from us. I briefly wonder if I could run fast enough to catch up with it. She doesn't seem at all mithered by any Bastard Chimp rampaging in her head, unlike the one who is now jumping up and down in mine. It's very clear to see that Karen is simply delighted with her decision to stick her bike on the roof of the bus and sit this part out. I envy her lack of self-flagellation.

'Right, guys! I'll be riding in the middle of the pack, and Carlos will be hanging at the back. Try to keep moving as much as possible throughout this section, and please let the more confident riders go in front. This is only fair for those who have more mountain biking experience and technical ability. The three of us will help as much as we can, but we can't ride it for you! JC is leading from the front. Let's go!'

With that, our rather subdued *non*-peloton gets back into action and rides away from the roadside hut with dirty plastic tables and matching chairs. It takes a few kilometres for us to lose all semblance of civilisation, but once we do, it soon becomes very clear why this section has been described as 'impassable'. I think back to the dusty, beige roller-coaster track from the early hours of this morning, and I laugh at the thought that, as difficult as it felt at the time, it was *a piece of cake* compared to this! THERE IS NO TRACK, PATH OR TRAIL HERE! The roller-coaster track may have meandered endlessly up, down and around in a million arduous combinations, but it was a track nonetheless. This? Some spiralling, deep grooves carved in the side of a volcano littered with loose boulders, tree roots that have been ripped up from the earth, and – well, the only thing missing is molten lava cascading down the mountainside, which we are supposed to be riding. It dawns on me that my ego may have forced me into a corner from which it is now impossible to escape. I simply have no option but to make my way along 20km of the most ridiculous – seemingly impossible – technical terrain on two wheels.

My mind has a flashback to just a few months ago, when the task of riding along the (ahem) 'bumpy' canal, avoiding extendable dog leads and low stone bridges was a challenge.

What the hell happened? How did I go from there to being here? What would the rest of the group say if they had any idea of my inexperience or ineptitude? Can I hide it from them all the way across Costa Rica? Four hundred and eighty kilometres right up to the Caribbean Sea? Is it possible for me to fake it for so long?

Cockney Luke with his breast-implant calves is nowhere to be seen. He and his small posse of real, Yorkie-bar-eating mountain-biking boys have cut loose and left us for dust. His power and confidence on the bike are surely enough to crush any boulders and vaporise the otherwise wheel-buckling tree roots churned up by the volcanic earth. I, on the other hand, must weave and gnarl my way up, over and around the same. My legs are caked in a thick paste of beige sand, sun cream, trails of sweat and dried salt. My padded shorts are as saturated as if they'd just been taken out of the washing machine's rinse-and-spin cycle. My arms and my back ache from holding myself in the same position on my bike since some ungodly hour of the morning, which feels like it was a fortnight ago. I've been topping up my metabolic fuel tank with protein bars, energy gels, electrolyte tablets dissolved in water, salty biscuits and watermelon, but my body is simply not used to this. It's like suddenly discovering there's a Mile 27 of the marathon: the shock and fatigue of this new place is all completely unknown. Basic survival instinct means that I simply must do whatever is necessary to deal with this unfamiliarity. I realise that I'm left with only two options: (1) I adapt to the circumstances, and slowly make my way to the Caribbean coast on two wheels, or (2) I crumple into a heap of sweat and tears, and crawl onto Coco's minibus for the remaining 440km. I choose option number (1) – to sit firm on my bike, and to keep pedalling.

I'm slowly grinding my way up the volcanic hillside, which looks to have been subjected to a recent landslide. I can see where water has cascaded down the deep channels in the ground, dragging all kinds of debris in its wake. The trenches are easily deep enough to catch my front wheel, and many times I simply hop off the bike before my nobbled tyres become wedged in a crevasse. *Fucking hell, not again!* I'm now muttering to myself, repeatedly. My head is bowed, and I'm focusing only on moving my wheels forwards – well, *upwards* – in whatever way I can. My words range from various frustrated expletives right through to desperate attempts at self-motivation.

Come on, Rach. Keep going, just keep going. There is absolutely no point in stopping, now. It will be over soon. The more effort you put in, the quicker you'll get to the end. Remember the last 5 per cent rule? This is it: it's the last 5 per cent.

'I can't ride over this,' I rasp to Sam, who is now riding right by my side, doing his best to keep the small splinter group of us inching ahead when it's clear that we are all ready to throw our bikes down the bastard mountainside, sit down and weep. A silence has descended, and there's no longer any chatter about jobs back home or previous cycling expeditions.

No, I haven't cycled across Peru, or paraglided off Mount fucking Kilimanjaro!

There are no words. Nothing can be said to make this any easier, or to make the route any more tolerable. I'm now so far away from the series of mini cycling challenges I set myself back home that I can barely bring myself to think back to my own apprehension at the prospect of riding five miles along a loose gravel path.

What the actual fuck was I worried about?

But the fear was real for me, then, just as the overwhelming task ahead is, now. The only thing the two have in common is the sure knowledge that they will both – at some point – come to an end. Eventually it will be over, and this time, I will have one MASSIVE, FUCK-OFF index card to place in my bulging box of mini 'YAY ME!' accomplishments. Or I might just begin a new box...

'Push the bike over the really tricky parts, Rach,' Sam says kindly, keeping his words succinct, as even he knows that he can't do a single thing to make it any better. 'And when you feel like you can, just start riding again. Look around you: everyone else is struggling on this section, not just you. This is highly technical, and it's nothing to do with fitness,' he continues.

I smile at him weakly and glance behind me. I can see Julie approaching, weaving her way up and over the impossible holes and unstable lumps on the ground. Her short, dark hair is glistening with sweat at the base of her cycling helmet, her sodden clothes vacuum packed onto her body with perspiration. She has a fixed stare which makes it appear as though she's in a trance. I watch her for a few moments longer as she continues to push, push, push down on her pedals – pedals just like mine – and she continues to force her bike to inch forwards, up and over the inhospitable terrain.

How is she doing it? How is she able to dig so deep, and just keep pedalling like that?

I think back to the things I've heard her say – and to the reason for her taking part in challenges such as this: she had her heart broken. When her husband left her five years ago, she was left staring into a deep void of lostness. That place caused her to set out on a quest to find herself. It led to her discovering things about herself – and about her own strength – which she hadn't known before. I can see how the pain and the struggle has morphed into something else: it has been magically transformed into inner strength. I realise that the same thing is true for me. Just like Julie, my struggle has become my strength.

I get back onto my saddle, and I turn to face the climb. *I can do this*, I tell myself, inspired by Julie's doggedness. *I can fucking do this!* We continue to silently crawl upwards, and the ground eventually breaks into a flatter, less severe, dusty track.

'Thank GOD for that!' I say to Julie as we are now pedalling side by side, finally able to break the desperate, exhausted silence. I look around and notice that the scenery is vastly different now: the ground is a deeper, burnt clay colour, and the sand is no longer beige. I shift the gears on my bike, and pick up my pace. We're rolling again. I'm so relieved to be moving forwards – not up mountains, or over large, insurmountable obstacles, just *forwards*. A mini rush of adrenalin floods my body and replenishes my earlier fatigue. Julie is still cycling with me, and she's making every effort to keep up with my increasing pace. As I put my foot down to speed up, she does the same.

'We can do it, Rach! Only 5km to go. We're almost there. We can do it!' she shouts across from the other side of the clay track.

I look over at Julie, with her face splattered in mud, dust – both beige and burnt clay colour – streaks of sweat, and traces of white salt, and I smile.

This woman is fucking incredible!

34

SICK

It's cycling Day #2. The camp waiting for us at the end of over 40 miles of mountain biking and 4,500 feet of climbing on Day #1 was … a large, empty room, not unlike an aircraft hangar, with a concrete floor. We moved our designated tent far away from the place it had been erected: next to one small toilet which didn't flush, and had never seen a splash of Toilet Duck. I think I slept, but I don't honestly know. Exhaustion, shock and anxiety over what lies ahead has completely over-ridden my ability to know *what* I think. Anyway, who cares if I slept or not? Even *I* don't care about that any more. All I care about is getting through whatever the hell we must cycle across, around, up and over, en route to the Caribbean coast. We had a hell of a day's riding yesterday, and some of the group can't comprehend that we might face the same again today: I'm one of them.

Cockney Luke is inhaling scrambled eggs and a rice dish with some indiscernible grey meat in it. I can barely stomach food, let alone warm rice with sloppy eggs, and so I'm back to my faithful peanut butter protein bars. I realise that I now hate them with a passion – I can't comprehend that these are my main nutritional sustenance for the coming days.

'OK, guys, listen up!' Sam interrupts the scraping of plates and chinking of cheap cups. 'We've got another big day ahead of us, but nothing quite as technically challenging as the last part of yesterday's ride!' Audible relief spreads amongst the group, and Julie makes a loud whooping sound. 'You all did so well yesterday, and I want to commend you for your amazing efforts.' He goes on complimenting us – presumably delivering a classic 'shit sandwich', this being designed to make the bad news slightly more palatable. Here it comes … 'Today, we have some more climbing in the morning, and then a long, flat road section after lunch.'

Fucking hell! I don't honestly know how much more climbing I can face. And this is only Day #2! A quiet acceptance has now fallen between me and my Other Half, who is still in a deep state of shock following all that has happened over the past twenty-four hours.

'Can you pass the chamois cream, please?'

'Sure.'

'Have you done with the electrolytes?'

'Yep.'

'Come on, guys, liven up! Let's get some tunes on!' Cockney Luke shouts through his perma-smile as the swarm of us hover nervously on our bikes outside the aircraft hangar campsite. It's 5:30 a.m. and we're ready for off. Music pumps loudly from Luke's iPhone as we roll away and onto the next part of our challenge. I smile to myself, as memories of shuffling up and down on the sticky Acapulco nightclub dance floor twenty years ago to Livin' Joy's 'Dreamer' momentarily distract me from my saddle-sore arse.

'I'm riding next to you and your nineties house music fun bus, today!' I declare to Luke, who laughs as I cycle alongside him singing house classics at full throttle. The funky tunes cheer me up, and I'm thinking, *I love this! I fucking love this! Movement, fresh air, freedom, heart thumping in my chest, and now, funky house tunes!* Finally, we're turning a corner.

* * *

I've had an epic morning riding alongside Luke's fun bus. 'Where Love Lives', 'Ride on Time', 'I Like to Move It' … we've sung along to endless retro tunes courtesy of Luke's mobile disco. What's more, I've managed to keep up with him (although I did fall behind during the Ultra Naté track – I was never a big fan of that one).

I hadn't noticed, but the sun has been blisteringly hot today and it's getting hotter. It's early afternoon now, and this section of the ride is very different to the meandering, sandy tracks of the morning. We're now cycling single file along a main road. Enormous articulated lorries thunder past as we roll mile after mile along the flat tarmacked motorway. That's what it is: it's a motorway. This would be illegal back home. Regardless of the minimalist Costa Rican health and safety laws, or non-existent traffic violations, it's good to be moving at a fast pace and eating up the miles.

This is flat … We're cycling on tarmac … Luke's playing his party tunes … What's not to like?!

But, crikey, that sun! And the pace ... Luke with his enormous calves is still pushing on ahead, with little old me pedalling like merry hell. I'm trying – and just about managing – to keep up. But it's so hot.

It's just soooooo hot.

There's no shade here. Gone is the lush vegetation of the volcanic mountainous climbs; there are no trees, just sky. Veronica has zero chance of spotting an orphaned sloth for the next 30km, unless one has sleep-walked far away from its usual treetop habitat or been abducted by a lorry driver.

'I hope you guys have covered yourselves in sun cream!' the ever-present, safety-conscious Sam shouts as he cycles at speed down the line, aware of the intense UV rays we are now subjected to. He knows that there will be no reprieve until the next pit stop in approximately 30km. My shoulders are bare. I'm wearing an all-in-one triathlon suit, comprising (very short) padded shorts, combined with a zip-up bodice. It has the look (and feel) of a swimming costume/nappy combination, and is perfect for these temperatures, but much of my skin is exposed. I hadn't realised it until now (largely because of my immediate shock and survival mode) but the sun is slowly baking my body. Sure, I slathered myself in Factor 50 at 4:30 a.m., along with the various other gloopy substances I'm required to coat myself in, preventing everything from nappy rash to insect bites. I'm like a lubricated condom on a bike.

Mile after mile goes by, and I wonder how much of my Factor 50 gloop is still effective. How much of it has been washed away by the constant streams of salty sweat running down the entire length of my body, and the water from my bottle which I douse myself in at any given opportunity? I can feel my exposed flanks burning in the relentless heat, and my shoulders are a clear ten degrees hotter than the rest of my body. I gulp electrolyte solution faster than my body can process the salt replacement, but I'm focused on just one thing: pedalling.

We're on our fifteenth rendition of Black Box's 'Ride on Time' when the vision of Coco and his bus appears in a lay-by.

'Thank God! It's the lunchtime stop,' I tell my cockney friend as we speed up to reach Coco's bus. Luke pushes on ahead, and I get another glimpse of his calves, which still stun me by their size and shape – I've seen racehorses with smaller thighs. The bus is tucked in just off the main highway, but there's *still* no shade here. Coco has brought out his pop-up table and has laid out some food and drinks for us, but the place is swarming with flies. Our salty, sweaty bodies don't help, as we stand side by side, swiping flying creatures away from our mouths so that we can replace some of the 4,000 calories we've just burned. Sadly, the heat – and the flies – are ruining my appetite. I feel hungry, but I can't stomach much food. My body has worked so hard, yet it feels too tired to cope with an injection of fuel.

Back to peanut butter protein bars, then ...

* * *

We've finished riding for the day and have finally rocked up at this, our *third* non-glamping location. Only this time, it miraculously *IS* a real campsite complete with showers, a

BAR AREA (I gasp in awe) and the most important thing of all: a flushing loo.

Ahhhhhh! This is more like it!

'Are you coming rafting with us, you two?' Sam asks, once we've had all of ten minutes to regain some feeling in our nether regions following another forty-four tough miles of riding up and over volcanoes. I wonder, have I heard him correctly? He's talking about GOING RAFTING? FFS! After the day we've had, who amongst us is in any fit shape to be careering down fast-moving water in an inflatable dinghy?

'No. Not for us, thanks,' I say definitively to Sam, before my Other Half has a chance to speak. I can tell from his sunken, hollow eyes that he'd rather sit motionless in the river and allow the cool water to numb everything from the waist down. And I'm right: the next few hours are spent doing precisely that. The few of us who are *not* derived from some superior gene pool sit in the cold river and reflect on all that has happened. Sometimes, we sit in comfortable silence listening to the unmistakable barking of the tree frogs and the constant singing from the giant grasshoppers as the cumulative tiredness washes over us. But this is frequently disturbed by random bursts of hysteria which – I can only presume – come from the utterly surreal experiences we have endured thus far and from our complete exhaustion.

Tonight's evening meal *should* be enjoyable. This place is, by all other standards we've experienced on the trip so far, sheer luxury. As per the normal drill, we congregate at a designated time around a collection of long tables. But I don't want to go for tea, tonight – I wish I could just stay in my tent. Cockney Luke and his posse are the first to order rounds of bottled beer, whilst large plates of food are hurried out from a hidden kitchen somewhere upstream.

'Are you not going to eat that?' my Other Half asks me, as I sit staring blankly at a white plate stacked high with varying kinds of beige stodge.

'To be honest, I'm not feeling too good,' I reply quietly, simply unable to force any of the pasta/rice/fried chicken/potato salad combination into my mouth.

I hadn't picked up on it earlier, but now I can sense that something is wrong. My head feels funny. *Is it dehydration?* I turn down the kind offer of a chilled beer and opt for a bottle of water instead. No, something *definitely* isn't right. I'm sitting listening to the laughter and chatter going on all around me. Everyone is so relieved to have arrived at this place. Many of the group are buzzing from their earlier rafting experience, whilst Julie and Karen are laughing about numbing their throbbing nether regions in the ice-cold river. I can't join in.

'I'm heading back to the tent,' I whisper to my Other Half, who is fast sweeping up the many leftover carbohydrates on my plate. 'Maybe I just need an early night.' I don't want to make a fuss. It's nothing – I'm probably just tired.

Thankful for some peace in the confines of our small tent, I've crawled into my sleeping bag. My head is thumping, and I can feel the heat radiating across my shoulders and down my flanks. It keeps making me shiver. *Fucking hell, I'm shivering!* Bedtimes are early here – unless you're Cockney Luke and his beer-drinking super-species, that is. I have my riding kit all ready for the morning but, more importantly, I've prepared myself for what I know instinctively will be a long night ahead. *Bottled water?* Check. *Paracetamol?* Check. *Ibuprofen?* Check. *Imodium?* Check. *Electrolyte tablets?* Check. *Peanut fucking butter protein bars (as I haven't replaced circa 4,000 calories from today, yet)?* Check.

'Right, I'm off to sleep,' I say to my Other Half, who has finished his second bottle of beer and has come back to the tent to check on me – and get some rest himself before *another* long day on the bikes, tomorrow.

'Jesus, you look pale, Rach! Are you sure you're OK?' he says before cocooning himself into his sleeping bag for the night. My tummy is aching. Gnawing pains are shooting across my abdomen, making the hairs on my arms stand on end. I grab my stomach, trying to comfort myself, and to make it stop.

'No. No, I don't think I am,' I squeak, before urgently unzipping my sleeping bag and dashing out of the tent, only just making it to the loo. This is where the night of horror begins. The pattern is this: I go back to the tent, crawl into my sleeping bag, try to sleep whilst sweating and shivering, roll around in pain, sip some bottled water, contort myself with yet another abdominal spasm, wake my Other Half (again) whilst squirming about reaching for the head torch and/or one of the many over-the-counter drugs I have lined up next to me, squeeze myself out of the tent, eject the remaining contents of my body. Most times, I make it to the loo. A few times, I don't. I don't get much sleep. Well, I don't get *any* sleep. My Other Half insists on going to talk to Sam when the group wakes at some ungodly hour the next morning.

'You've got heatstroke, Rach,' Sam says, poking his head into our tiny, and now stinky two-man shelter. 'I really don't think you should ride today.'

What? What has he just said?

'No! I'll be fine to ride, Sam. I've had some rehydration salts, and I'm eating again. Honestly, I'll be fine.'

I make a determined effort to rally myself, shoe-horning my aching limbs into an unforgiving triathlon suit, and I step outside the tent to go to the bathroom (well, the single toilet cubicle which has a mirror in it), but I feel shaky, as though I could collapse onto the floor at any moment.

'I think Sam is right,' I splurt, crying breathless tears onto the shoulder of my Other Half, who is equally exhausted. 'I can't ride today, I just can't do it.'

* * *

It's Day 3 and I'm lying listless on a bus seat, with bottled water and small amounts of bland food being forced into my mouth at frequent intervals.

I can feel the bus pull up for lunch. I'm still lying in the recovery position with my body curled up on one bus seat, my legs spanning the aisle and propped up onto the seat opposite. The rest of the group begin to trickle onto the bus to pick up various bits and pieces from their hand luggage.

'Oh, Rach, you poor thing. You look like death!' one of the Marks says as he gingerly steps over my legs, which are blocking the aisle of the bus (it's one of the problems with being longer than 2'11" – the width of a standard bus seat). I don't reply; I can hear him, but I'm completely zoned out.

With some help, I'm managing to force down tiny sips of water, and even the occasional nibble of a salty biscuit, but my body is in virtual shut down. The previous two days of relentlessly *push, push, pushing* myself up and over the roller-coaster tracks of volcanic mountains, whilst trying in vain to keep up with Cockney Luke and his nineties house music fun bus – combined with the intense and prolonged heat of yesterday's motorway section – has finished me off. I've lost more body fluids than I can possibly replace, and all I can do is sleep. I don't even care about the fact that I'm the one who has been forced to utilise Coco's mobile safety bus as a means of emergency transport, because I'm simply unfit to ride the bike. Thankfully, the severe heatstroke has wiped out my Bastard Chimp as well as myself.

The group are about to visit a local primary school, where – we've been told – we will be entertained by the throngs of young children, who I can hear whooping and cheering outside.

'Are you coming to see the kids, Rach?' my Other Half asks quietly, as he is getting ready to join the gang for this welcome break from the relentless riding. He has been sitting with me on the bus for the entire morning, holding the water bottle up to my mouth at frequent intervals and breaking off small sections of food for me to eat.

'No, I'm good here, thanks,' I say, still unable to bring myself to a seated position after approaching six hours of horizontal rocking and rolling on Coco's converted ambulance. 'But I would like to speak to Tilly. Please could you pass me my phone?' I ask weakly. 'I just want to hear her voice.'

Ring ring … Ring ring …

'Hello, Mummy!' an excited little voice on the other end of the phone answers.

Silence. I cannot speak because I'm sitting by myself, on a bus in a strange country, in floods of tears: I'm broken.

'Mummy, are you there?' the voice continues – she sounds so far away.

'Tilly. Tills, it's me!' I gulp desperately, but I'm struggling to string more than three monosyllabic words together. 'Oh, Tills!'

'Why are you crying, Mummy?' she asks.

'Oh, erm [gulp] I, erm [gulp harder], I'm just so tired, Tills. And I miss you – that's all.'

'Are you all right, Mummy?' she says, sounding concerned.

I pull myself together, whilst silent tears continue to stream down my face.

If only you could see me, Tills.

I try to think of something interesting to tell her, because I'm very aware that a long-distance phone call with a parent has the excitement factor of a bag of salad for a seven-year-old girl.

'We've cycled around two volcanoes!' I say, wondering if this will hit the 'vaguely interesting' vibe.

'Oh. I've been to the park,' she replies.

I feel more tears welling up and stinging my eyes through my snotty, spontaneous laughter.

My phone call with Tilly has made all the emotions pour out of me: the build-up of anxiety, the apprehension, the extreme fatigue, the sleep deprivation, the aching limbs, and the disappointment that I am here – sitting on the bus – and not out there, on the bike.

Have I failed? Why has this happened? Why do I feel so weak?

'Rach, I've been thinking. I reckon we should stay in a hotel tonight. You've been so poorly, and I can't imagine you'll be much better after another night sleeping on a concrete floor,' my Other Half says as he steps back onto the bus after his *Costa Rica's Got Talent* experience. I can't tell if I feel ridiculous or relieved at the suggestion.

Julie, Karen, Veronica and Sally are all still managing to ride across Costa Rica. Why can't I?

'Yeah, I think you might be right.'

The silent tears are still streaming down my face.

* * *

It's *sooooo* good to finally be in a bed! My heatstroke + complete exhaustion combo brought me to my knees. One full day spent riding on Coco's minibus-turned-emergency-ambulance was unavoidable in the circumstances, and I was – at that point – in no fit state to concern myself with any bruising to my cycling ego. Even my Bastard Chimp couldn't be arsed to join in with his usual mocking diatribe, so I *know* without any doubt whatsoever that I was really quite poorly.

So far on this trip, I've been existing on a diet of predominantly peanut butter protein bars and packets of salty biscuits (with a few slices of watermelon thrown in for my one-a-day vitamin requirements), but I've struggled to eat proper meals. Today, for the first time, my appetite has returned … AND. I. WANT. FOOD!!

'Hi. Could I order two chicken club sandwiches with fries for Room 211, please,' I say to the non-English-speaking person on the other end of the phone. This feels like complete, unadulterated luxury.

It arrives and is quite simply the best thing I have ever tasted. I look over at my Other Half, who is in a deep trance-like state, unable to engage in any kind of conversation because he too is busy focusing on mopping up all the greasy remnants on his plate with his last remaining fries. I've never known either of us eat so much, so quickly. My tummy feels kind of bloated and is now protruding like a small child's after eating too much cake at a birthday party. But I can already feel the energy flooding back into my system. It feels weird, like being plugged in, recharged. The listless shell of a person I was only a matter of hours ago is about to be replaced by a living, breathing, fully-functioning human being!

In my head, I'm processing the miles I've missed riding on the bike and I'm rationalising the contributing factors that have led me here. The rest of the group have been nothing but supportive, offering to help in any way – not that they can do much about my ongoing 'Power of Yet' versus 'The Curse of Enough' tightrope walk. Now and again, the strive to push myself tips over into something dangerous and potentially damaging, and kicking my own arse cycling up and over volcanoes whilst trying to keep up with Cockney Luke certainly falls within this bracket.

'We don't have to go back tomorrow, you know,' my Other Half says sheepishly, once he emerges from his carbohydrate-induced coma.

What? What is he talking about?

'We don't have to prove anything to anybody, Rach,' he adds in response to my continued, bemused silence.

'What are you talking about? Why wouldn't we go back and finish the ride? What do you mean?' I honestly don't know where to begin processing what he's quite clearly suggesting.

'You've been completely wiped out, Rach,' he says. 'And I'm worried if we carry on with the ride, you'll push yourself too hard, and you'll become *really* poorly.'

I can't believe what I'm hearing: he thinks I'm not fit to continue, and complete the cycle ride to the Caribbean!

'But I'm eating real food again,' I say, gesturing to my empty plate, which has just a few oily smears left as evidence of my recent calorific intake. 'I've got my appetite back, and I feel tons better for having some proper food.'

My Bastard Chimp is quick to jump onto this apparent vote of no confidence and chaotic thoughts begin to swirl around in my head about the feasibility – or not – of my continuing with this epic cycling challenge. I know that I've been poorly, and I'm very aware that my body has been pushed to its limits. Admittedly, I feel weak. But, surely there's an element of bad luck at play here? Yes, the first two days of inconceivably tough mountain biking has kicked my arse good and proper, but the heatstroke? I know that I'd be better prepared next time. I'd cover up any exposed areas and take greater care slathering myself in Factor 50+ … *absolutely everywhere*. I'd make a determined effort to eat proper meals rather than rely on my God-awful protein bars for sustenance, and I'd perhaps think twice about trying to keep up with Cockney

Luke on the relentless roller-coaster climbs, allowing myself to settle a little further back in the pack.

I would learn to PACE MYSELF on the bike, too. Because you know what? I'm new to this – I'm still a learner, here. Sure, one who's been on a hell of a steep learning curve, but I'm undeniably wet behind the ears when it comes to two wheels. I need to accept this fact and be kind to myself about the predicament I'm now in. Hear that again: *I need to be kind to myself.* This feels like a strange and uncomfortable notion and it makes me slightly nauseous. All I've ever done is buy into the 'DIG DEEPER, TRY HARDER, DO MORE, BE BETTER' mantra. This feels wimpy, and as though I'm giving myself an excuse to be shit.

Is that what I'm doing? Giving myself permission to just be shit?

'I'm going to have to think about it,' I say to my OH who has now snuggled down into his feathery-light, duck-down 10-tog duvet for the night. I don't feel like launching into a big discussion about this, just now. I'm busy having my own internal battle, which is enough for me to manage. And as hard as the last twenty-four hours have been, I keep coming back to one thing: I desperately want to complete this challenge and reach the Caribbean coast on my garish green Trek mountain bike with the rest of the group in just a few days' time.

BEEP BEEP BEEP BEEP ... The offensive alarm on my iPhone sounds. It might as well be a person standing over my head, banging on a large pan with a wooden spoon. It's 4:30 a.m., and *I've slept!* We've BOTH slept like babies being rocked gently in Moses baskets. But it's still objectionably early, and it's time to break the bad news.

'WHAT?! You want to ride again? TODAY? Are you serious?'

My Other Half doesn't mean to sound so utterly incredulous at my decision, but he can't help it. After days of trashed travel plans and a thorough arse-kicking on bikes with minimal sleep, one fried chicken sandwich (with delicious salty fries) plus a single night's sleep in a bed of any description is more than enough to make any sane person want more of the same and to politely refrain from partaking in any further ludicrousness. Surely, enough is enough? And he's right ... to a degree. We *don't* have to prove anything, to anybody; this is *our* cycling challenge, and we're doing well to just be here and place ourselves amongst these 'real' riders. Plus, this is meant to be fun, right? It's supposed to be an adventure, and anyone would be pushed to consider that twenty-four hours suffering the effects of heatstroke (nine of which were spent lying in the recovery position on a minibus) could constitute 'fun' of any description. But, despite all these undeniable truths, the fact is I HAVE enjoyed many aspects of this trip, and I don't want it to end. Not here. Not like this.

I contemplate all that we have done so far and a wide smile spreads across my face at the realisation that the most meaningful, satisfying and even *enjoyable* parts of this adventure have also been the most challenging: facing my fears and riding through them – literally up and over them, being fully immersed in uncertainty but embracing it anyway. Realising that just because something is scary and alien to me doesn't mean that it's too big for me to face. Even when the best laid plans go to pot, even when there are NO WASHING

FACILITIES OR MIRRORS available for days on end, then I can still be OK. Realising that I *don't need those things*, when – at one time – just like the daily Prozac happy pills, and later, just like my running – I firmly believed that I did.

'Yeah,' I reply, feeling bad that I may well have ruined my Other Half's dreams of three days' relaxing on a sun lounger by the terraced pool, 'I'm sure. I'm going to send Sam a text. Coco can pick us up on the way to the start of today's ride.'

That's it, decision made. Thanks to one chicken club sandwich and salty chips, and a bed for the night, it's game on: we're getting back on the bikes.

35

BACK ON THE BIKE

WOO HOO! This is *I-N-C-R-E-D-I-B-L-E*! I'm intoxicated by the rush of endorphins as we ride up and over the Costa Rican trails, making me feel alive again. I'm *so glad* that I didn't bail out when I had every opportunity to take an 'easier' option. But four nights spent lounging by the pool of a luxury hotel with the best fried chicken and chips in the world couldn't come anywhere close to compensating for this. I'm back riding, and everything feels to be flowing. My strength and confidence have returned, and I feel more settled, having finally managed my Bastard Chimp, with his pathetic chuntering about me not being 'good enough' or 'fast enough' or 'whatever ... enough'.

Bore off, Chimp!

'Hey, look! Up there!' Julie hollers as she screeches her bike to a dramatic halt. Those of us riding closer to the front wonder if she's had a mechanical malfunction and make an about turn. Luke and one of the Scots have ridden too far ahead, so they will miss out this time.

'Oh, my goodness, it's a sloth!' Veronica screeches in her high-pitched West Counties accent. I look up and see a small furry ball hanging motionless in a tree. We stand around in a huddle, gaping up at the high branches in silence. No one knows what to say, other than 'Wow, it's a sloth!' but the group is patient and kind, and we know what this moment means to Veronica. To be fair, this is what sloths do – they hang around motionless in trees – but there's something special about knowing that we are on their turf, and this is their backyard. We are riding our bikes across Costa Rica, apparently in the middle of nowhere, on desolate, rough tracks, and I'm just so happy to be here. I feel proud of myself for not giving up; for turning my adversity and disappointment into fuel for getting up, and back on the bike. I look across at Julie and think how watching her over these past ten days has inspired me to keep going, and – regardless of circumstances – find my inner strength. And I think about how Karen has reminded me that superheroes come in all different shapes and sizes – there isn't a one-size-fits-all. Veronica's joy at seeing her mystical sloth is enchanting. Right here, right now, there's nowhere else I would rather be than in this incredible place, with these incredible people. Finally, I am learning to live in the 'now' and see the beauty right where I am. I've been freed from waiting for some unspecified time in the future when everything will be perfect: when *I* will be perfect. It *IS* perfect – right here, right now.

The sky rumbles and then belches loudly, reminding me of my upset tummy from the previous day. We're standing around admiring the sedentary sloth snoozing in his penthouse when everything changes. The air is suddenly filled with foreboding. A thin slash of sunshine pierces through the heavy raincloud, which has just placed itself directly overhead. Within seconds, the gash of sunlight has disappeared, leaving only the swollen cloud, now spewing out relentless, warm rain.

'Let's get moving, guys!' Sam shouts from the front. 'And say "hello" to your first taste of a tropical rainstorm!' he giggles, riding away with both arms out wide as though he is catching water in his open palms.

How does he do that? I have no idea.

The warm, swollen droplets make it feel like we're riding through a hot shower rather than the cold, piercing stuff back home. And it doesn't make any difference to the oppressive heat. It feels as though the earth has absorbed all the warmth it could from days of baking under the blistering sun and is now smouldering like a hot massage stone. We have all brought our waterproofs on this trip – as per the suggested 'list of essential items' – but the mere thought of wrapping ourselves up in long-sleeved cagoules is akin to a chicken voluntarily jumping into a bag and being roasted in the oven.

Instead of the usual discomforts of riding in a cold downpour back in the UK, the challenges are very different here. The main – undesirable – effect I notice is that of my now entirely drenched padded shorts and the impact on my already saddle-sore arse. The warm, wet skin all around my legs and upper thighs – and, well, *absolutely everywhere* – is now rubbing against the sodden fabric. I can feel these areas beginning to burn and chafe, without any lubrication to protect the most badly affected parts. Nothing is dry. No part of my clothing, shoes, undergarments, Camelbak (or contents thereof) is unaffected. Any items such as iPhones or other mobile electrical devices are tightly encased in dry bags. This is one opportunistic airport lounge purchase that I'm *very* grateful for.

We continue riding in the hot, sticky rain for what feels like hours. I'm hypnotised by the sound of the water falling, bouncing off the trees and hitting the ground. Puddles develop on the uneven, bumpy track, making it more fun to navigate our way around – and more often through – the muddy pools. Miles tick by, and I'm getting used to the way the bike feels riding over the increasingly saturated ground. I can feel my speed increasing as I'm growing in confidence.

'Hey, HEY! Coming through!' I shout to my Other Half, who is riding along, chatting away happily to one of the non-Scots. I look to my left and then my right: there's nowhere for me to go. I have no option but to ride *between* their two bikes, it's too late for me to consider slowing down. This is NOT mountain biking etiquette. This is NOT how to overtake a rider – or riders, plural. This is NOT going to end well.

My Other Half is stunned by the sudden appearance of my front wheel between his and Non-Scot's bike. He instinctively turns his head to look, but unfortunately for me, he swivels the front wheel of his bike as well.

'SHIIIIIIT! WATCH OU—'

But it's too late. His front wheel has collided with mine, and I hit the floor: my knees, elbows and palms skid along the scree, picking up small stones and leaving much of my skin behind. Fortunately for him, he has landed on top of me.

I'm stunned.

'SAM ... SAM!' my Other Half hollers over audible gasps from the group as I lay splayed out on the gravel. Like a homing pigeon, our group leader makes an abrupt U-turn and I can hear his wheels skid up to where I lie face down on the ground.

'Bloody hell, Rach! You're determined to make me earn my corn this week, aren't you? Do you think you can move? Can you stand up?' he asks, reaching down to help scrape me up from the gravel track. I suddenly feel very alert and tingly all over. Aided by Super Sam, I do a quick scan of the most vulnerable, bony areas: knees, ankles and wrists. I figure that at least I haven't broken any bones. My body is throbbing, and is now completely flooded with adrenalin. Blood gushes from both knees, and there's a large flap of skin hanging loosely over a gaping wound on one knee. I can't feel any pain. It probably needs stitches, but I don't have that option available to me. Instead, Sam and I slowly make our way to the steps of Coco's emergency bus, where I sit down as he opens the large First Aid box, preparing to assess me for damage. I can feel my entire body stinging, as though I've just been harangued by a mob of very angry bees. The stinging is all over my body, because the impact areas are quite evenly spread – my knees (which have suffered the worst of the impact), both elbows and the palms of my hands, both of which are severely grazed, and my palms now have indented, bloody pieces of gravel embedded in them.

Sam has his medical gloves on, and methodically works his way around my battered and bruised body, doing his best to clean up the mess I've made of myself. Saline solution cleans the more superficial wounds, but we both know that my knees will need more comprehensive treatment later – we've still got another twenty-five miles of riding to complete today. If he can bandage me up so that I can at least get through to the end of today, then we will deal with the bloody carnage later. Above all else, I DO NOT WANT ANOTHER DAY TRAVELLING HORIZONTALLY ON COCO'S MINIBUS.

I want to get back on my bike. I want to ride.

'God, Rach! What is it with you on this trip?' Mark asks, looking concerned as I bite my lip, grimacing through the reality of making my bloodied limbs pedal again. The nauseating pain hasn't kicked in yet, just throbbing and tightness. My skin has been shredded from both my knees and I've packed them tightly with a pair of adapted compression socks (with the feet cut out), covered by Sam's First Aid bandages. The tightness I can feel is my body trying to protect itself from any further damage. My knees have stiffened up completely, but I've no option other than to force my limbs to bend and to move again. Stinging, tingling, throbbing, aching, and flashes of acute pain follow me along the next twenty-five torturous miles. Blood seeps through my compression sock/bandage combination, and I don't honestly know how I'm still moving forwards.

Why me? Why this?

After the dreadful experience of heatstroke, I made the firm decision to get back on the bike, and complete this challenge. And now this.

WHY?

'Watch out, guys! There's a large pit of water coming up around the next corner. It's quite deep with rocks in it, and there's a sharp rise out onto the banking on the other side,' Sam shouts, riding back towards the group of us. Luke and the fast boys have forewarned him of this unhelpful obstacle, so that he can pass the word on to the rest of us. I'm struggling to process how much more difficult this day can possibly become. Riding through this murky – *dirty* – water and submerging my now-shredded, bandaged knees in a pit of filth is simply too much for me to comprehend: how can I possibly get myself through this? I can feel that my head has gone into survival mode.

Just stay calm, Rach. Keep calm, and breathe.

'You OK, Rach?' Sam asks quietly, riding up alongside me before we reach the dreaded corner. 'You can get off the bike and just push, you know. You don't have to ride this.'

I stay close to the back and watch as one after the other take turns in riding through the deep, muddy pit, scrambling up onto the banking on the other side. Cockney Luke and his fun bus pals have been there for a while already. They stand whooping and cheering as they video everyone riding through the obstacle, making it safely across to the other side in whatever way they can.

'WOO HOO! Go, Mark!'

'HEYYYY! You made that look TOO EASY, Sally!'

'NICE ONE, KAREN! LOOKING GOOOOOD!'

'OMG, JULIE, YOU LEGEND! Through in one go!'

Two of the non-Scots didn't make it through the muddy pit and Veronica decided to push her bike in the end, after her Ironman husband was one of those who didn't successfully navigate his way across. Being in the wrong gear, and therefore not being able to maintain sufficient torque (this being the force applied to the pedals) proved problematic. In the murky, muddy water, being in a gear that is too low, i.e. 'granny gear' (no offence to any arse-kicking, cycling grannies intended, this is a familiar term used in cycling), there was not enough force to push through the water, mud or any obstacles, and so the wheels slipped and spun around, making the bikes wobble uncontrollably. This is exactly what happened to Ironman and one of the non-Scots (it may have been PJ or Duncan, I can't recall) to the delight and amusement of Luke, who caught it all on camera.

And now it's my turn. I can feel the sweat trickling down my neck, and the throbbing and oozing of my bandaged – and now increasingly swollen – knees. But I want to give this a go. I want to be like Sally, Julie and Karen; I want to at least *TRY* to ride my bike through the murky pit. I don't want to be that person who was too scared to give it a shot – despite my very convenient (and very visible) – Get Out of Jail Free card.

'Come on, Rach, you can do it!' Luke shouts across from the other side of the muddy pit. I look across the banking, and I can see that the whole group is standing, watching and willing for me to make it through.

'Yeah, go, Rach! We know you can do it!' Julie shouts, whilst Karen whoops and pumps her fists above her head.

My confidence has been severely dented by the collision and I'm still in a state of shock that I'm having to ride the rest of today's already challenging route with painful, open wounds. But in a way, it helps me to focus, because really, how much worse can it possibly get? Even if I don't make it across the muddy pit and I fall foul of the same mistakes as Ironman and PJ (or Duncan), resulting in me being buck-aroo'd off the bike and into the stagnant filth, so what? It can't possibly be any worse than a day on the minibus with heatstroke, or an unfortunate bike collision and subsequent face-plant onto bumpy gravel.

So, what the actual fuck have I got to lose?!

My gears are high enough to stop me from sinking into the pit (I think), and I've ridden back a little way to get a decent run-up. I've chosen my line (this being my preferred route through the muddy filth) and there's nothing left for me to do but pedal. I push down hard, gripping tightly onto the handle-bars, knowing that I will be riding over some invisible loose rocks, stones and debris lurking underneath the burnt-orange water. The only thing I can do is to hold tight and pedal. I can feel my compression socks and bandages becoming saturated as my wheels spin in the water, dousing my legs. But the water feels cool, and it has an incredibly soothing, anaesthetic-like effect on my shredded flesh. My handlebars jerk as I can feel the wheels weaving and dodging their way over and around small, moving rocks underneath the water, but I *push, push, push* down on the pedals and ride over them.

I WILL MAKE IT TO THE OTHER SIDE.

I'm through the deepest part of the pit and I can see the incline of the banking on the other side. One of the Scots shouts at somebody to make room for me to come through, and I know then that I've done it: that I'm safely across. I'm elated. I'm in pain, and the most physical discomfort I can recall ever experiencing, but inside I'm dancing around, setting off fireworks in celebration of ... riding through a muddy pool of water. It doesn't seem like very much, but to me, in this moment, it is everything. I had a plethora of fears – *real* fears – about cycling through the murky, filthy pit and my ability to get to the other side. And after falling off my bike and hurting myself so badly only hours before, I had every possible reason to opt out and take the easier route. But in choosing to commit to at least *trying* to ride across, I caused my Bastard Chimp irreparable damage, from which he may never recover. This is what I had absolutely no idea I had come here for. I had no clue when taking on a challenge like this, that in one single, victorious moment, it would all make sense. This is that moment. Despite all the pain, and the struggle that has gone before, I *chose* to ride through the deep, muddy, filthy pit – and I made it to the other side.

* * *

It's our last day of cycling through Costa Rica and we're into the last 25km. Over the past two days, we have ridden for miles along tiny, narrow tracks through banana plantations. We have seen men wearing harnesses, sweating profusely as they drag hundreds of harvested bananas on pulleys behind them. We have been transported across crocodile-infested rivers, our bikes piled high on rickety old wooden boats, with zero thought to health and safety, and minimal confidence that either ourselves or our bikes would reach the other side. We have slept (and I use the word liberally) in an eclectic range of distinctly unglamorous locations. But these last few days – ever since making the decision to return to the group, and to get back on the bikes – have by far been the best.

On the evening of the bicycle collision incident, I did end up having to bite down onto a towel whilst Sam scrubbed my open flesh clean with lint and hot water. Riding the bike since then has been far more challenging – my knees wanting to seize up and heal, rather than be forced to pedal for mile after mile. But, the tightness eventually loosened, and I'm now accustomed to the pain. Of course, I would far rather have avoided this particular part of my experience, but then again, what doesn't kill you …

And so here we are … Approaching the final 25km of riding up to the Caribbean coast. I simply cannot believe that we've made it this far – that now, we are so close.

'OK, guys!' Sam shouts over the general murmurs and conversations going on between the newfound friends. 'We're going to be turning onto a train track shortly. It's a long section of about 15km. But please know that this is perfectly safe, you don't have to worry. JC will be leading from the front, and it is very narrow, so it will mean that you will need to ride in SINGLE FILE, and you must give each other SPACE. If one of you stops suddenly, then it will be like dominoes. You all good with that? Right then, let's go!'

Cycling along train tracks? OK, that doesn't sound too bad. And 15km? That seems perfectly feasible – it's only another 10km from there to the Caribbean coast.

FUCKING ACE! Yes, I can do this. I can do this, Sam.

We turn into the start of this next section of the ride, and I decide to hover close to the back of the pack. Sam's message about riding in single file hits home: I do not want the pressure of somebody cycling up my backside when my now-scabbing-over, pustulating knees are doing their very best to continue pedalling, to keep my bike moving forwards. I'm happy with my decision. The train track isn't what I expected, although I'm not quite sure *what* I had in mind. These are traditional, old-fashioned railway sleepers. Large blocks of timber laid out horizontally, with wide gaps of fresh air in between. Pedalling along these horizontal tracks, it soon becomes apparent to me that the next 15km may be the worst of the entire trip, or possibly my entire life. Why? Because the rhythmical bouncing and sharp jarring over the sleepers and the spaces in between feels like being repeatedly punched in my most sensitive female parts. And there's simply no way to escape the pain. *Punch, punch, punch. Punch, punch, punch.* It's not like feeling 'a little bit sore down below' or '*slightly irritated downstairs*', this is a full-on assault on my female genitalia, and it's simply the worst physical torment I have ever experienced. My knees are torn to shreds, but pain? What pain? THERE IS NO PAIN COMPARED TO THIS.

I let the two people behind me move past, so I'm now riding at the very back of the group. Only Sam is left behind me, metaphorically holding my hand as he knows how much this is killing me. Physically, I'm in such agony that tears are streaming down my face with every revolution of the wheels. Yes, I'm crying – no, *sobbing* whilst continuing (only just) to move forwards along the wretched tracks. At times, I try to stand up on my pedals, but the track keeps narrowing and then we ride over several high, exposed bridges (still on the railway sleepers) so I don't dare to do anything other than keep my bottom firmly on the seat and inch forwards despite my pain and my terrified tremors (I don't do heights).

I stop and get off my bike – the agony is just too much to bear. I'm even berating my external female genitalia, which now feels to be protruding – bright-red and swollen like a baboon's anus. I can only hope that there are no male baboons lurking, as they would no doubt mistake me for one of their species who is clearly demonstrating that I am 'in oestrus'. I'm not: I'm just a very tired, very broken – and now a very swollen novice cyclist who wants to reach the coast.

I take some (more) high-strength Ibuprofen, slather myself in yet more lubricant and other seemingly ineffective anti-chaffing goo, and sob loudly on the shoulder of the ever-patient Sam before mounting my bike with the *only* goal being to reach the end of this wretched train track.

When will it end? I want it all to end.

* * *

'Guys!' Sam shouts above the rising, excitable chatter. 'You all know that we're now just TEN KILOMETRES away from the Caribbean coast.' Loud cheers and whoops spread amongst the group. I'm standing quietly beside my Other Half, silent tears running down my grubby, salty face. My nether regions are throbbing. 'So, listen up. The final track we're taking will be very twisty and turny. It weaves in and around trees – so watch out for hidden tree roots – and it's mostly on sand. Please be careful, because sand can be tricky to ride on. Stay in a low gear, and try to keep moving: stopping and starting in sand will be difficult and frustrating, especially when riding in a group like this. Give each other plenty of space. And finally, keep your focus and concentrate on steering: it can be more difficult to handle the bike on this kind of terrain.'

I'm not an overtly religious person, but from my early years of Sunday School teachings, I vaguely recall the story of the Ten Plagues of Egypt, when God sent down plagues of frogs, flies, hail and locust (amongst other insufferable things) to send some message or other to the kings of Egypt (I'd stopped listening by this point. I was only seven). And I wonder, is this my equivalent? I count the intolerable conditions I've been faced with thus far, which are gargantuan considering my mental health challenges. Flunked travel plans, sleep deprivation, zero access to basic hygiene amenities, heatstroke, bike collision and face-plant onto gravel, being injured, riding through deep, murky filth with seeping wounds, suffering potential long-term damage to my female genitalia ...

Are we at ten, yet? No. So, we can't be at the end – or in my case, the Caribbean Sea.

I listen to Sam's preamble, but in all honesty, nothing matters now. All I want is to get back on the bike and ride the last ten kilometres to reach the Caribbean coast. Nothing he – or anyone else – says will alter the fact that we must still mount our godforsaken chameleon-green Trek mountain bikes and pedal some more, until we reach the end of our journey.

Warn us all you like about the perils of riding on sand, and tricky, gnarly tree roots, Sam, but we've still got to ride over and/or around them.

I take a large swig of electrolyte solution from the now-battered, filthy water bottle mounted on my bike, and a reluctant bite of my last remaining peanut butter protein bar.

I FUCKING HATE THESE BARS!

I'm pumped, ready to go. We set off riding in our usual non-peloton (nope, we're *still* not that good) and I've pushed my way to the front. Just like the first few days (which feel like they were a decade ago), I have Luke's bulging calves within sight. I'm pushing down hard on my pedals, and enjoying the challenge of weaving in and out of the sandy track. Having to focus and concentrate on the ever-changing terrain, and moving at speed across ground which shifts momentarily from hard to soft, wet to dry, and rough to smooth is taking my mind off any of the pain I'm in. The goal – the ONLY goal – is to cycle this last ten kilometres and arrive at the Caribbean coast on two wheels. Not on Coco's minibus, not by taxi, not limping whilst pushing the wretched bicycle: I want to arrive at that coastline on two wheels, despite all of the biblical calamities I've endured over the last ten days. This is the reason I came here: to prove that I can do this. And now, I can smell the sea. I have visions of Levi Roots cooking up some jerk chicken with Reggae Reggae sauce for us on the beach.

This is happening, we're almost there.

I grip tightly on my handlebars and push down harder on my pedals. I'm concentrating on reading the track ahead, and picking my line. My mind is solely focused on moving forwards as fast as possible. Nothing else matters. No pain, no discomfort, just focus on reaching the end. The track is narrow, and just as Sam said, it weaves around tight corners. Handling the bike on various types of sand takes some getting used to, but hey, where's the surprise on this trip? Unlike the days of riding the volcanic up, round, down roller-coaster trail as we set off from the Pacific Coast, this isn't a wide, open expanse – it feels like we are enclosed here. But then, the sky widens as though someone has just turned the dimmer switch up.

'IT'S THE SEA! I CAN SEE THE SEA!' I shout to anyone who will listen. 'WE'RE HERE! IT'S THE CARIBBEAN SEA!'

The group of us rush to abandon our bikes at any reasonable location. Mine has been unceremoniously dumped next to a tree. We remove our shoes and socks, and like a stampeding herd of turtles, stagger down to the sea and immerse ourselves in the cold, salty water. Everything is numb. The cold water washes away my pain, as the brightest, bluest Caribbean sky lifts my broken spirits. *We've made it!* I stand with my arms raised high in the air, making a victory pose on the wet sand, the vast ocean behind me. People in the group take photos of the evidence that we are here. We have cycled just over 480km, and we're at our finish line: we are standing in the Caribbean Sea.

I don't care how I look. I've forgotten about anything relating to my own image, and I've stopped picking myself apart on the endless quest for imperfections. My body dysmorphia doesn't exist. There's no place for it here. It has been swept away into the sea, and carried by the waves to a different place. It's no longer my burden to carry, as the focus of pedalling on my bike and surviving this trip has usurped anything my Bastard Chimp can possibly throw at me.

I have arrived here, and I feel like Superwoman.

EPILOGUE

I've erupted in large, ugly cold sores, I'm bandaged up heavily on both knees and one elbow, and I have visible dark bags under my eyes. Not the imaginary ones from a few months ago, but *real* ones. I have baboon's arse genitalia, and I'm struggling to sit down, walk, move – or do *anything* without wincing in pain. I've written my future sex life off as a bad job, and resigned myself to a relationship of hand-holding and companionship – and possibly *The Times* crossword – going forward.

This cycling adventure was always meant to challenge me; it was supposed to force me to look in another direction to realise what I was capable of, both physically and mentally. And as I sit here, reflecting on the experience of not only cycling for 480km across another country, but the months beforehand of self-discovery and learning, I know without a shadow of a doubt that I would go through it all again. The enormous cold sores on my face will eventually disappear, my battered knees will heal. My nether regions will (I hope) return to some reasonable proportions. My body will recover from the serious bashing it has endured over the last ten days, but my mind will never be quite the same again.

I have faced so many of my anxieties in the run-up to this trip and all the way across Costa Rica, and my ability to cope with those challenges without the need for medication or running is now indisputable. The body dysmorphic disorder therapy earlier in the year enabled me to access a mental health tool box which has undoubtedly made an extraordinary difference to the way my mind selects, interprets and accepts thoughts as being the truth, whilst this epic cycling challenge has made me see myself and my own physical capabilities in a whole new light. And it's for these reasons that losing running back in 2017 was quite possibly the best thing to happen to me, because I've finally learned how to manage my anxiety and how to tackle the Dream Stealer.

What does anxiety feel like?

It's a daily battle with the Dream Stealer.

It rears its ugly head like one of the bullying, meat-head giants who trample across the BFG's hillside.

It's a cat pawing at a cornered mouse, a bully taunting the vulnerable kid at school. It's always there, lurking in the background, ready to rouse and pounce, paw and taunt – you just don't know when.

It laughs and says, *'You can't!'* when otherwise, you might have – just possibly – dared to consider that you could.

It prepares you for the worst, even when the worst is unfeasible.

It paints a picture of a scary, doomed outcome on the brightest and sunniest of days.

It makes you fear the outcome, kyboshing the journey to even get there.

It's your heart suddenly beginning to race in a super-market aisle, your chest pounding when sitting motionless, that nobody sees.

It's fight or flight that won't switch off – on constant repeat. Only there's no one to fight, and no need to take flight.

It's teetering on the edge of a cliff, about to jump off. But jump where? Into some invisible, non-existent place where only fear lives.

It's standing, sword drawn, opposite an invisible opponent – a permanency of '*en garde*'.

It's all these things, and a million more. And it can never, *EVER* win.

Here's why …

The silent, daily battles, the mini-victories.

Pushing yourself out the front door when it would be so much easier not to.

Refusing to allow the world to shrink, whilst the Dream Stealer feeds on the remnants of your joy.

Smiling, and faking confidence when you're terrified inside.

Starting a conversation with the quiet mum in the school playground.

Saying '*Yes*' when every ounce of your being wishes it were a '*No*'; saying '*No, thank you*' when compulsion and obligation try to steer you to go.

Standing on the start line with a dry mouth, wishing it were the finish.

Entering 'Destination: Unknown' into your internal satnav and revving up the engine.

Pressing that 'send' button and risking rejection.

Clicking 'submit' because there's ever such a small chance that you might win.

Taking part when you doubt you have much to contribute.

Walking into a room when it feels infinitely safer to stay outside.

Picking up the phone when you'd rather switch it to silent.

Asking the question you've tried hard to swallow.

Not listening to the small talk, or the ones who just gossip. Or to those who are jealous because their dreams have already curled up and died.

Walking past the crowd, with your head held high.

Meeting up for a coffee, regardless of the panic rising inside.

Asking for help when you can't face it alone, despite the only comfortable place being by yourself.

All these are what will keep the Dream Stealer away from your door.

I know, because I've done them all many, many times before.

ACKNOWLEDGEMENTS

As with the evolving journey I've been on since *Running For My Life* was published in January 2018, life moves on – everything changes. And so, with this – my second non-fiction book, my life has shifted and morphed into a different shape. None of us can plan for these things. Nobody can account for the sliding doors and the transient nature of this rollercoaster ride we call life. But this rather unexpected chapter of my personal story has heralded some incredible memories, and some amazing people who have all been a part of the adventure. And that's what it is – an amazing adventure.

When things threw me off track in the early part of 2017, I wasn't entirely sure what to do or where to find my 'safe place'. Things fell apart, and many people have played a part in helping me to piece together the fragments that were left from a dark place, and to help me turn towards the sunshine again.

I am indebted to all those people – those close to me for loving and supporting me through the carnage of life's upheaval; to my mum for standing and cheering me on whatever the circumstance. To the friends – both old and new – who have been there to walk and talk, laugh and cry with. Sean, Rhiannon, Steph and Emma. Thanks for making the difference in massive – and tiny – ways. And to JF, my BFF from a long time ago. To rediscover your friendship after all these years has been like an infusion of pure happiness into my life.

Getting my old mountain bike out and pushing past my fear was as steep a learning curve as I would care to imagine. But I have met the most incredible people on my journey – people who showed me that real, ordinary folk can and do cycle across countries like Costa Rica(!). My deep thanks to all those incredible people who have crossed my path along the way. Jackie, Caroline, Sarah and Vanessa, Luke and the boys – you were and are my heroes! Trixie, Karen, Steph, both Emmas and the guys who I was lucky enough to meet – the same is true for our adventures cycling across Vietnam. And to Sam – the best guide with the biggest heart who bandaged me up in Costa Rica, and made me believe that I could do it – that I could get to the finish. Thank you so much for all your kindness, and for making this world a little bit brighter.

It goes without saying that the continued support, encouragement and guidance of my agent, Jo Bell, and editor, Beth Eynon, has continued way beyond the first book, and in fact beyond any book. Thank you for your friendship and your constant, unfailing belief in my ability to somehow pour words – and my heart – onto the page.

I must also thank all the people who have contacted me since reading *Running For My Life*. Over a period of two years, I have received hundreds of messages from people who can relate to some aspect of my story. I have received selfies of my book in far-flung places, from remote Africa to Antarctica, and I have heard deeply personal accounts from those who have experienced similar issues to my own. To every one of those people, thank you for reaching out, and for making me believe that my story was worth sharing. I know, now, that I was never alone.

Finally, to my beautiful girl, Tilly. You are my joy and my sunshine. You are the reason I continue to battle with the bastard chimp every single day. Thank you for challenging me in ways I couldn't even imagine, and for bringing me the deepest possible joy. This book – and all the lessons I have learned – wouldn't have been possible if it wasn't for you.